STRATEGIC MARKET TIMING

Robert M. Bowker

D1202060

New York Institute of Finance

Library of Congress Cataloging-in-Publication Data

Bowker, Robert M.
   Strategic market timing / Robert M. Bowker.
      p.   cm.
   Includes index.
   ISBN 0-13-504754-4 :
   1. Investments. 2. Business cycles.   I. Title.
HG4521.B634 1989
332.63'2--dc20   89-32648
                                                      CIP

This publication is designed to provide accurate and authoritative information in regard to the subject matter covered. It is sold with the understanding that the publisher is not engaged in rendering legal, accounting, or other professional service. If legal advice or other expert assistance is required, the services of a competent professional person should be sought.

From a Declaration of Principles Jointly Adopted by a Committee of the American Bar Association and a Committee of Publishers and Associations

Printed in the United States of America

10 9 8 7 6 5 4 3

New York Institute of Finance
(NYIF Corp.)
70 Pine Street
New York, New York 10270-0003

To my wife Judith and my children Matthew and Sarah, whose love, comfort, support, and patience made this book possible.

And to all of those investors who needlessly got caught in the crash of October 1987 and who, by understanding the true nature of business cycles, should never be similarly misled again.

Contents

Acknowledgment

I wish to express my sincere thanks to Ms. Lisa Gaskins, whose dedication, editorial skill, and word-processing magic allowed this manuscript to be completed on schedule.

Introduction

SEPTEMBER 1986

After rising from 1500 in January to 1900 in September, the Dow Jones Industrial Average suddenly plunged 141 points on September 11 and 12. An analysis of our position in the business cycle at that time led us to issue an unequivocal recommendation in the *Business Cycle Monitor*, a monthly advisory letter: *"Buy!"*

SEPTEMBER 1987

After rising for the rest of 1986, the Dow rose to over 2700 in August 1987. Then, in September, it fell back by about 150 points. On September 15, the same advisory letter contained another unequivocal recommendation based on our analysis of the business cycle: *"Sell!"* A month later, the world was stunned by the infamous 508-point crash of October 19, 1987.

What was the difference? In both 1986 and 1987, the market rose by 25–35 percent. In September of each year, the market declined by 6–7 percent. But in 1986, the September decline was a temporary pullback in a strong bull market, while in 1987, the

September decline foreshadowed the largest single market decline in history.

The pure action of the market itself did not provide any clues that one was just a momentary setback while the other was a major stock market peak. But a *significant fundamental difference lay beneath the surface of the stock market itself:*

- In September 1986, we were at the wrong point in the business cycle for a major stock market decline. Conditions necessary for a major downturn had not yet occurred.
- But in September 1987, we were at exactly the right point in the business cycle for a market downturn. All of the conditions necessary for a significant decline were precisely in place. In addition, the market was outrageously overvalued by mid-1987—running on a euphoria of its own with blatant disregard for all known investment fundamentals. Additionally, given the realization that we were poised for a downturn and that the market was extremely overvalued, several short-term indicators gave decisive sell signals—well before the crash.

Two critical points can be seen from this comparison:

- *It is not possible* to tell where the stock market is going by looking at the stock market in isolation.
- *It is possible* to tell where the stock market is going by understanding the relationships between stock prices and other predictable turning points contained in the business cycle.

In this book, we provide all of the information on business cycle analysis, stock market valuation, and market signals that investors need to recognize the difference between minor oscillations and major stock market turning points and to avoid stock market crises such as the crash of 1987.

But this is *not* a book about short-term trading, speculation, arbitrage, stock picking, or technical market timing. We do *not* talk about mysterious "waves," "time cycles," or chart formations, which are predominantly fictitious and highly misleading.

This book is about a long-term investment strategy that allows conservative investors to capitalize on the major upswings in stocks, bonds, and gold that occur in every business cycle and then to exit those markets during the major downturns that also occur in each business cycle.

The foundations of this investment strategy are rooted in:

- Proven cause-and-effect relationships in our economy and our financial markets
- A defined business cycle that consists of a prescribed series of events that occurs in the same basic sequence over and over again (including tops and bottoms in stock, bond, and gold prices)
- Over 80 years of supporting historical evidence
- A definitive way of measuring the degree of overvaluation or undervaluation of the stock market at any time
- A few selective market indicators that, when used correctly, provide the final signals of major stock market tops and bottoms
- A complete portfolio management system that is timed to the business cycle and can be managed and executed by any investor with a minimum of time, effort, and cost

The financial rewards to be derived from this approach are quite spectacular (see Chapter 1). More important, these significantly higher rewards can be achieved without a commensurate increase in risk because the investor never has to invest money in anything more risky than the market itself.

The debacle of October 1987 left many investors in total financial ruin. Others were seriously injured. Millions of other conservative investors, along with people who had simply put money away in pension funds, individual retirement accounts (IRAs), or their children's education funds, saw a substantial part of their future plans, hopes, and dreams go up in smoke. It is extremely disheartening to realize that these financial losses were, in fact, avoidable. It is the author's sincere hope that this book will provide investors with a clear and understandable set of facts, principles, insights, and analytical tools so that similar situations in the future can be *clearly recognized and acted on* in advance.

Part I

THE PURPOSE OF THIS BOOK

"The years teach us much that the days never knew."
—*Ralph Waldo Emerson, "Experience,"* Essays,
Second Series, *1844*

Chapter 1

The Value of Strategic Market Timing

This book was developed to meet three specific objectives:

- To present a completely new and original set of insights and perspectives concerning the nature and structure of business cycles
- To show that long-term movements and *major turning points* in the economy, inflation, interest rates, and our financial markets (including the stock market) are driven by known, proven, and predictable cause-and-effect relationships
- To demonstrate that a fundamental knowledge of the dynamics of business cycles, coupled with sound economic and financial theory, can be translated into a long-term investment strategy that has a proven track record of generating much higher than average returns without a commensurate increase in risk

The methodology described in this book was developed from an extensive analysis of long-term historical data obtained primarily from the U.S. Department of Commerce and the Standard and Poor's Corporation. These data were used to confirm a conceptual model of business cycle behavior that synthesizes several well-accepted individual laws and principles of economic and financial theory.

THE LESSONS OF 80 YEARS OF HISTORY

Over the course of our research efforts, we drew several important conclusions about business cycles, current methods of forecasting, and some basic "truths" about investing that are, in fact, false. Some of these key conclusions are listed below:

• Economic models are generally based on regression analysis, which simply projects the past into the future in a straight line. They are not designed for—nor do they succeed at—predicting major turning points.

• Psychological indicators and investor sentiment indexes are valid measurements of how people feel about *the past* and *the present,* but do not provide any useful information as to where financial markets are headed in *the future*—which is all that really counts from an investment standpoint.

• Technical analysis may work sometimes, but it does not work on a consistent, reliable basis. Moreover, it is geared to short-term ups and downs—not long-term major turning points.

• Time cycles and wave theories are interesting to study, but have no logical or economic foundation. It would be a wonderful world indeed, if investors could make money on a consistent basis by doing nothing more difficult than referring to a calendar. But if you believe that the world is driven by a rational system of real causes and real effects, as this author does, then you must view simplistic time-cycle systems with a critical and skeptical eye. There is simply no known reason why financial markets should move in 6-week cycles, 39-week cycles, 54-year cycles, or any other fixed time cycle unless stock prices are believed to be directly connected to sunspots, phases of the moon, or other periodic, external forces.

• Some absolute "truths" about investing are, in fact, false. Consider the following well-accepted "truth": *When interest rates go up, the stock market goes down, and when interest rates go down, the stock market goes up.* As shown later, history proves that this statement has been true *only* 55 percent of the time since 1920.

- Business cycles are driven by *real, known, cause-and-effect* relationships that can successfully be used to predict major tops and bottoms in the stock market, interest rates, inflation, and the economy.

   Example: A change in the inflation rate will *cause* a change in interest rates, which in turn will *cause* a change in the economy. And all of these will *cause* changes in the stock market in highly predictable ways, based on 80 years of business cycle history.

- Stock market movements are *not random* and do not take place in a vacuum. The stock market is a *part* of our overall economic and financial system in which movements and changes in the supply of money, the economy, inflation, interest rates, and stock prices *are all interrelated*. (See Figure 1-1.)
- These interrelated movements form a "Primary Business Cycle" in which the major turning points in stock prices, interest rates, inflation, and several specific economic indicators have occurred in the *same basic sequence* for *the last 80 years*. Therefore, once an investor knows where we are in the business cycle, he or she knows when to look (and when not to look) for the next major turning points.
- Changes in the *fundamental direction of the stock market* are caused by actual or perceived fundamental changes in other parts of the system, and the key to identifying major stock market turning points lies in understanding how these relationships work.

CHANGING THE RULES OF RISK AND REWARD

Every student and teacher of financial theory tells investors that the rules of risk and reward are clearly defined: High rewards can only be achieved by taking high risks, and low-risk investments can be expected to produce low rewards. An analysis of the performance of any individual security—whether a common stock, a convertible stock, a Treasury bond (T-

Figure 1–1.

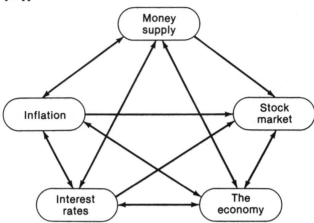

bond), or an ounce of gold—over any long-term period of time shows that these rules of risk and reward are absolutely true.

However, no rule holds that an investor must select a given security with specific risk/reward characteristics and hold it for an indefinite time period. The primary thesis of this book is that the rules of risk and reward can be altered in favor of the investor with a knowledge of business cycles and the use of professional money managers. The methodology presented in this book is designed to alter the rules of risk and reward in three specific ways.

Reducing Market Risk

We can reduce the primary risk—the systematic risk of the stock market itself—by using the principles of business cycle analysis to allow investors to move money *into* the stock market *only at major bottoms* and to take money out of the market *only at major tops*. When the market undergoes major declines of 20 or 30 percent, investors' money will be safely out of the stock market, earning the going rate for short-term money market instruments. Then, at the next bottom, investments can be made to capture the full benefit of the next market upswing. In other words, we create a new type of security that we call the business cycle–timed (BCT) portfolio.

The difference between this approach and many short-term, technically based market-timing systems is that the major buying and selling actions in the BCT portfolio occur, on average, only once every $3\frac{1}{2}$ years and generate dramatically superior long-term returns over the market averages. In addition, the portfolio actions are based on proven, fundamental relationships as opposed to quasi-reliable technical factors that tend to ignore economic fundamentals.

Reducing Portfolio Risk

In addition to reducing the systematic market risk, we can reduce the inherent portfolio risks of having money deployed in any single stock, any single industry, or any small group of stocks that are particularly sensitive to a single influence, such as oil prices, takeover speculation, or interest rates. This can be done by using mutual funds that are similar in size and structure to the S&P 500 Stock Index itself.

There are hundreds of mutual funds and mutual fund families that allow investors to move money into or out of stock or bond portfolios at little or no cost, and these funds offer investors the ideal way to participate in major market upswings without exposure to the volatility and uncertainty of individual stocks or industry sectors.

Reducing Information/Research Risk

To evaluate properly the quality of any given stock, an investor must devote a great deal of time and effort to studying the industries and markets in which the company participates, national and international competitors, new product developments, balance sheet structure, technology, financial strength, growth potential, and many more aspects of the company and its management. And to construct a relatively well-balanced portfolio of stocks, an individual investor would have to perform this type of analysis for several stocks in several industries on an ongoing basis.

Well-informed investors should have access to many sources of information pertaining to each industry and each company in their portfolios. But information such as industry outlooks, new technological developments, recent company financings, or the market potential of new products would be available only to individual investors who expend considerable time and money.

By letting the professional portfolio managers of mutual fund companies perform this research and select the companies to be put into their stock portfolios, the individual investor can eliminate the risk of poor portfolio construction that can result from lack of time or information.

Therefore, in managing the BCT portfolio, the investor (1) *chooses when to be in the market* based on the business cycle analysis presented in this book; (2) *moves money into a mutual fund stock portfolio* at that time, allowing professional managers to determine the stocks that compose the stock portfolio; (3) *chooses when to exit the market,* again based on the status of the business cycle; and (4) *moves money out* of the mutual fund's stock portfolio into a money market or cash portfolio where it can earn the going short-term market interest rate until the business cycle provides the next opportune time to buy.

PROFIT POTENTIAL

The potential profitability of the approach described in this book can be more fully appreciated by examining the last half-century of the performance of the stock market, as measured by the broadly based S&P 500 Stock Index.

In April 1942, the S&P 500 index stood at 7.84.[1] By March 1988, the S&P index was 265.7, after falling from the August 1987 peak of 329.3 during the famous crash of October 1987. If an investor had put $1,000 into the stock of an average company on the S&P 500 list in April 1942, that stock would have grown at

---

[1] Monthly average of daily prices.

a compound annual growth rate of 8.59 percent; the original $1,000 invested in 1942 would be worth $33,890 by March 1988.

The system described herein would have performed in a far superior manner. Specifically, the same $1,000 investment in 1942 would have been worth $345,605 if the investor had exited the stock market and moved into cash on only *seven occasions* in the *last 45 years* and then bought back into the market at the six major bottoms that followed.[2] These few timely exits and re-entries into the stock market would generate a 1988 portfolio value *over ten times* the ending value of the unmanaged S&P 500 stock portfolio. This system represents the BCT portfolio performance if it had been perfectly managed—hitting the month of the exact top and the exact bottom for each of 13 major buy and sell points that have occurred since 1942.

Since perfection is an unreasonably high standard of performance, we should manage our expectations by providing for a margin of error in the management of our own BCT portfolio. By selling stocks at the seven market peaks but missing the top by 5 percent and then buying back in at the next major bottom but missing the bottom by another 5 percent, this portfolio would convert the $1,000 initial investment in 1942 to $171,522 by March 1988—*over five times* the value of the unmanaged S&P Stock Index. And if an investor could have moved into and out of the market to miss these major tops and bottoms by as much as 10 percent, his 1988 BCT portfolio would still be worth $84,826—*two and a half times* the value of the S&P 500 Stock Index.

Figure 1-2 shows the results of these portfolio performances from 1942 to 1987. The calculations for Figure 1-2 are given in Appendix A.

This analysis reveals two very significant facts:

• The entire difference between the unmanaged $33,890 end result and the $345,605 or $84,826 end results can be attributed

---

[2] In each case, the investor would also have had the additional benefit of a stream of annual dividends, but since some investors would actually reinvest those dividends while others would not, we have excluded the dividend stream from the comparison.

Figure 1–2. *BCT Portfolio Versus Unmanaged S&P 500 Index*

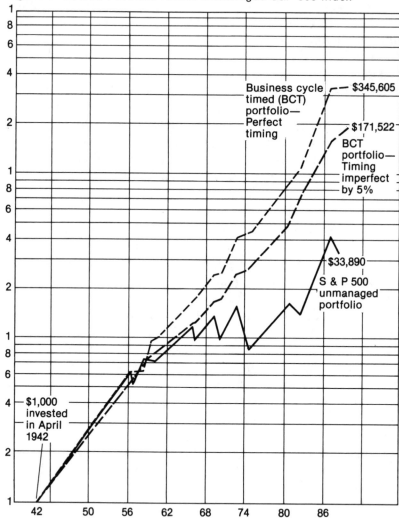

to the investor *simply being out of the market for seven brief periods over the last 45 years.* In fact, to achieve this result, the investor had to be out of the market for a total of only 109 of the 551 months between April 1942 and March 1988—or 19 percent of the total time elapsed.

• This tenfold increase in the value of the "perfectly managed" BCT stock fund over the "unmanaged" portfolio was obtained without ever buying a security with a risk level higher than that of the market itself.

The obvious conclusion is that the singular ability to identify major tops and bottoms every few years is sufficient to increase dramatically the rewards of investing, while never taking on any specific high-risk additions to a portfolio.

IDEAL ASSET ALLOCATION

These results reflect only the proper long-term timing of major buying and selling decisions with respect to the stock market. But the evolution of each business cycle involves major upturns and downturns in interest rates, inflation, and the entire level of economic activity; this means that major cyclical movements in bond prices and gold prices, as well as stock prices, will accompany every business cycle.

As discussed in depth later in this book, each of these financial markets (stocks, bonds, and gold) moves in its own distinctive cycle as it is affected by the cause-and-effect relationships that drive each business cycle. This offers investors the opportunity to construct an ideal portfolio (the BCT portfolio), which consists of an allocation of funds to stocks, bonds, gold, or cash, as dictated by the current position of the business cycle. Only a select group of mutual fund families is equipped to manage this type of portfolio, and these funds, along with the ideal BCT portfolio, are discussed later.

OTHER SYSTEM FEATURES

In addition to higher returns and lower risks, this methodology provides conservative, long-term investors with a practical, usable portfolio management system that:

• Screens out the useless, emotional, nonfactual, ill-founded, uninformed, or misinterpreted investment information that

dominates the media and usually confuses or misguides serious investors
- Allows investors to recognize the news events and economic indicators that truly matter in terms of portfolio management actions
- Provides a logical analytical framework within which economic and financial trends and events can be interpreted; this analytical framework is exclusively based on:
  —Proven cause-and-effect relationships
  —Proven laws of supply and demand
  —More than 80 years of historical validation
- Allows investors to begin with as little as $1,000 as an initial investment
- Generates buy and sell signals that are *decisively clear* and *timely* enough to act on
- *Excludes* all of the high-risk investment vehicles that are normally associated with high-return investment strategies—specifically, options, futures, commodities, margin buying, short selling, and arbitrage techniques

THE BOTTOM LINE

The essential message of the strategic-market-timing investment strategy is that it is not necessary to take excessive investment risks to gain superior investment returns. There is no need to gamble on volatile equity issues or speculate on short-term, technical market swings; it is also not necessary to do extensive research on individual stocks.

Individual investors can implement a very successful, high-return, low-risk, long-term investment strategy by:

- Understanding the true nature of business cycles
- Analyzing proven cause-and-effect relationships
- Identifying the major tops and bottoms in the financial markets
- Managing money in a structured, unemotional, and disciplined manner over the course of every business cycle

However, to do this confidently and consistently, the investor must have a *firm understanding* of the system of relationships that drives the business cycle and causes these major tops and bottoms. Developing this firm understanding has two implications: First, in this book, we must delve into the world of economics and finance in sufficient depth to explain clearly these relationships. Second, the investor must take the time to study the material and gain the understanding and confidence required to *act with conviction* at the critical turning points of future business cycles as they unfold. *Knowledge without action has no profit potential.*

Part II

THE STRUCTURE OF BUSINESS CYCLES

"It is not certain that everything is uncertain."

—*Pascal,* Pensées, *1670*

What Is a Business Cycle?

DEFINING THE BUSINESS CYCLE

Virtually everyone with a passing interest in investments or the economy is familiar with the term "business cycle." But if a number of people were to define a business cycle, a wide variety of answers would result. For example, *Barron's Dictionary of Finance and Investment Terms* defines a business cycle as a:

". . . recurrence of periods of expansion (recovery) and contraction (recession) in economic activity with effects on inflation, growth, and employment. One cycle extends from a GNP base line through one rise and one decline and back to the base line, a period averaging about $2\frac{1}{2}$ years. A business cycle affects profitability and cash flow, making it a key consideration in corporate dividend policy, and is a factor in the rise and fall of the inflation rate, which in turn affects return on investments."

A popular reference book, *The A to Z of Investing,* describes a business cycle as:

". . . a more or less continuous pattern of alternate expansion and contraction in the entire economy. During the period of expansion, industrial production increases, and with it, employment, prices, wages, interest rates, and profits all rise. After the cycle reaches a high point, it gradually begins to contract, with production shrinking and employment, prices, wages, interest rates, and profits all declining. After a low point is reached the economy begins to recover and business activity again increases. Although the general pattern holds true, the duration of each phase, the precise high and low points, and the overall duration of the cycle vary. Moreover, economists frequently disagree about exactly what state of the business cycle the current economy is in.''

The common theme in these and several other definitions is that business activity and financial markets seem to go up and down over time, and the common characteristic of these definitions is that they are quite vague.

In this book, we explicitly define the term "business cycle" as follows:

- A business cycle is a repeating schedule of economic and financial events that occur in the same basic sequence, cycle after cycle.
- These events recur in the same basic sequence because they are driven by proven cause-and-effect relationships that force the events to happen in a prescribed order.

To introduce this concept of the business cycle, we begin with an example of another, more familiar cycle.

THE SEASONAL CYCLE: EXAMPLE

You live in Boston, Massachusetts. The date is December 10 and the temperature has fallen steadily for the last two months. But on December 11, the temperature soars to 86°. The next day it rises to 90°, and on the following day it hits 94°.

Now suppose it's your job to forecast the temperature through the remainder of December and all of January and February. Will you forecast a continuation of 90° temperature or a further increase in temperature because it has risen for the last three days? Of course not. And the reason is that you *know* that the *fundamental forces* of physics that govern the relationship between the sun and the earth will cause the temperature to decline over the winter months. Even though you may not be a physicist, you can confidently predict that the temperature will drop in the next few months because:

- You know that the decline in temperature through the winter phase of the *seasonal cycle* is *consistent* with the *basic laws* of *physics*.
- You have a *long record* of *historical data* to show that the seasonal temperature decline in the winter is reliable.

Therefore, even if the temperature remains in the nineties for several more days, you can be confident that the fundamentals will ultimately prevail. In other words, *you will not be fooled by an aberration because you know where you are in the seasonal cycle.* By the same token, you may not know the exact date on which the warming trend of spring will begin next year, but when certain *signs* of spring begin to appear (birds flying back north, flowers blooming, etc.) you can be sure that spring is not far away.

This concept is identical to the business cycle concept. When a cycle can be defined that is consistent with the basic laws of economics and is backed by several decades of historical data, *you won't be fooled by short-term movements in the stock market, interest rates, or the economy because you will know where you are in the business cycle.* You will also be able to read the signs that foreshadow the next real phase of the cycle.

TRACKING AND MONITORING A CYCLE

Continuing with the seasonal example, how would you track and graphically show our progress through the cycle? If you were interested only in the temperature throughout the four seasons of the year, you could simply plot the temperature at 12 o'clock noon every day and display the data graphically, as shown in Figure 2-1.

But this type of graph displays only one component of the cycle—in this case, the temperature. And if you didn't have a calendar or didn't know how long the cycle of the four seasons might last, you would have a difficult time in finding the seasonal turning points. It might be well into September or October before you could be confident that summer was over, based only on the temperature readings.

Instead, suppose that you could define the seasonal cycle in terms of a predetermined, historically proven schedule of events that always happens in the same basic sequence, as illustrated in Figure 2-2.

Given these predetermined, time-tested events in the seasonal cycle, we could track the progress of each cycle by using a Gantt chart. In Figure 2-3, the "events" of the seasonal cycle are listed on the left side and time is shown on the horizontal axis. When an event is seen to occur, a black dot is placed on that date in the chart.

By connecting the black dots, we can see just where we are in the cycle and what the next events will be. As indicated in the chart, even for something as well defined as the seasons of the year, events might not happen in the exact order defined by long-term history [e.g., Event 4 (flowers blooming) happened a

Figure 2-1. *Average Daily Temperature*

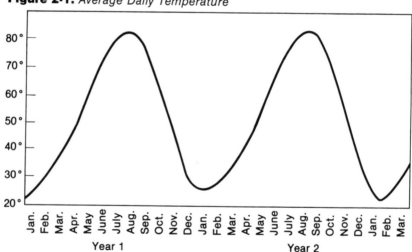

Figure 2-2. *Components of the Seasonal Cycle*

1.	Coldest day of year	Winter
2.	First thaw	Spring
3.	Birds flying north	Spring
4.	Flowers blooming	Spring
5.	Leaves turning green	Summer
6.	Longest day of year	Summer
7.	Hottest day of year	Summer
8.	Flowers wilting	Autumn
9.	Leaves turning brown and falling	Autumn
10.	Birds flying south	Autumn
11.	First frost	Winter
12.	First snowfall	Winter
13.	Shortest day of year	Winter

little before Event 3 (birds flying north) in the first cycle]. But when you are familiar with all of the events of the cycle, you can clearly see what season you are in and what season will soon follow at any point in the cycle.

This seasonal cycle analogy is a close approximation of the concept pursued in this book. The business cycle that we develop consists of several economic and financial events that occur in the same basic sequence again and again. Although we don't know how long each cycle will take to complete, we don't need that information as long as we know what "season" of the business cycle we are in and what the next events will be.

The events of the business cycle consist of major tops and bottoms in several economic and financial indicators. The sequence of these turning points is determined by the time-tested laws of supply and demand and the universal principle of cause and effect. When we complete the development of the components and sequence of events in the business cycle, the result appears in the Gantt chart format shown in Figure 2-3.

BUILDING BLOCK APPROACH

The remainder of this book is devoted to the step-by-step development of a complete investment strategy that is based on the fundamental structure of business cycles. The resulting

Figure 2-3. *Gantt Chart: The Seasonal Cycle*

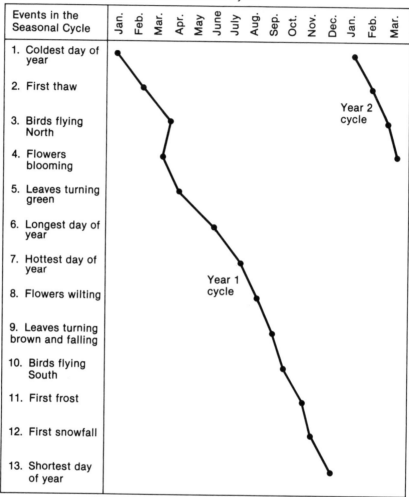

Events in the Seasonal Cycle	Jan.	Feb.	Mar.	Apr.	May	June	July	Aug.	Sep.	Oct.	Nov.	Dec.	Jan.	Feb.	Mar.
1. Coldest day of year															
2. First thaw															
3. Birds flying North															
4. Flowers blooming															
5. Leaves turning green															
6. Longest day of year															
7. Hottest day of year															
8. Flowers wilting															
9. Leaves turning brown and falling															
10. Birds flying South															
11. First frost															
12. First snowfall															
13. Shortest day of year															

strategy allows investors to capitalize on the ability to recognize in advance the major tops and bottoms in:

- The stock market—For obvious reasons
- Interest rates—For buying and selling bonds
- Inflation—For buying and selling gold
- The economy—For business planning and forecasting

We develop this total investment strategy through a series of logical building blocks by:

- Creating a simplified but conceptually accurate model of the economy.
- Reviewing the fundamental cause-and-effect relationships that drive our economy and shape the movements in our financial markets.
- Developing—from the proven laws of supply and demand—a new framework for analyzing, understanding, and predicting changes in the economy and our financial markets. This analytical framework is the Primary Business Cycle: a proven, predictable, repeating sequence of economic and financial events.
- Reviewing the competitive investing environment that we now face, dispelling some popular investing myths, and developing some new approaches to market analysis.
- Building the ideal portfolio of investments between stocks, bonds, gold, and cash at each defined stage of the business cycle.
- Providing a set of investor-friendly mutual fund telephone switching systems that allows investors to manage long-term portfolios throughout each business cycle at virtually no cost.
- Reviewing the underlying causes and the analytical basis of the author's early warning of the crash of 1987.
- Presenting the economic outlook and investment recommendations based on our present position in the Primary Business Cycle.

Chapter 3

A One-Page Model
of the U.S. Economy

We begin by developing a simple but accurate and useful model of our economy and then putting the final result on a single page. Once we can see the dominant driving factors and relationships behind our economy within a logical framework, the pieces of the economic puzzle can be analyzed one by one and then reassembled into a sensible, practical, and profitable framework for a successful investment strategy.

BUILDING BLOCK 1: GOODS AND MONEY

You hear it on the news every day: Consumer spending is up, housing starts are down, interest rates are up, stocks are down, durable goods are up, the money supply is down, real gross national product (GNP) is up, leading indicators are down, and so on. Enough economic statistics are being tracked and reported to fill a book. In fact, one of the most valuable and useful sources of economic information *is* a book entitled the *Business Conditions Digest*, printed by the Department of Commerce. The problem in understanding the economy is not a lack of data. The problem is sifting through the thousands of available numbers and determining what is important and meaningful and what is not. This is the purpose of the model that we are about to construct.

When you cut through all of the details, it becomes clear that the entire economic world is based on only two things: *goods* and *money*.

- *Goods*—These are all the products and services offered by individuals, companies, institutions, or the government. Cars, dishwashers, plumbing services, the U.S. Postal Service, and your morning newspaper are all goods for which you must pay, one way or another.
- *Money*—This is all of the cash, checks, IOUs, securities, or credit used to pay for all of the goods.

When you think about it, every economic transaction involves the exchange of:

- *Goods for money*—Buying and selling
- *Money for money*—Lending, borrowing, or investing
- *Goods for goods*—Bartering

So we begin our model by dividing the entire national economy into two sectors: goods and money, as illustrated in Figure 3-1.

Figure 3-1.

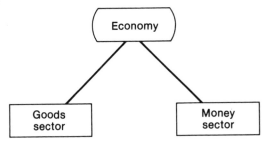

BUILDING BLOCK 2: SUPPLY AND DEMAND

In both the goods and money sectors of the economy, the basic laws of supply and demand are always operating. We define these laws specifically in the next section, but for now it's enough to say that proven and well-known relationships control:

- The supply, demand, and prices of goods
- The supply, demand, and prices of money (where the price of money is the interest rate that you pay to borrow it)

We can now take into account the operation of the laws of supply and demand in both sectors of the economy by adding them to the model, as shown in Figure 3-2. It can also be shown that interest rates can directly affect the demand for goods, such as houses, and that the prices of goods (inflation) can directly affect the prices of money (interest rates). So we can connect the goods and money sectors in Figure 3-2 to show that changes in either sector can cause changes in the other.

Figure 3-2.

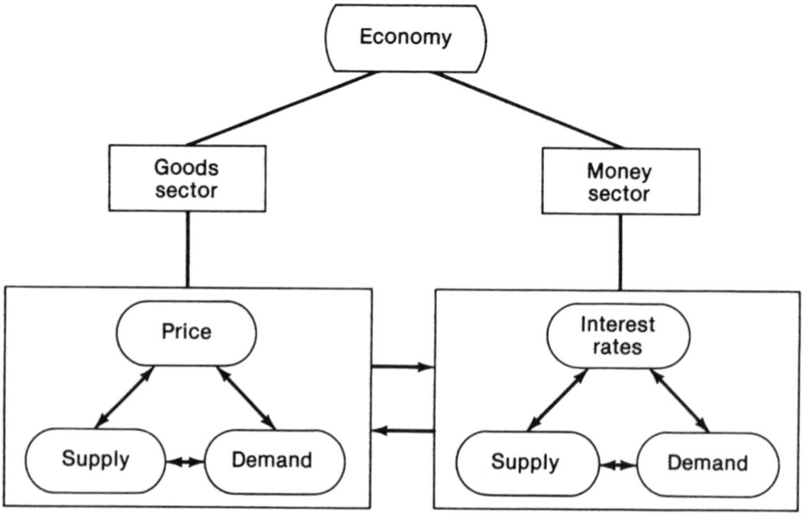

BUILDING BLOCK 3: THE ROLE OF THE GOVERNMENT

If we lived in a totally free economy, we could stop developing the model right here. But the truth is that we live in only a quasifree economy, in which the government plays a very active role. The government's accepted role is to "help" the economy by taking specific actions to meet one or more broadly defined economic or political goals. In general, the goals of our government are usually stated as shown in Figure 3-3.

To achieve these desirable but difficult goals, the government has only two primary sets of tools: *fiscal policy* and *monetary policy*.

Fiscal Policy

Within the domain of fiscal policy, the government has two fundamental levers that it can pull to try to fix, change, or help the economy at different times during the business cycle.

Fiscal Lever 1: Tax Policy. The government can raise or lower taxes at its discretion, subject only to the potential political implications of new tax provisions. A change in the tax laws can obviously affect the economy in many ways. Consumer spending levels, savings rates, business investment, and corporate profits, which can affect employment levels, can all be changed significantly by a change in tax policy. More important, the *directional effects* of higher or lower taxes on all or specific

Figure 3-3. *Broad Goals of the Government*

Economic growth
Full employment
Stable prices
A favorable balance of trade
A reasonably low budget deficit (a recent addition)

parts of the economy and financial markets are *highly predict-able*. For example, higher taxes will obviously leave less money for consumer spending, and a windfall profits tax will reduce incentives to drill for oil and gas.

Fiscal Lever 2: Government Spending. With or without regard for the amount of tax revenues coming into government coffers, Congress can choose to increase or decrease the amount that it spends on government programs. The government is the largest single customer of the private sector of our economy, and every dollar that it spends directly affects the economy by employing people, creating a need for new factories, building highways, or putting spending money into the hands of under-privileged citizens. Cutting back on spending obviously affects the same sectors of the economy, but in the opposite way. Here, too, the *effects* of increased or decreased levels of government spending are *predictable* and easily defined.

Monetary Policy

The control of the nation's monetary policy rests in the hands of the Federal Reserve Board (the Fed), an independent government agency that controls the U.S. banking system. The Fed's primary responsibility is to manage the liquidity (the supply of money) and interest rate structure of the economy to meet the government's goals listed in Figure 3-3. The Fed can do this in one of two ways.

First, it can directly change the interest rate that commercial banks must pay to borrow money from the Fed (the discount rate). This causes other, related interest rates to change in the same and, therefore, *predictable* direction. Second, it can increase or decrease the supply of money. When the supply of anything (including money) increases, the price of it (in this case the price of money, or interest rates) decreases based on the laws of supply and demand. Therefore, an increase or decrease in the supply of money directly affects interest rates in a *predictable* way.

FINAL ASSEMBLY OF THE
ONE-PAGE ECONOMIC MODEL

To complete our one-page model of the economy, we need only to add the responsive role of the government, which can be succinctly stated as follows.

Responsive Government

The various branches of government continuously monitor the condition of the economy (and their own political situation) with respect to economic growth, unemployment, inflation, interest rates, the trade balance, and the federal deficit or surplus. As one or more of these economic factors start to get out of line and become a problem, the government responds with some combination of fiscal or monetary policy actions. When these actions are taken, they trigger changes in the supply, demand, or prices of goods and/or money. Sometimes these actions help and sometimes they don't, but as we will see later, *every governmental action causes a predictable economic reaction,* which can represent either a boom or a bust for businesses and can create either a windfall or a wipeout for investors, depending on where they happen to have their money invested at the time.

With the government playing such an important role in shaping future economic conditions, knowing how to read the implications of government policy changes is obviously a key success factor in building a long-term investment strategy. Yet, amazingly, the vast majority of stock market forecasting "systems" fail to take the government's role into consideration. For example, technical analysis ignores all external events, and most stock-oriented methods focus only on the action of the stock market itself. But the stock market is only a *part* of our overall economic and financial system, which can be dramatically affected in many ways by governmental decisions and actions. Any forecasting approach that does not consider the effects— the *predictable* effects—of fiscal and monetary policy changes is very likely doomed to failure in the long run.

Figure 3-4. *The One-Page Economic Model*

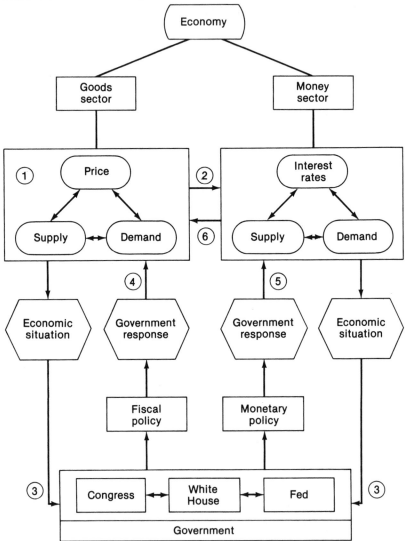

The One-Page Model

Figure 3-4 is our final one-page model of the economy, which reflects the role of the government, and following is a step-by-step description of the sequence of actions and reactions.

---

*Economic and Political Action Sequence of
the One-Page Model*

1. Economic conditions change in the goods sector of the economy.
2. These changes, which may have been the *result* of previous changes in the money sector, are now the *cause* of new changes in the money sector (e.g., inflation in the goods sector triggers higher interest rates in the money sector).
3. The economic situations in both sectors are assessed by various branches of government.
4. New tax or government spending policies are implemented, which alter the economic situation in the goods sector.
5. New monetary policies are put into place, which change the money supply and interest rate situation in the money sector of the economy.
6. The changes in the money sector caused by (5), above (e.g., higher interest rates), now change the economic situation in the goods sector. And with these changes in the goods sector, we are back to Step (1), above.

This one-page model really shows a defined, repeating cycle or *sequence of events* that is driven by known cause-and-effect relationships between the goods sector, the money sector, and government policy actions. We can now explore each part of this model to find the specific cause-and-effect relationships that drive each sector and then collectively produce a surprisingly predictable sequence of events that we call the Primary Business Cycle.

Chapter 4

All You Really Need to Know About Economics

Like everything else in the world of economics, the business cycle is driven by the time-tested laws of supply and demand. Therefore, the first step in discussing business cycles in a structured way is to establish this foundation of proven supply and demand relationships. We hope to do this in a brief and relatively painless way—by defining the laws of supply and demand for goods (the left-hand box in our one-page economic model). We exclude the equations and charts that normally accompany discussions of supply and demand and instead focus on the concepts and principles behind these laws.

THE IMMUTABLE LAWS OF SUPPLY AND DEMAND

"If you laid all of the world's economists end to end, they would not reach a conclusion."

—Anonymous

Economists from Adam Smith to Karl Marx to Milton Friedman have taken widely differing approaches to the study of various aspects of economics and of the social implications of economic policies—and they have developed many varied opinions on these subjects. The anonymous quote above is seen to be glaringly true about almost any complex aspect of the economy. But no school of economic thought has ever departed from the absolute, basic, immutable laws of supply and demand. In an uncertain world, it is a great comfort to be able to identify some principles and rules that *are always right* and can be trusted in *any* situation. Such are the laws of supply and demand described below.

Supply and Demand: Eight Laws in One

The "law of supply and demand" is a widely used term but, in fact, there is not just a single law that relates supply to demand. The term really refers to eight specific relationships between the supply of, the demand for, and the price of a product, a service, or a security at any point in time. These laws are listed in Figure 4-1.

These basic laws have been proven in every Economics 101 textbook in the world and have been tested over centuries of economic history. The absolute truth and common sense of some of these statements are immediately obvious; however, in some cases, the logic behind the relationship may not be readily

Figure 4-1. *The Laws of Supply, Demand, and Price*

1. If the *price* of something goes *up*, the *demand* for it will go *down*.
2. If the *price* of something goes *down*, the *demand* for it will go *up*.
3. If the *price* of something goes *up*, the *supply* of it will go *up*.
4. If the *price* of something goes *down*, the *supply* of it will go *down*.
5. If the *demand* for something goes *down*, the *price* of it will go *down*.
6. If the *demand* for something goes *up*, the *price* of it will go *up*.
7. If the *supply* of something goes *up*, the *price* of it will go *down*.
8. If the *supply* of something goes *down*, the *price* of it will go *up*.

apparent. Although it is not necessary to derive these laws from scratch, they are too important to pass by without ensuring that the fundamental logic and truth of these eight relationships are both understood and fully accepted. They are not only the foundation for everything that follows in this book, buy they represent the *only* things that investors need to know about economics to understand the financial world in which we live.

The Relationships Between Supply, Demand, and Price

Following are a brief explanation and illustration of each of the laws of supply, demand, and price as they apply to goods and services.

How Price Affects Demand.

"Bargains are better than rip-offs."

—An astute consumer

Demand is defined as the *quantity* of a product—let's say Gadgets—that consumers will buy at a given price. The relationship between demand and price is visibly and constantly displayed to consumers across the country at every factory warehouse sale, department store sale, or inventory clearance sale: *Consumers will buy more Gadgets at a lower price than they will at a higher price.*

Based on this well-founded principle, which is incessantly advertised to the consuming public, we can confidently state the first two laws of supply, demand, and price:

Law 1: *If price goes* ***up****, demand will go* ***down****.*
Law 2: *If price goes* ***down****, demand will go* ***up****.*

How Price Affects Supply.

"Big profits are better than little profits."

—An astute businessperson

Supply can be defined as the *quantity* of Gadgets that will be offered by Gadget producers at a given price. While everyone is a consumer and is, therefore, familiar with the price and demand side of the equation, most people do not manage manufacturing companies, so the relationship between supply and price is less obvious than it is between price and demand. However, it is equally logical. Let's take a look at the Gadget industry, which has three producers in the United States.

- Producer A can make a Gadget for a cost of $10; it is the low-cost producer.
- Producer B is not as efficient, and it costs it $14 to make each Gadget.
- Producer C has a factory on top of a mountain in Wyoming, where it costs a fortune to bring in raw materials and to ship its products to New York, the largest market for Gadgets. It costs Producer C over $18 to make each Gadget.

If Gadgets are selling for $20 apiece, all three producers will operate at full capacity to sell as many as they can. Producer A makes a handsome $10 profit per Gadget, Producer B makes a $6 profit per Gadget, and even Producer C can make a $2 profit per Gadget; therefore, the entire industry will run at full speed.

But if prices were to drop to $16 per Gadget, Producer C would lose $2 per Gadget and would probably stop producing them. If prices fell further to $13, Producer B would suddenly begin to lose money; if prices remained at this level for very long, Producer B would also have to cut its losses and stop making Gadgets. The principle is now clearly established: As prices decline, more and more producers will drop out of the business because they can't make a profit by producing Gadgets.

As these producers stop producing, the supply of Gadgets goes down. In other words:

"If you're losing money on every item you sell, you can't make it up on volume."

—An astute producer

Conversely, two years later, if the price of Gadgets starts to rise again, many of these producers or new producers will open up their factories and start making Gadgets again as soon as it becomes profitable to do so. Therefore, the basic relationship between supply and price is the exact opposite of that between price and demand: *Producers will make (supply) more Gadgets at a higher price than they will at a lower price.*

This logic provides the basis for the next two laws of supply, demand, and price:

Law 3: *If price goes **up**, supply will go **up**.*
Law 4: *If price goes **down**, supply will go **down**.*

How Demand Affects Price. The U.S. automobile market is a good example of the effects of changing demand patterns on prices. A division of an American car maker, General Engines, Inc., is producing 5,000 cars every month and is selling 5,000 cars every month at the price of $10,000. Their car competes with a Japanese imported car, the Saki; 2,000 of these cars are made and sold per month at the same price. But when the major automobile magazines and the *Consumer Guide to Japanese Imports* come out with a barrage of articles that proclaim the unbelievable quality of the new Saki, consumers rush to the nearest dealer to get one. Two things happen immediately.

First, the Saki dealer gets 5,000 orders for new cars against a supply of only 2,000 Sakis. It will take several months for the

Japanese car producer to gear their production level up to 5,000 cars per month, even if they start immediately. In the meantime, a shortage exists.

What will happen to the price of Sakis? The price will rise and will continue to rise until it hits a point at which some other car represents a better deal for the consumer. If $10,000 was a good price before the Saki's new quality image became widely known, consumers may now think the Saki is still a bargain at $12,000—maybe even $13,000. But if the price climbs up to equal the price of a BMW, the Saki won't compare very well anymore and the price will stabilize somewhere below that level. But until that price is reached, *increased demand will cause the price to rise.*

The second result isn't so pleasant. General Engines just lost 3,000 customers to the new Saki. Although General Engines has a constant flow of 5,000 cars per month coming from the factory, they have only 2,000 orders for their new car, the McVette. The American factory cannot adjust their production volume down any faster than the Japanese factory can adjust their volume up. Therefore, there is a significant excess of McVettes due to sharply lower demand.

What will happen to the price of McVettes? The dealers, whose lots are now filled with unsold inventory, will immediately start to discount the prices of McVettes to generate some additional sales. "Cash-back" deals, 2 percent financing, the elimination of "dealer prep" charges, and real price reductions will abound to stimulate sales. This discounting will continue until the price reaches a point at which the McVette is viewed as a bargain compared with other cars at the same price. But until that price is reached, *reduced demand will cause the price to fall.* This leads us to the next two laws of supply, demand, and price:

Law 5: *If demand goes down, price will go down.*
Law 6: *If demand goes up, price will go up.*

How Supply Affects Price. The actions of the Organization of Petroleum Exporting Countries (OPEC) and the worldwide reactions of the oil industry represent the most vivid, real-life examples of the relationship between the supply and price of a commodity. To set the stage, the United States is the largest oil consumer in the world, but does not produce enough oil to meet its own demand. Therefore, the United States must import foreign oil from several countries, including the countries that belong to OPEC.

This story of supply and price begins in 1973, when the Arab nations of OPEC placed an embargo on oil to the United States. The United States no longer had access to oil from the OPEC nations; in other words, our supply had been cut off. The obvious result was a shortage of oil.

In the automobile example in the last section, a shortage was created when a surge in Saki demand outstripped the existing supply. In this example, a shortage was created when the supply was cut back to a point well below the demand. But the effect of a shortage on price is the same whether the shortage develops from too much demand or too little supply: The price goes up until consumers can find a suitable substitute.

In the case of the OPEC embargo, there were no immediate substitutes for oil on the horizon. Thus, the price quadrupled from about $3 per barrel in 1973 to over $12 per barrel by 1979. In 1979, the Iranian revolution produced another "supply shock." Iran's instability actually caused the supply of oil to be cut off to the rest of the world, but the *fear* of an even greater supply shortage sent oil prices from $12 in 1979 to over $30 per barrel in 1980.

In recent years, we have also witnessed the opposite happen to the oil supply. The OPEC nations continued to produce too much oil for the existing market demand. As the world became flooded with oil and buyers could meet their needs from many sources, OPEC had to compete in the market to sell their oil and the price came tumbling down.

We can now complete the list of the laws of supply, demand, and price by including the last two laws: the laws of supply and price, which OPEC forgot in their desire to maintain high prices while increasing the supply at the same time:

Law 7: *If supply goes up, price will go down.*
Law 8: *If supply goes down, price will go up.*

These are the laws of supply, demand, and price. They can be trusted in any economic situation and represent the foundation of everything an investor needs to know about economics. When the newspaper or the evening news features a story on anything from a war to a foreign trade policy, the impact of the event on different parts of the economy or on financial markets can be assessed by asking:

• What will this do to supply?
• What will this do to demand?
• What will this do to price?

In the next section, we show that if any one of these questions can be answered, they all can be answered. This can be done by linking the laws of supply, demand, and price together into a chain of predictable events.

THE BASIC BUSINESS CYCLE: A MATTER OF PUTTING THE LAWS TOGETHER

The oil example in the last section poses some fascinating questions. In the 1970s, OPEC curtailed supply, raised oil prices, and was clearly in control of the world markets. By the mid-1980s, the world was awash with oil, prices had plummeted to $12 per barrel, and OPEC was scrambling to keep their member nations from cheating on production quotas and driving prices down again. What changed the oil world so dramatically?

The answer lies in the eight laws that we just described. As oil prices soared and then collapsed, we went through a complete business cycle in the oil industry that can be defined exactly by these eight laws. We can walk through this cycle step by step, using the laws as guideposts.

- *Step 1:* OPEC curtails the supply of oil to the United States, and the price of oil goes up. (Law 8: If supply goes down, price goes up.)

- *Step 2:* When the price of oil goes up, the potential profit from exploration for oil in the United States goes up. Thus, money comes out of the woodwork to finance oil well drilling, and U.S. oil producers find and supply much more oil. (Law 3: If price goes up, supply goes up.)

- *Step 3:* At the same time, when the price of oil soars, consumers take action to save money. They conserve energy by driving less, buying more fuel-efficient cars, and turning down thermostats. Higher oil prices also throw us into a recession, which reduces the industrial demand for oil. In addition, substitute energy sources (solar heating, wood stoves, etc.) are installed. The result is a lower level of demand for OPEC oil. (Law 1: If price goes up, demand goes down.)

- *Step 4:* The combined economic forces of higher supply (Step 2) and lower demand (Step 3) finally push oil prices down. (Law 7: If supply goes up, price goes down; and Law 5: If demand goes down, price goes down.) At this point in the cycle, oil prices fall sharply, as they did in early 1986, when the price of oil dropped from $28 to less than $12 per barrel in just a few months. But then the remaining laws come into play.

- *Step 5:* The sharp decline in oil prices makes almost all exploration ventures unprofitable, and drilling activity in the United States comes to a standstill. Oil that was discovered earlier in the cycle is kept in wells and is not brought to market at such a low price. The supply of oil is sharply reduced. (Law 4: If price goes down, supply goes down.)

- *Step 6:* With prices falling and gasoline prices below $1 per gallon for the first time in years, conservation efforts are discarded or severely cut back: "No need to conserve now!" Solar projects are abandoned, racy cars come back into fashion, the economy picks up because people have more money to spend on things other than gas and oil, and demand for oil starts to rise again. (Law 2: If price goes down, demand goes up.)

- *Step 7:* The combined pressures of a lower supply of oil (Step 5) and a higher demand for oil (Step 6) cause oil prices to begin

Figure 4-2. *The Business Cycle for Oil*

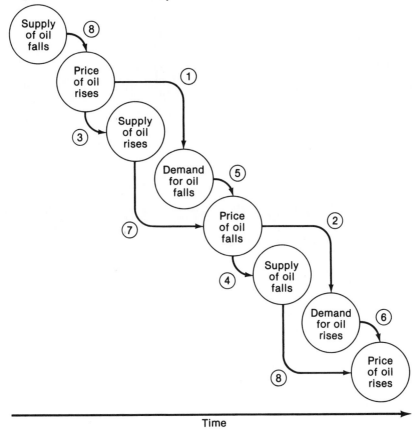

Time

to rise again. (Law 8: If supply goes down, price goes up; and Law 6: If demand goes up, price goes up.)

This completes one full business cycle; we are now right back where we started, with oil prices rising. But there is one big difference. Now when the price of oil starts to rise, we can clearly see and *predict* the basic sequence of events that is certain to follow because of the absolute reliability of the laws of supply, demand, and price.

Figure 4-2 depicts the sequence of events described in the oil cycle. The numbers on the chart represent the pertinent laws behind the cause-and-effect relationship.

Chapter 5

The Goods and Services Cycle: The Laws of Supply, Demand, and Price in Action

We can now define the basic business cycle for any good or service that is bought or sold in any market environment in which the laws of supply, demand, and price are free to operate.

First, we can redraw Figure 4-2 to apply to all goods by substituting "supply of goods falls" for "supply of oil falls," and so on. Then we replace the words "rises" and "falls" with arrows (↑ ↓), as appropriate. Figure 5-1 now shows the preliminary business cycle for goods.

Next, we need to define the terms "demand" and "supply" when applied specifically to goods produced in a free and competitive business climate.

THE DEMAND FOR GOODS

Demand for goods represents the total quantity of a good that consumers will buy if there is sufficient supply at the right price. Demand generally has two components: *consumption* (or *usage*) and *inventory change*.

Consumption

The consumption component is the quantity that customers will actually use for its designed purpose—for example, the

Figure 5-1. *The Business Cycle for Goods: Preliminary*

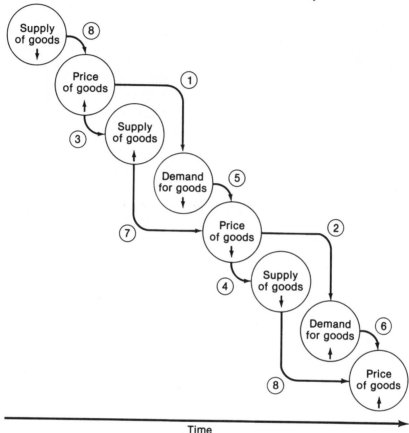

number of tires that will be installed on automobiles actually coming off an assembly line.

Inventory Change

The inventory change component is the quantity of goods (let's say tires) that Ford orders from Goodyear that is over or under the actual quantity needed to meet the automobile production schedule. Suppose that Ford needs 12,000 tires for 3,000 cars, but Ford's management wants to have an extra inventory of 4,000 tires on hand because they are predicting a sudden surge in Taurus orders or think that tire prices are going up. Ford's demand for tires from Goodyear will be 12,000 tires for immediate use on cars plus 4,000 tires to build up their inventory—or 16,000 tires.

But two months later, when Ford sees that the Taurus surge has failed to materialize, they may decide to reduce their inventories. So, their next order to Goodyear will be 12,000 tires for immediate use on cars, less 4,000 tires that they will use out of their own inventory—or 8,000 tires. So, Ford was trying to manage its inventories by first building and then reducing its inventory of tires. But while Ford was simply adjusting its inventories, Goodyear's managers were tearing their hair out. Their stable production plan for 12,000 tires per month had just increased by 33 percent to 16,000 tires, even though the demand for cars hadn't changed at all. Then just as Goodyear geared up for higher production, their orders dropped by 50 percent to 8,000 tires.

Although this is a hypothetical example, it is easy to see how demand for a particular product or an entire industry can undergo significant periods of expansion and contraction based only on buyers' decisions to build or reduce inventory. When an industry gets overheated and everyone builds inventory at the same time that consumption increases, total demand moves up sharply. At the end of the boom, if people cut back on their inventories and consumption falls at the same time, total demand falls off very significantly from the twofold decline. This psychology of building inventories while consumption rises and reducing inventories to save money when consumption falls represents the basic core of the business cycle for goods.

The general equation for demand can be expressed as shown in Figure 5-2.

Figure 5-2.

Total Demand		Usage	+ or −	Change in Inventory
16,000 tires	=	12,000 tires	+	4,000 tires
8,000 tires	=	12,000 tires	−	4,000 tires

Economists refer to this definition of demand as Apparent Consumption.

THE SUPPLY OF GOODS

The Supply concept is often misunderstood, so it's important to distinguish between apparent supply (the amount provided to meet today's demand) and true supply (the available capacity to produce), which is the supply that is used in the laws of supply and demand.

Apparent Supply of Goods

Every month in which some quantity of products (let's say cars) is bought, that same quantity of cars is obviously sold or supplied by someone. Apparent supply is the number of cars provided by producers to meet the demand, or Apparent Consumption. Since sales must equal purchases, apparent supply always equals Apparent Consumption.

The apparent supply of a product generally has three components: *domestic shipments, imports,* and *exports.* For example, if the U.S. market demand for steel was 6 million tons per month, U.S. steel producers might make and *ship* 5 million tons, sending 4 million tons to the U.S. market and *exporting* 1 million tons to foreign countries. The remaining 2 million tons needed by the U.S. market would be fulfilled by steel that was *imported* from foreign countries. Figure 5-3 shows the composition of apparent supply in this example.

The important point is that demand and apparent supply are always equal, since apparent supply represents the sources of supply of those products that were actually provided to meet

Figure 5-3.

Apparent Supply	=	Total Shipments	− Exports	+ Imports
6 million tons	=	5 million tons	− 1 million tons	+ 2 million tons

demand. The term "supply" as used in our business cycle analysis is a completely different economic concept.

The True Supply of Goods: Capacity Plus Net Imports

The true supply of any product is the total potential supply of that product. It usually means the physical capacity, or production limit, of the manufacturing plants of an industry. However, true supply can be defined by other means as well.

If OPEC jointly commits to produce no more than 18 million barrels of oil per day and the world believes that OPEC will stick to that limit, that becomes the supply of oil. And if demand exceeds that supply, the price will rise in accordance with the laws of supply and demand.

If the United States put up a trade barrier restricting the importation of certain products, the supply of those products would be constrained until someone in the United States put up a new plant and added capacity (supply) to the industry. Under the laws of supply and demand, this sequence of events would produce a very predictable pricing scenario. When the United States put up the import restriction reducing the supply of those products, the price of the products would rise (Law 8). Later, when U.S. producers thought that they would make a fortune from the outrageously high price of the products and added capacity (and increased supply), the price would fall when the new plants opened for business (Law 7).

The true supply of any product made available to the U.S. market (or any other market) can be defined as having two components: domestic capacity and net imports allowed. To clarify this concept, imagine a world with only two nations: the United States and Foreign Country X, which represents the sum of all other foreign countries with which the United States trades goods and services. In this hypothetical situation, the supply and demand for cars is summarized in Figure 5-4, and is graphically depicted in Figure 5-5.

Starting at the bottom left-hand corner of Figure 5-5, the United States has the capacity to produce 130,000 cars, but at the moment has idled the capacity for 50,000 cars and is only

Figure 5-4. *The Supply of Cars: Illustration*

U.S. market demand	100,000 cars
Foreign market demand	40,000 cars
U.S. production capacity	130,000 cars
Foreign production capacity	100,000 cars
Maximum imports allowed into the United States	30,000 cars
Maximum U.S. exports allowed into Foreign Country X	10,000 cars

producing 80,000 cars. Of the 80,000 cars produced and shipped, 70,000 go to the U.S. market and 10,000 are exported to the Foreign Country X market.

At the top right-hand corner of the chart, we can see that Foreign Country X has the capacity to make 100,000 cars, but is now producing only 60,000 cars and has idle capacity to make 40,000 more cars. Of the 60,000 cars made in Foreign Country X, 30,000 cars are shipped to its own market and 30,000 are sent to the U.S. market.

The U.S. market demand for 100,000 cars would be met with 70,000 cars from the United States and 30,000 cars from Foreign Country X. The foreign demand for 40,000 cars would be met with 30,000 cars from Foreign Country X producers and 10,000 cars from the United States. U.S. producers would operate at a capacity utilization rate of 61.5 percent (80,000 ÷ 130,000), and Foreign Country X producers would operate at a utilization rate of 60 percent (60,000 ÷ 100,000).

It becomes clear that if we were to combine the U.S. and Foreign Country X production capacities, that total capacity (230,000 cars) represents the total possible supply to the combined world markets. Of course, this total must balance the individual supply totals for the United States and Foreign Country X, respectively. If we recognize that each country may have import trade restrictions in place at any time, the total supply available to each country is the sum of its own internal capacity plus the imports allowed into that country at any given time, less the cars that the country chooses to export to the other country.

Here, the total or true supply of cars to the U.S. market is

Figure 5-5. *The Supply Flow of Cars: Illustration*

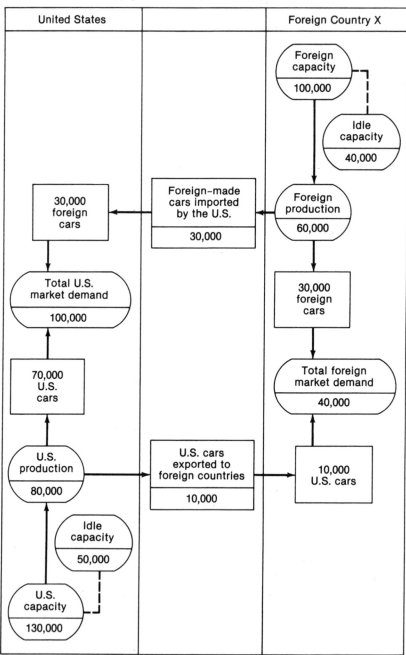

the U.S. capacity (130,000 cars) plus allowed imports (30,000 cars), less U.S. exports of 10,000 cars—a total supply of 150,000 cars.

The total supply of cars to the foreign market is the Foreign Country X capacity (100,000 cars) plus the limit of U.S. cars that Foreign Country X allows to be imported (10,000 cars), less the cars that Foreign Country X chooses to export to the United States (30,000 cars)—a total supply of 80,000 cars. The total supply schedule for each country is given in Figure 5-6.

From this example, we can see that the United States could *increase* the total supply of a good to our market in any one of three ways:

• By expanding our domestic capacity
• By restricting exports to other countries
• By allowing more imports from foreign countries

Since we know that when supply increases, prices tend to decrease, all of these actions would have to be considered *deflationary* actions.

Similarly, we could *decrease* the supply of a product into our market:

• By reducing our domestic capacity
• By creating incentives to export more products abroad
• By restricting foreign imports into the United States

By reducing supply, these actions are *inflationary* and tend to drive up U.S. prices for this product. We expand on this concept when we discuss international trade and the value of the dollar.

Total Supply Equation. The total supply of a product to the U.S. market can be expressed as:

$$\text{Total True Supply} = \text{Capacity} + \text{Imports} - \text{Exports}$$

Figure 5-6. *World Total Supply of Cars*

	The United States	Foreign Country X	World Total
U.S. capacity	130,000	—	130,000
Foreign capacity	—	100,000	100,000
U.S. exports to Foreign Country X	− 10,000	+ 10,000	0
Foreign imports to the United States	+ 30,000	− 30,000	0
Total supply	150,000	80,000	230,000

Another insight can be gained by examining the total supply equation more closely.

The U.S. balance of trade can be defined by the equation:

U.S. Balance of Trade = Exports − Imports

If exports minus imports is a positive number, the trade balance is positive and we have a trade *surplus*. If imports exceed exports, the trade balance is negative and we have a trade *deficit*. A *trade deficit is defined as imports minus exports,* and a *trade surplus is defined as exports minus imports.* Using these definitions, we can now substitute the trade surplus or deficit into the supply equation:

• *Condition 1*—If we are running a trade deficit:

Since: Total Supply = Capacity + (Imports − Exports)

Then: Total Supply = Capacity + (Trade Deficit)

• *Condition 2*—If we are running a trade surplus:

Since: Total Supply = Capacity + (Imports − Exports)

Then: Total Supply = Capacity − (Exports − Imports)

And: Total Supply = Capacity − (Trade Surplus)

These two equations help to explain why politicians are not always horrified by a trade deficit. When the United States runs an increasing trade deficit, the supply of goods into the United States *increases,* which helps keep prices low (Law 7: If supply goes up, price goes down). Conversely, when we run an increasing trade surplus, the total supply of goods into the United States decreases and puts upward pressure on prices (Law 8: If supply goes down, price goes up).

Two More Laws for Goods Only

To finalize the business cycle for goods, we'll make just two additions to our eight laws of supply and demand:

Law 9: *If demand goes up, supply will go up.*

It takes more than a price increase for their products to cause management of manufacturing businesses to invest in new plant capacity. Management must be convinced that the quantity of their product demanded by the market will increase substantially in the future and will provide enough volume to use the new plant efficiently and justify the investment. Since we are a society of big businesses, venture capitalists, and entrepreneurs seeking profit opportunities, an increase in demand that appears to be a long-term trend is usually met by new plant capacity that is added by some producer in a fairly short time frame.

Law 10: *If demand goes down, supply will go down (but later).*

When a recession takes place either in a single industry or in the entire U.S. economy, demand for products falls off and the apparent supply falls off in lockstep as producers cut back production to avoid being stuck with inventories of products that they cannot sell.

But the supply of goods—the physical capacity of producers' manufacturing plants—usually remains the same for quite some time after demand has fallen off. There are several reasons for this:

- Managers are eternally optimistic and are usually certain that the downturn is temporary and that demand will rise again soon.

- There are real exit costs in closing down a facility that often make it more profitable to leave a plant idle than to close it down permanently.

- In many cases, manufacturing facilities are convertible in the sense that they can be modified to produce alternative products for markets that may not be undergoing a recession at the time. For example, steel products used in drilling oil wells could be dropped when oil prices fall and drilling levels decline; instead, steel products that are used in cars or planes—industries that would benefit from lower oil prices—could be made.

- If the plant is relatively new and modern, managers will simply "mothball" the facility until the recession is over rather than give up on a relatively recent investment decision.

So when demand begins to fall, the true supply of goods remains the same. Since this idle capacity represents a latent supply of goods that can enter the market at any time—if the price is right—industry pricing remains depressed for a prolonged period of time. Any small increases in demand and price will be quickly met with the reopening of an idle facility, which will push prices down again.

If the recession lasts long enough, the industry will eventually "rationalize" their facilities—that is, systematically close down the most inefficient plants, sell off the equipment, and reduce the true capacity of the industry. Then, with supply and demand for the industry back in balance, the business cycle is ready for the next upturn.

Development of the Business Cycle for Goods

We can now complete the picture for the business cycle for goods by making two changes to Figure 5-1, which was shown in the beginning of this chapter.

Figure 5-7. *The Business Cycle for Goods*

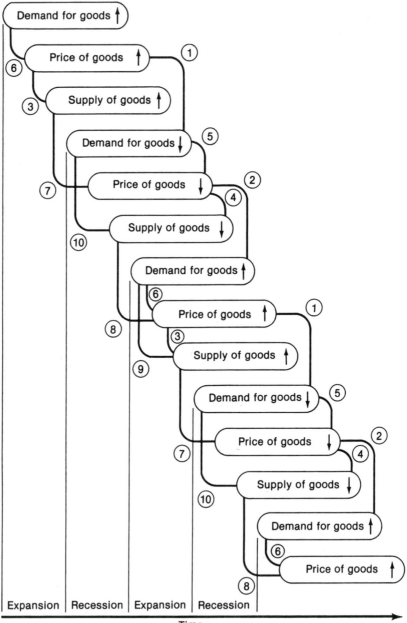

- We add Laws 9 and 10.
- We can identify periods of economic expansion and economic recession by defining these periods as follows:
  - —An expansion begins when the demand for goods hits bottom and begins to turn *up*.
  - —A recession begins when the demand for goods peaks out and begins to turn *down*.

The result is shown in Figure 5-7, which displays two complete business cycles for goods using the first ten laws of supply and demand.

Chapter 6

The Money Cycle: Enter the Fed

DEFINITIONS

As we will shortly see, most but not all of the basic laws of supply and demand also apply to the business cycle for money. But first, some additional definitions are in order.

The money available to finance all of the country's economic activities is known as the nation's *money supply*. The total money supply is usually referred to by the abbreviations M1, M2, and M3, which represent different portions of the money supply.

The M1 money supply is the extremely liquid cash in the system, such as the money in checking accounts and traveler's checks. This accounts for about 20 percent of the total money supply. The M2 money supply consists of the M1 supply plus the bulk (another 60 percent) of the remaining money in our financial system. M2, which includes the money in savings accounts and money funds, represents approximately 80 percent of the total. M3 is the total money supply, which comprises the M2 total plus some additional specific pockets of money, such as large savings deposits, institutional money funds, and government savings bonds.

A breakdown of the money supply that shows the specific

components of, and the amounts of money in, each category as of September 1988 is shown in Figure 6-1.

In our studies, we have found that M2 is the best indicator of changes in the money supply; all specific references to historical changes in the money supply will refer to M2.

The "price of money" is a general term that refers to the price, or interest rate, that you have to pay to borrow that money for some specific purpose and length of time. Taken together, several interest rates reflect the interest rate structure of the economy at any point in time. They range from the rates on overnight bank loans to large businesses with fluctuating daily cash needs, to long-term T-bond rates and 30-year home mortgage rates. Municipal bonds offer tax-free rates, and banks all over the country compete on certificate of deposit rates. Later, we will use seven specific interest rates to track our position in the final business cycle for the purpose of managing investment portfolios.

Figure 6-1. *The U.S. Money Supply and Its Components ($ Billions)*

Currency	$ 207.2	
Traveler's checks	7.2	
Demand deposits ($ in checking accounts)	290.0	
NOW accounts	278.1	
M1 total	$ 782.5	20%
Savings deposits	$ 433.9	
Small time deposits	985.3	
Money market deposit accounts	517.2	59%
Money market funds	230.9	
Overnight repos (repurchase agreements)	65.6	
Overnight Eurodollars	15.9	
M2 total	$3,031.3	79%
Large time deposits	$ 515.8	
Term repos	121.0	21%
Term Eurodollars	99.5	
Institutional money funds	84.0	
M3 total (total liquid assets)	$3,851.6	100%

Source: Barron's, September 19, 1988.

The *demand for money* is simply the monetary expression of the aggregate need or desire to finance the national demand for goods. It is reflected in the amount of money borrowed by all consumers, corporations, and government agencies.

DEVELOPMENT OF THE BUSINESS CYCLE FOR MONEY

If money were similar to goods—that is, produced by many suppliers, bought and sold in a free market environment, and driven by a profit incentive—all of the first eight laws of supply and demand would apply to money, as well as goods. Then we could simply substitute the word "money" for the word "goods" in Figure 5-7 to show the business cycle for money. However, economic reality is not that simple.

There is one significant conceptual difference between money and goods. Money is created, managed, and controlled by an absolute monopoly known as the Fed, so it is far from a free market commodity. In addition, the motivation of the Fed's participation in the system is not to make a profit, but to steer the economy in the appropriate direction to achieve one or more of our national economic goals (economic growth, full employment, stable prices, a favorable balance of trade, and a reasonable budget deficit).

The price of money, or interest rate, is still determined by supply and demand. However, while the demand for money is generated by everyone in both the private and public sectors of the economy, the supply of money is driven by motivating forces different from those that govern the supply of goods. With this in mind, we can now develop the laws of supply and demand as they relate to money.

The Laws of Supply and Demand for Money

Law 11: *If the price of money goes **up**, the **demand** for money will go **down**.*
Law 12: *If the price of money goes **down**, the **demand** for money will go **up**.*

These two laws parallel Laws 1 and 2 for goods. Are you more interested in financing a house when mortgage rates (the price of money) are 13 percent or 8½ percent? Enough said.

Law 13: *If the **demand** for money goes **up**, the **price** of money will go **up**.*
Law 14: *If the **demand** for money goes **down**, the **price** of money will go **down**.*

Laws 13 and 14 are identical to their counterparts for goods, except that the seller of money is your banker, savings and loan association, or car dealer. When the demand for what they have (money) goes up, you can be sure that the price (the interest rate) will also go up.

Law 15: *If the **supply** of money goes **up**, the **price** of money will go **down**.*
Law 16: *If the **supply** of money goes **down**, the **price** of money will go **up**.*

These two laws match laws 7 and 8 for goods. Even though the Fed controls the supply of money, the *effect* of any changes in money supply on the money cycle will be identical to the *effect* of an increase or decrease in the supply of goods on the goods cycle—that is, an excess of money will push the price (interest rates) down, and vice versa.

These six laws are conceptually identical to the laws that apply to goods. The major difference between the goods cycle and the money cycle is that the Fed's actions are the primary cause of increases or decreases in the money supply, whereas the free market controls the supply of goods.

Causes of Changes in the Money Supply

If the supply of money behaved as the supply of goods, the supply of money would rise when the price of money rose and would fall when the price of money fell. However, this is not the case. In fact, the money supply is not linked to either the demand for money or the price of money. Instead, it is controlled by the Fed's response to changes in the business cycle for goods. The Fed generally operates under one of two distinct monetary policies, depending on our economic situation at the time.

Monetary Policy 1: Fighting Inflation. When the economy overheats, demand exceeds supply, and prices begin to rise at a rapid rate, the Fed steps in to reduce inflation. It does this by *reducing the supply of money,* since the classical definition of inflation is "too much money chasing too few goods." This definition is a variation on Law 17, which states that, all other things being equal, a reduction in the money supply will reduce the demand for goods and, thus, the price of goods will decline because there is less money to spend on available goods.

Law 17: *If the **supply** of money goes **down,** the **demand** for goods and the **price** of goods will go **down.***

We can now add Law 17 to our model. We can also add the Fed's monetary policy for fighting inflation.

Monetary Policy 1: *If the **price** of goods goes **up** too fast, the supply of money goes **down** (by Fed policy).*

Monetary Policy 2: Fighting Recession. When we enter a recession, demand for goods falls off, inflation and interest rates come down since no one is investing or buying houses or cars, and thousands of people are laid off. The Fed then steps in to stimulate economic growth and put people back to work. The Fed *increases the supply of money* by injecting money into the banking system and providing easy credit at attractively low interest rates to encourage people to buy goods and services. Here, again, the supply of money is driven by a part of the business cycle for goods—specifically, the demand for goods or, in this case, the lack of it. Therefore, the Fed's second policy is:

Monetary Policy 2: *If the **demand** for goods goes **down** too far or for too long, the **supply** of money goes **up** (by Fed policy).*

The Fed takes this action in acknowledgment of Law 18, which is the mirror image of Law 17.

Law 18: *If the **supply** of money goes **up**, the **demand** for goods and the **price** of goods will go **up**.*

We've referred to the actions of the Fed as policies—*not* laws of supply and demand. The laws that we've described are immutable and will always dominate any economic market. On the other hand, the Fed's policies are a function of the Board of Federal Reserve Governors and, as such, are subject to political influences, external pressures, and the collective wisdom of many economists who provide the Fed with multiple points of view and recommendations. Therefore, the Fed's policies are subject to the human errors of overestimating or underestimating a situation and/or the economic response to policy actions that the Fed takes.

Over the last 40 years, many of the Fed's policy responses to economic conditions have been fairly appropriate under the prevailing conditions. However, serious errors have occurred in the past and may well occur in the future. For example, the

Figure 6-2. *The Business Cycle for Money*

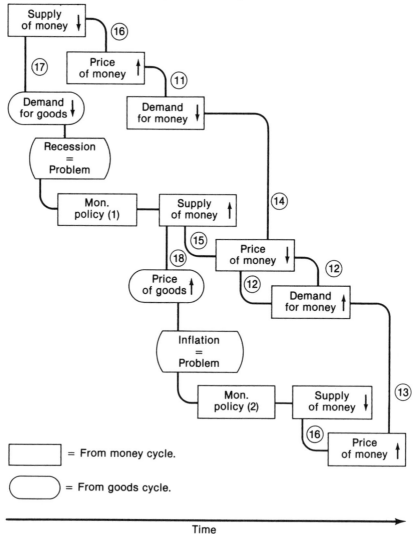

depression after the crash of 1929 was prolonged for years because the money supply was not increased sufficiently until 1933.

Using these new laws and monetary policies, we can now construct the business cycle for money. It is identical to the business cycle for goods, with two exceptions: (1) There is no cause-and-effect relationship between the price and supply of money, as there is for goods, and (2) there are now two cause-and-effect linkages between the business cycle for goods and the business cycle for money, as shown in Figure 6-2.

Chapter 7

Putting the Cycles Together

We just established two relationships that link the business cycle for goods with the business cycle for money. To assemble the combined business cycle, we now have to include a few more linkages or connecting relationships. Some of these relationships involve events in the goods cycle that *cause* changes in the money cycle, and some involve events in the money cycle that *cause* changes in the goods cycle. We discuss each linkage separately and then build a new business cycle chart that combines the goods and money cycles.

CONNECTIONS BETWEEN THE GOODS AND MONEY CYCLES

Monetary Policies 1 and 2 showed that the Fed raises or lowers the money supply to fight either inflation or a recession. Whenever this happens, a number of other events are triggered throughout both the goods and money cycles. The easiest way to develop these interrelationships is to track the step-by-step consequences of both a period of high inflation and a recession.

The Inflation Chain of Events

The inflation chain of events proceeds as follows:

1. An overheated economy produces an inflation rate that is unacceptably high, so the Fed cuts back on the money supply (Monetary Policy 1).

2. The reduced supply of money causes interest rates (the price of money) to rise (Law 16).

3. When interest rates rise, several things happen in the goods cycle. First, *demand for goods falls* along with the demand for money (Law 11) because consumers can't afford or simply don't want to pay higher rates for homes, cars, appliances, or furniture. In addition, the *supply of goods is negatively affected* because new manufacturing facilities are usually large investments, and higher interest rates will cost millions in extra interest payments. Thus, both the demand and supply of goods are reduced as a result of higher interest rates, as stated in the following two laws:

Law 19: *If the* **price** *of money goes* **up,** *the* **demand** *for goods goes* **down.**

Law 20: *If the* **price** *of money goes* **up,** *the* **supply** *of goods goes* **down.**

---

4. When consumers feel the pinch of tighter money and slow down their spending activities, the prices of goods start to fall (Law 5). The chairman of the Fed, who took a lot of heat because he drove interest rates up, now starts to see the fruits of his efforts: a lower inflation rate, which was his ultimate goal in cutting the money supply.

5. When consumers stop buying cars and houses, the national need for money to finance those items, or total borrowing, declines, which gives us the next law:

Law 21: *If the* **demand** *for goods goes* **down,** *the* **demand** *for money goes* **down.**

When the demand for money declines, the price of money quickly declines (Law 14). So the Fed's cutting of the money supply, which initially raised interest rates, now produces a decline in both inflation and interest rates by lowering the demand for goods and money.

6. There is still more good news about interest rates. Not only do interest rates decline because of a lower demand for goods (which lowered the demand for money), but they also decline because of a decline in inflation. The fact that interest rates tend to follow inflation—both up and down—is one of the key relationships that drives the business cycle. As such, this relationship deserves a more in-depth explanation.

Suppose that you are trying to eke out a living as a banker. You are currently lending money to your customers at the competitive rate of 7 percent per year. You forecast that your operating costs at the bank will escalate about 4 percent next year—your economist's forecast for inflation next year. Thus, you will make a *real* profit of 3 percent on the money that you lend out—your 7 percent interest profit, less the extra 4 percent that it will cost you to run the bank next year.

The 3 percent profit figure happens to be the long-term "real" interest rate, or interest rate before considering inflation, that lending institutions have averaged over the last several decades. It is considered the "real" price of money that the banker earns for going to the trouble and taking the risk of lending money to people who may or may not be creditworthy. In this case, by lending money at 7 percent, you have made your "real" interest profit of 3 percent and covered your 4 percent cost increases projected for the next year.

But what happens if inflation starts to accelerate rapidly, as it did in 1979 and 1980, to an annualized inflation rate of over 15 percent? In this situation, you have two choices. Knowing that your costs will go up by 15 percent, you can continue to lend money at 7 percent, which will give you (and your unhappy shareholders) an operating loss of 8 percent, or you can raise your lending rate to a level that will give you the 3 percent "real" interest rate and will also cover the costs of the higher inflation rate.

You don't have to be Donald Trump to make this decision. You will raise your lending rates to 3 percent (real rate) plus 15 percent (anticipated inflation rate)—or 18 percent. Although this seems to be an exaggerated example, for most of 1980 and 1981, the prime lending rate fluctuated between 16 percent and 21 percent. Similarly, when inflation rates drop down to 5 percent or 6 percent, lending institutions cannot justify 18 percent or 20 percent interest rates on the loans that they make; interest rates fall accordingly.

In our inflation-fighting scenario, when the Fed curtails the money supply and drives the inflation rate down, the higher interest rates seen earlier are no longer justified and competitive pressures in the money-lending industry pull interest rates down to 3 percent plus the new *lower* inflation rate. This is a demonstration of Law 22.

Law 22: *If the **price** of goods goes **down**, the **price** of money goes **down**.*

When faced with high inflation, the Fed cuts back on the money supply, which eventually reduces inflation and interest rates. However, the reduced supply of money and higher interest rates also reduce the demand for goods. In other words, the actions necessary to slow inflation have the unfortunate effect of driving the economy into a recession. So now the Fed must deal with the problem of ending the recession to get the economy going again.

The Recession Chain of Events

As you would expect, this chain of events is the mirror image of the sequence of events triggered by inflation.

1. An economy that is in a deep recession produces low demand for goods, lower prices, a soaring unemployment rate, and

federal budget deficit problems as tax revenues fall and unemployment and social costs rise. As the administration is under severe political pressure to "do something," the Fed eventually increases the money supply (Monetary Policy 2) even though it is an independent government agency and is not officially subject to political pressure.

2. The increased supply of money causes interest rates to decline still further (Law 15).

3. The availability of money at increasingly attractive interest rates, coupled with prices for goods that have been driven down by the recession, begins to take hold; people begin to buy goods again. Demand for goods begins to rise, as does the demand for money (Law 12). Businessmen finally find interest rates attractive enough to begin to reinvest in their businesses.

Law 23: *If the **price** of money goes **down,** the **demand** for goods goes **up.***
Law 24: *If the **price** of money goes **down,** the **supply** of goods goes **up.***

---

4. When consumers start buying again, they exert upward pressure on prices (Law 6); the new surge in demand and prices for goods allows production companies to begin hiring people again. The Fed is rewarded for its efforts by increased employment, higher corporate profits, and increased tax revenues.

5. When consumers start buying again, the demand for money (borrowing) increases to finance their pent-up desires to purchase things.

Law 25: *If the **demand** for goods goes **up,** the **demand** for money goes **up.***

---

6. Finally, as the economy moves into a full-fledged recovery, inflation will begin to resume its upward trend. When this happens, our lenders will simply raise their lending rates to cover the anticipated new inflation rate, as described earlier.

Law 26: *If the **price** of goods goes **up**, the **price** of money goes **up**.*

THE COMBINED BUSINESS CYCLE

This completes the basic set of relationships between the goods and money sectors of the economy. By adding this group of linkages, we can complete the combined business cycle for goods and money, as shown in Figure 7-1.

What Does It All Mean?

If you look past the connecting lines and identification numbers, which are included here only to validate the cause-and-effect connections, and focus only on the events shown in the boxes of the chart, you will see a remarkably well-structured, orderly, and *repeating sequence of events,* as shown in Figure 7-2.

Since this sequence of events was derived entirely from proven economic laws and established governmental policies, we really have a *predictable,* repeating sequence of events, or *business cycle,* that is based on known cause-and-effect relationships. We can now convert the events of this business cycle into a Gantt chart similar to that used for the seasonal cycle (Figure 2-3). This transformation requires only two steps.

First, we can list the events in Figure 7-2 down the side of a chart and mark with dots when they occur, as we did for the seasonal cycle. The result is a preliminary Gantt chart of the business cycle, as shown in Figure 7-3.

Given this Gantt chart, we need to make only one more change. To set the stage for the analysis of major tops and

Figure 7-1. *The Combined Business Cycle*

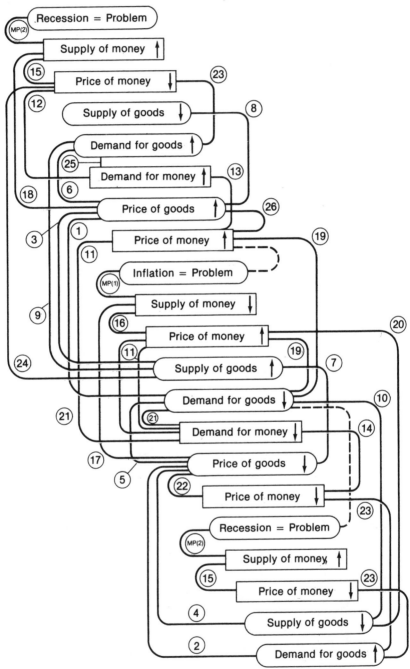

Figure 7-2. *Repeating Sequence of Events in the Combined Business Cycle*

1.	Recession becomes a problem
2.	The supply of money turns *up*
3.	The price of money falls
4.	The supply of goods turns *down*
5.	The demand for goods turns *up*
6.	The demand for money turns *up*
7.	The price of goods turns *up*
8.	The price of money turns *up*
9.	Inflation becomes a problem
10.	The supply of money turns *down*
11.	The price of money rises
12.	The supply of goods turns *up*
13.	The demand for goods turns *down*
14.	The demand for money turns *down*
15.	The price of goods turns *down*
16.	The price of money turns *down*
1.	Recession is a problem again and a new cycle begins

bottoms, or turning points, in the economy and financial markets, we need to change the names of the events in the business cycle to indicate tops (peaks) and bottoms (troughs) in each of the components of the cycle. Whenever an event "turns up," that component was previously going down, hit bottom, and then turned up. Every event in the cycle that is labeled "turns up" reflects a bottom for the component. Similarly, whenever an event "turns down," that component was previously going up, hit a peak, and then turned down. Each event labeled "turns down" signifies a peak for the component.

We can now refer to each event in the business cycle as a peak or a bottom.[1] The first event, "the supply of money turns up," will be replaced by "supply of money bottom"; the event labeled "the supply of money turns down" will be replaced by "supply of money peak"; and so on. We can also show periods of economic expansion and recession: "Demand for goods

---

[1] In later sections, we will talk about indicators that bottom out with some frequency. The author has used the term "bottom" here because of a personal dislike for the phrase "troughing out."

Figure 7-3. *Preliminary Gantt Chart*

Repeating Sequence of Events in the Combined Business Cycle	The Business Cycle
	────────── Time ──────────►
1. Recession becomes a problem	
2. The supply of money turns *up*	
3. The price of money falls	
4. The supply of goods turns *down*	
5. The demand for goods turns *up*	
6. The demand for money turns *up*	
7. The price of goods turns *up*	
8. The price of money turns *up*	
9. Inflation becomes a problem	
10. The supply of money turns *down*	
11. The price of money rises	
12. The supply of goods turns *up*	
13. The demand for goods turns *down*	
14. The demand for money turns *down*	
15. The price of goods turns *down*	
16. The price of money turns *down*	
1. Recession is a problem again and a new cycle begins	

bottom" indicates the beginning of an expansion, and "demand for goods peak" reflects the beginning of a recession.

The new business cycle chart is shown in Figure 7-4.

Next Steps

Although the sequence of events in the combined business cycle has been proven from a theoretical standpoint, it is not yet a practical tool for forecasting or making investment decisions. It is still cast in the economic terminology of the supply, demand, and prices of goods and money. But having established the validity of this business cycle, we can now convert it into a usable form. To do this, we need to (1) translate these economic events in the cycle into terms that we can recognize and

Figure 7-4. *Turning Point Gantt Chart*

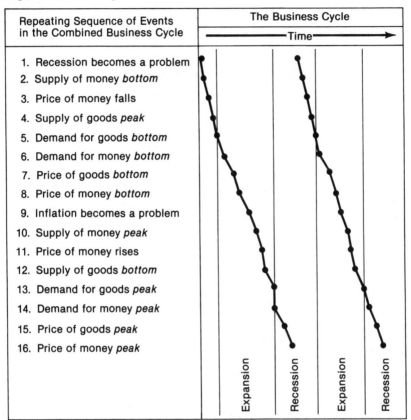

Repeating Sequence of Events in the Combined Business Cycle	The Business Cycle ——————Time—————→
1. Recession becomes a problem	
2. Supply of money *bottom*	
3. Price of money falls	
4. Supply of goods *peak*	
5. Demand for goods *bottom*	
6. Demand for money *bottom*	
7. Price of goods *bottom*	
8. Price of money *bottom*	
9. Inflation becomes a problem	
10. Supply of money *peak*	
11. Price of money rises	
12. Supply of goods *bottom*	
13. Demand for goods *peak*	
14. Demand for money *peak*	
15. Price of goods *peak*	
16. Price of money *peak*	Expansion Recession Expansion Recession

(2) convert them into specific indicators that are measured and reported on every month so that we can track our position in the business cycle at any time. We make this conversion to measurable indicators in the next chapter. Following that, we discuss the relationships that link the repeating sequence of events of the business cycle to the major tops and bottoms of the stock market, the bond market, and the gold market.

Chapter 8

Tracking the Complete Primary Business Cycle

To translate the business cycle developed in the last chapter (which we call the theoretical business cycle) into a practical business cycle that can be tracked and monitored on a monthly basis, we turn to one of the greatest sources of information in the world: the U.S. government. Virtually all economic and financial data of any relevance are reported by some branch of the government. For our purposes, we have used the Commerce Department as the prime source of economic data.

The Commerce Department publishes updated tables and charts for several hundred economic variables every month in a publication entitled the *Business Conditions Digest*. This publication, which is available for an annual subscription of $44 per year, is rich with economic and financial data. Unfortunately, data have no meaning unless they can be cast into a framework that allows analysis to be performed and conclusions to be reached.

The economists at the Commerce Department have constructed a basic economic framework for tracking and reporting hundreds of *actual, recorded* economic and financial statistics. In the first seven chapters of this book, we have constructed a proven, theoretically sound business cycle framework based on the supply, demand, and price relationships for goods and money. The objective of this chapter is to marry these two frameworks to produce the Primary Business Cycle—a proven method of charting our position in the business cycle by tracking factual statistics within a sound theoretical framework.

CONVERTING THEORY TO STATISTICS

In the last chapter, Figure 7-4 listed the events of our theoretical business cycle. Two of these events, "inflation becomes a problem" and "recession becomes a problem," are intermediate events that cause the Fed to take action on the money supply and interest rates. These are not trackable events that can be recorded per se, but are situational events that trigger other events in the cycle.

The remaining events are explicitly defined turning points that consist of the peaks and bottoms of the six fundamental components of the theoretical business cycle, as shown in Figure 8-1.

First, we convert the turning points in each of these theoretical variables into their statistical counterparts, which are tracked and reported monthly by the government. We can then reconstruct the business cycle in terms of indicators that we can monitor every month.

The Supply of Money

We can begin our conversion from theoretical variables to trackable indicators with the supply of money. Earlier in the book, we discussed the various measurements of money supply: M1, M2, and M3. Our research has shown that the M1 money

Figure 8-1. *Theoretical Business Cycle Components*

The supply of money
The demand for money
The price of money
The supply of goods
The demand for goods
The price of goods

supply is too narrow to capture what is happening in the business cycle but that M3 is so broad that it masks cyclical events. However, the M2 money supply is an excellent cyclical indicator that is tracked every month by the Commerce Department. Thus, we can directly substitute M2 for the theoretical supply of money in the business cycle, as shown in Figure 8-2.

Figure 8-3 shows the history of the M2 money supply since 1952.

Figure 8-2.

Theoretical Cycle Event	Trackable Indicator Event
Supply of money peak	M2 money supply peak
Supply of money bottom	M2 money supply bottom

Figure 8-3. *The M2 Money Supply*

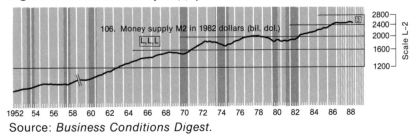

Source: *Business Conditions Digest.*

The Demand for Money

The Commerce Department tracks several monthly indicators that reflect both the level and the rate of change in the demand for money. These include such items as the amount of commercial loans, industrial loans, consumer loans, and money borrowed by state and local governments. However, there is an indicator of the demand for money that is particularly meaningful in terms of business cycle analysis: the ratio of consumer installment credit to personal income.

The ratio of consumer installment credit to personal income represents the degree to which consumers are borrowing against their annual income. Implicit in this ratio is the amount of confidence that consumers have in the future of the economy, as well as the irresponsibility that may be involved in overbor-rowing against one's income. This ratio is an excellent measure of the consumer's financial needs and can be used as a trackable indicator of the demand for money. (See Figure 8-4.)

The history of this indicator is shown in Figure 8-5.

Figure 8-4.

Theoretical Cycle Event	Trackable Indicator Event
Demand for money peak	Consumer credit ratio peak
Demand for money bottom	Consumer credit ratio bottom

Figure 8-5. *History of the Consumer Credit Ratio*

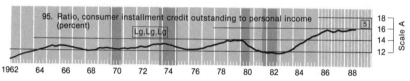

Source: *Business Conditions Digest.*

The Price of Money (Interest Rates)

The Interest Rate Structure. Conversion of the price of money variable to measurable indicators is a very straightfor-ward matter. These are several interest rates that are reported monthly and even weekly or daily in publications such as *Barron's* or the *Wall Street Journal.*

The only issue is selecting the interest rates to monitor. We have performed an extensive study on historical interest rates that produced some unusual findings, which are discussed more fully in a later section. However, one of the key findings was that focusing on only one interest rate, such as the prime rate or the T-bond rate, can generate very misleading signals. Another key finding was that in every business cycle, all fundamental interest rates reach peaks and bottoms together in a systematic pattern.

For example, if we were tracking only three interest rate measures, they would follow the pattern shown in Figure 8-6 in every full business cycle.

The sequence in which the interest rates reach peaks and bottoms and the time period in which they all reach turning points may not be the same in any two cycles; however, in every cycle, they *all* reach peaks and bottoms together. We have found that the interest rate situation can be assessed and that turning points can be clearly seen by tracking seven interest rates that are reported by the Commerce Department every month. These seven interest rates involve both long-term and short-term rates, government bonds, and private sector bonds. These seven interest rates are as follows:

- The federal funds rate
- The 91-day T-bill rate
- The prime rate
- The corporate bond rate
- The long-term T-bond rate
- The municipal bond rate
- The Federal Housing Administration (FHA) mortgage rate

Figure 8-6. *Illustration*

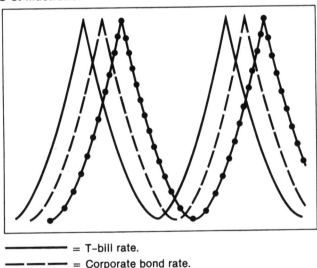

——————— = T–bill rate.
— — — — = Corporate bond rate.
—●—●—●— = Prime rate.

Figure 8-7, which shows the history of these seven interest rates, clearly reflects the fact that they all reach major peaks and bottoms at the same time.

Figure 8-7. *History of Interest Rates*

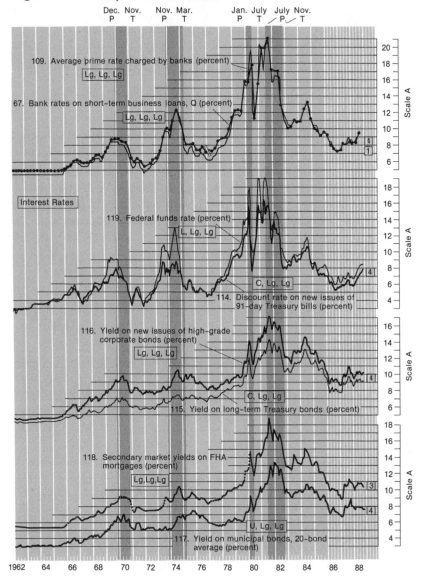

Source: *Business Conditions Digest.*

In addition to these seven rates, another indicator of interest rate pressure is largely unrecognized by investors, but has historically served as a consistent confirming indicator of interest rate turning points. It is known as the velocity of money.

The Velocity of Money: The Unrecognized Interest Rate. The *velocity of money* is defined by economists as the ratio of personal income to the money supply. In theory, it represents the amount of economic activity generated by each dollar of the money supply. While this is interesting, it is not the most useful way of viewing this indicator.

In fact, the velocity of money is a broad, national interest rate. Personal income is a very close approximation of the GNP, which represents the overall demand for goods. Since goods cost money, it is also a good measure of the demand for money. Thus, the velocity of money can be viewed as a measure of the demand for money (personal income) compared with the supply of money. And since interest rates are obvious indicators of the demand for money compared with the supply of money, it is logical to predict that the velocity of money will behave exactly like interest rates over any length of time.

Historical evidence shows that this is true. Figure 8-8 shows the history of the velocity of money and the long-term T-bond rate since 1951. The correlation of turning points is clear.

The velocity of money can be used as a final confirmation of major interest rate turning points in our business cycle analysis. Velocity tends to reach a turning point, just as the last of the seven interest rates reach turning points.

We can now replace the price of money variable with eight measurable indicators that are reported on a monthly basis, as shown in Figure 8-9.

The Supply of Goods

Earlier, we defined the supply of goods as the total U.S. plant capacity plus net imports into the United States (if we are running a trade deficit, as we are now). The trade balance is an exogenous (external) economic factor that is not a permanent component of the Primary Business Cycle. Although the trade balance can be measured, it is treated here as an outside

Figure 8-8. *Velocity and Interest Rates: 1953–1988*

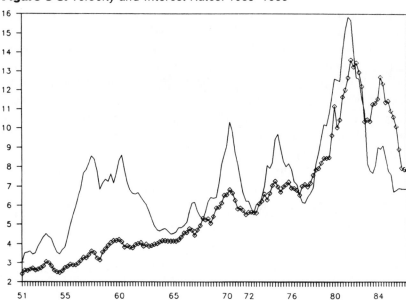

◇   LT BOND RATE   —— VELOCITY ^ 7

Note: The velocity index has been uniformly adjusted through mathematics to put it on the same scale as the T-bond rate. Source of raw data: *Business Conditions Digest.*

Figure 8-9.

Theoretical Cycle Event	*Trackable Indicator Event*
Price of money peak	The federal funds rate peak
	The 91-day T-bill rate peak
	The prime rate peak
	The corporate bond rate peak
	The long-term T-bond rate peak
	The municipal bond rate peak
	The FHA mortgage rate peak
	The velocity of money peak
Price of money bottom	The federal funds rate bottom
	The 91-day T-bill rate bottom
	The prime rate bottom
	The corporate bond rate bottom
	The long-term T-bond rate bottom
	The municipal bond rate bottom
	The FHA mortgage rate bottom
	The velocity of money bottom

influence with predictable effects on the business cycle; it is not a part of the business cycle itself in that it does not necessarily reach a peak and a bottom in every business cycle. It is a part of the whole international trade and foreign exchange system, which is discussed in a later chapter.

However, U.S. capacity is a distinct part of the business cycle; while actual numbers representing the total productive capacity of the United States are not available, the amount of available capacity relative to demand can be obtained by examining the capacity utilization figures that industry provides to the Commerce Department.

Capacity utilization, which is the measure of the degree to which existing production capacity is used, can be defined arithmetically as:

$$\text{Capacity Utilization (\%)} = \frac{\text{Capacity Used in Production}}{\text{Total Capacity Available}}$$

Therefore, capacity utilization is a percentage—not an absolute number—that represents the portion of total production capacity that is needed to meet the demand for goods. Capacity utilization can also be viewed in another way. If the total capacity of a steel mill is 100,000 tons per month and that mill is currently producing 65,000 tons per month, it is running at a capacity utilization rate of 65 percent. The excess capacity, or unused portion of the mill's total capacity, is obviously 35 percent.

$$100\% \text{ of Capacity} = \% \text{ Being Used} + \% \text{ Not Being Used}$$

or

$$\text{Total Capacity} = \text{Capacity Utilization} + \text{Excess Capacity}$$

If we view capacity in this way, it is clear that if the percentage used (which is the same as capacity utilization) is very high, excess capacity is very low and not much extra capacity is available. Thus, the supply of goods available to meet any new demand is very low.

Similarly, if the percentage used (capacity utilization) is very low, excess capacity will be very high and a lot of extra capacity will be available. Therefore, the supply of goods available to meet any new demand will be high. Stated more succinctly:

- When capacity utilization is high (e.g., 90 percent), excess capacity is low (10 percent); therefore, the supply of goods available to meet new demand is *relatively low.*

- When capacity utilization is low (e.g., 60 percent), excess capacity is high (40 percent); therefore, the supply of goods available to meet new demand is *relatively high.*

We can track the turning points in the relative supply of goods by equating the peak in the supply of goods with the peak in excess capacity, which is the bottom in capacity utilization. The bottom in the supply of goods tracks with the low point in excess capacity, which would be the peak in capacity utilization. (See Figure 8-10.)

The history of capacity utilization is shown in Figure 8-11.

The Demand for Goods

The Economy. The term "demand for goods" is just another way of saying "the economy," which is generally measured by the "real" GNP. The GNP is the aggregate sum of the dollars generated by all the sales of goods and services in the

Figure 8-10.

Theoretical Cycle Event	Trackable Indicator Event
Supply of goods peak (or maximum excess supply)	Capacity utilization bottom
Supply of goods bottom (or minimum excess supply)	Capacity utilization peak

Figure 8-11. *History of Capacity Utilization Rate*

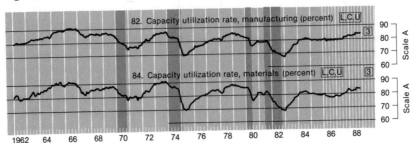

Source: *Business Conditions Digest.*

country, and the real GNP is the GNP minus the effects of inflation. If the GNP grew by 8 percent in a given year but inflation averaged 5 percent throughout that year, the economy as measured by the real GNP grew at a rate of 3 percent.

However, the real GNP is calculated quarterly and is reported several weeks after the end of the quarter that it measures. In addition, preliminary GNP figures are often revised at later dates, which makes the GNP a relatively useless figure with respect to understanding our current economic situation or forecasting the future of the economy.

The economy is said to be growing or in an expansion phase as long as the real GNP is growing at some rate. Whenever the real GNP is shown to decline for two or three consecutive quarters, the economy is said to be in a recession. Of course, the problem is that, under this definition, the official declaration that we are in a recession can only be made after we have been in the recession for a considerable period of time.

Composite Indicators. Thanks to the Department of Commerce, there are other ways to determine where the economy is and where it is going. Since the late 1940s, the government's economic analysts have studied and categorized hundreds of economic and financial indicators. These cyclical indicators have all been placed into three primary categories based on when they reach turning points as compared with officially declared turning points in the economy.

- *Coincident indicators*—These have historically been proven to peak out almost exactly at officially declared economic peaks and to bottom out just at the bottom of a recession.
- *Leading indicators*—As the name suggests, these have been shown to reach turning points ahead of the coincident indicators and the economy.
- *Lagging indicators*—These reach tops and bottoms some time *after* the coincident indicators and the economy reach tops and bottoms in each business cycle.

Of the hundreds of indicators and time series monitored by the Commerce Department, the three most famous statistics that the Commerce Department publishes every month are the composite indexes of leading indicators, coincident indicators, and lagging indicators. Figure 8-12, which is taken from the *Business Conditions Digest,* shows all three of these indexes from 1952 to 1988. The darkly shaded areas are periods of recession, as officially defined after the fact. In any recession—for example, the recession of 1974–1975—the timing characteristics of these composite indexes become quite clear. The leading indicators clearly peaked out well before the recession began, the coincident indicators peaked out just as the recession began, and the lagging indicators didn't peak until the recession was almost over.

In early 1975, which marked the end of the recession and the beginning of the 1975–1980 expansion, the same timing patterns held true. The leading indicators bottomed out first, the coincident indicators hit bottom almost exactly at the end of the recession, and the lagging indicators didn't bottom out until mid-1976—more than a year after the recession ended and economic expansion began. Of course, this timing pattern is to be expected, since the components of each composite series were selected based on their consistent historical tendency to either lead, coincide with, or lag behind major turning points in the economy as a whole. Historical data and charts detailing the components of these three composite economic indicators are provided in Appendix B.

Figure 8-12. *History of Economic Indicators*

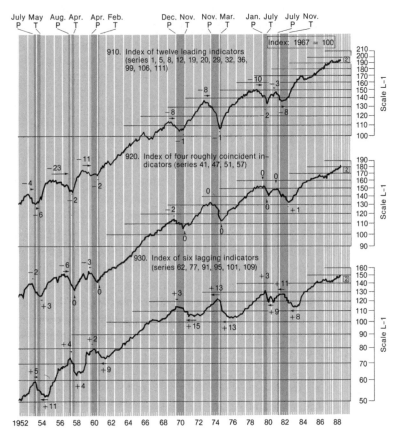

Source: *Business Conditions Digest.*

Tracking the Demand for Goods. Associating these indicators with a theoretical variable, the demand for goods, is a bit trickier than doing so with some of the others because we have to deal with the leading, coincident, and lagging economic indicators. The indicator that best relates to "the demand for goods" is the index of coincident indicators. This index comprises four meaningful measures of the economy and the actual demand for goods: sales, production, employment, and personal income. People buy goods and services (sales) that are produced (production) by companies that employ people (employment) and pay them (personal income) so that they can buy more goods and services. The index of coincident indicators is a good measurement indicator of the demand for goods in the business cycle.

The index of leading indicators has been developed to track the indicators that *foreshadow* major turning points in the coincident indicator index. Leading indicators of economic peaks and bottoms can be developed in one of three ways.

One method captures and records paperwork that precedes changes in the business environment. For example, before goods can be *produced* and *shipped* (coincident indicators), those goods must be *ordered* by someone; thus, a decline in orders would be a natural leading indicator of a decline in production or sales. Several leading indicators have been developed by tracking business data pertaining to orders, permits to build, and authorization for expenditures that consistently peak or bottom out before shipments, construction activity, or spending actually take place. Such indicators make up a large percentage of the index of leading indicators (see Appendix B).

A second way to construct a leading indicator analyzes the rate of change of a coincident indicator. The rate of change of most cyclical indicators will tend to reach tops and bottoms before the indicator itself does. For example, in Figure 8-13, the indicator reaches a peak in the eleventh month, while the six-month rate of change reaches its peak in the ninth month. The Commerce Department has developed several leading indicators based on the rates of change of other economic indicators.

The third way to find a leading indicator simply examines hundreds of indicators to see which ones reach their turning points ahead of the coincident indicators; the Commerce Department has several indicators that fall into this category.

Leading indicators developed in this way are interesting, but should not be assumed to be valid unless one can explain the *reason* that a particular indicator should lead economic turning points.

One such indicator is the stock market, as measured by the S&P 500 Stock Index. The Commerce Department has defined the stock market as a leading indicator because it has consis-

Figure 8-13. *Example of Rate of Change Turning Points*

Month	Indicator	% Change from Indicator Reading 6 Months Earlier
1	100	—
2	104	—
3	105	—
4	112	—
5	120	—
6	130	—
7	138	38.0
8	145	39.4
9	150	42.8 (peak)
10	154	37.5
11	155 (peak)	29.1
12	153	17.7
13	150	8.7
14	145	0.0
15	140	−6.6

tently reached turning points ahead of the economy. However, it has also reached turning points when the economy has moved straight up. This is the basis of Nobel laureate Paul Samuelson's famous quip, "The stock market has successfully predicted 9 out of the last 5 recessions."

For the moment, we will insert the stock market into our business cycle as a leading indicator; in a later chapter, we develop the cause-and-effect relationships that logically place the stock market at this position in the business cycle and show why it often mistakenly predicts recessions. Figure 8-14 shows the last 35 years of stock market history relative to the economy.

As one would guess, the index of lagging economic indicators is a composite of indicators that lag behind or follow the economy. Detailed information on this index is found in Appendix B. Since this index reaches turning points well after the economy has turned, it is of little interest from a forecasting standpoint; by itself, it is useful only as another measurable milepost to help us see where we are in the business cycle. However, the index of lagging indicators can be used in conjunction with the coincident indicators to produce a very spe-

Figure 8-14. *History of the S&P 500 Stock Index*

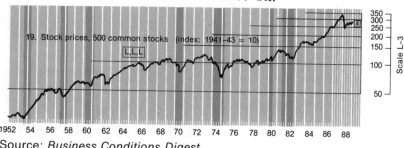

Source: *Business Conditions Digest.*

cial leading indicator, known as the ratio of the coincident to lagging (C/L ratio) indicators.

The C/L Ratio. This ratio has some very interesting characteristics:

• It is not a widely known indicator among investors.

• Those who use the ratio as either an economic or stock market forecasting tool tend to use it incorrectly.

• Used properly, this ratio is a key leading indicator that is extremely useful in identifying major tops and bottoms in both the economy and the stock market.

• This indicator gives clear signals at economic bottoms.

• This indicator first gives *false* signals of economic tops and later gives *true* signals of economic tops.

Figure 8-15 shows the historical movements of the C/L ratio since 1952.

Figure 8-15. *History of the C/L Ratio*

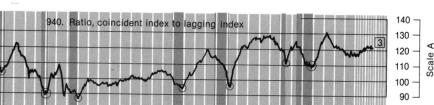

Source: *Business Conditions Digest.*

First, compare the clear bottoms of this ratio with the shaded recessions. In each case since 1952, this indicator has turned up before the end of recessions. But now let's look at the tops of this ratio in Figure 8-16.

Figure 8-16. *True and False Signals in the C/L Ratio*

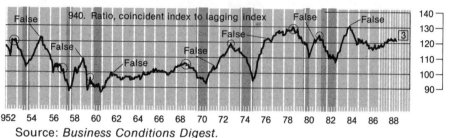

Source: *Business Conditions Digest.*

The peaks that are circled are *true* signals of an upcoming recession. However, this indicator also reached several peaks that were, in fact, *false* signals. To understand why those *false* peaks are generated, we must look at the mathematical nature of the ratio itself. This ratio has coincident indicators in the numerator and lagging indicators in the denominator.

$$\text{C/L Ratio} = \frac{\text{Coincident Indicators}}{\text{Lagging Indicators}}$$

By definition, the timing of turning points of these two indicators must look something like Figure 8-17, with the lagging indicators reaching peaks and bottoms after the coincident indicators do.

Figure 8-17.

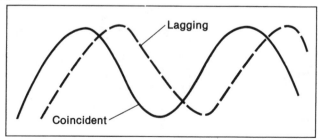

If we return to high school arithmetic for a moment, we remember that a ratio of two numbers will go up or down if either of two things happen, as shown in Figure 8-18.

Figure 8-18.

If:	Then:
The numerator increases *or* The denominator decreases	The ratio will *rise*
The numerator decreases *or* The denominator increases	The ratio will *fall*

Consider the examples in Figures 8-19 and 8-20.

Figure 8-19. *Causing the Ratio to Rise*

Starting Ratio	Ratio If Numerator Increases	Ratio If Denominator Decreases
$\frac{5}{8} = 0.625$	$\frac{6}{8} = 0.75$	$\frac{5}{7} = 0.714$

Figure 8-20. *Causing the Ratio to Fall*

Starting Ratio	Ratio If Numerator Decreases	Ratio If Denominator Increases
$\frac{5}{8} = 0.625$	$\frac{4}{8} = 0.50$	$\frac{5}{9} = 0.535$

Joining these ideas, we can state the following rules concerning the C/L ratio:

• The C/L ratio will bottom out and *rise* if the coincident indicators (the numerator) rise or if the lagging indicators (the denominator) decline.

• The C/L ratio will peak out and *decline* if the coincident indicators fall or if the lagging indicators rise.

Let's now look at what happens to these indicators during a recession, as shown in Figure 8-21.

The peak (A) and bottom (C) of the coincident indicator index coincide exactly with the beginning and the end of the recession, as you would expect. The index of lagging indicators doesn't peak (B) until midway through the recession and then doesn't bottom out (D) until well after the recession is over.

Notice what happens just before we reach Point A in Figure 8-21. The coincident indicators are beginning to *flatten out*, while the lagging indicators are rising rapidly toward their peak. The result is that the C/L ratio will peak out and decline *before* we hit Point A, because the denominator (lagging indicators) is rising while the numerator (coincident indicators) is flattening out. This decline in the C/L ratio is the *true* leading indicator of the upcoming recession because the decline in the ratio is *caused* by the flattening out of and subsequent decline in the coincident indicators, which truly measure economic activity.

Now look at what happens at Points C and D as the recession ends. As we move from Point C (coincident bottom) to Point D (lagging bottom), the coincident index *rises* while the lagging index still falls. This produces a twofold effect on the C/L ratio, which rises very sharply (in accordance with Rule 1) as a result of both a rising numerator and a declining denominator. But at Point D, when the lagging index finally turns up, the C/L ratio peaks out and declines (as per Rule 2); at this point, we can see the *false* peak in the C/L ratio, which marks the *end of the last recession. This false peak is caused by the lagging indicators reaching a bottom and rising rapidly from that bottom point.*

After some time, during which both the coincident and lagging indexes rise (during the next expansion), the C/L ratio will decline again shortly before Point E, just as it did before Point A—*sending another true warning signal of the next recession, which is caused by the next peaking of the coincident indicators.* Figure 8-22 shows the plot of the C/L ratio with the coincident and lagging indicators in our example, and a review of Figure 8-16 will show the history of *true* and *false* peaks in their proper perspective. The *false* peaks occur just *after* a recession has ended, but the *true* leading indicator peaks occur just before each recession begins.

While we will discuss the stock market in detail in a later chapter, it's important to note that the false peak that occurs

Figure 8-21. *Coincident and Lagging Indicators During a Recession*

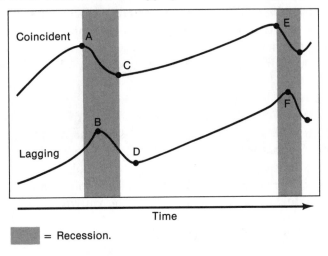

= Recession.

Figure 8-22. *Coincident and Lagging Indexes and the C/L Ratio*

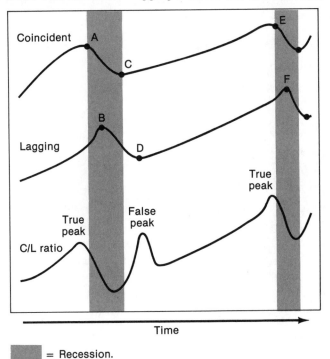

= Recession.

shortly after the end of a recession is often misread by influential technical analysts. The result is often a stock market sell-off. However, by tracking the C/L ratio indicator, investors can foresee this market decline. In addition, investors will know that the decline is only temporary, and represents a buying opportunity for stocks, which will then proceed to rise until the onset of the next recession.

We can now complete the translation from the "demand for goods" to trackable indicators by (1) equating the index of coincident economic indicators with the "demand for goods" and (2) using the other indicators as presignals and postsignals that are visible before and after the turning points in the demand for goods during each business cycle, as shown in Figure 8-23.

The Price of Goods (Inflation)

The price of goods can be easily translated into measurable indicators. Although the Commerce Department maintains several price indexes, we have found that the inflation picture can be seen clearly by looking at only three:

• The index of raw material prices
• The producer price index
• The consumer price index

Figure 8-23.

Theoretical Cycle Event	Trackable Indicator Event
Demand for goods peak— Presignals	C/L ratio peak Leading indicators peak
Demand for goods peak— Actual	Coincident indicators peak
Demand for goods peak— Postsignals	Official: "Recession has begun" Lagging indicators peak
Demand for goods bottom— Presignals	C/L ratio bottom Leading indicators bottom
Demand for goods bottom— Actual	Coincident indicators bottom
Demand for goods bottom— Postsignals	Official: "Expansion has begun" Lagging indicators bottom

These three prices are logically related to each other. Increases in raw material prices will directly affect the production costs of manufactured goods. Trying to protect their profit margins, manufacturers will pass raw material price increases along to producers that make the final end products for consumers. And those companies will naturally pass their cost increases along to consumers. This would be called "supply-push" inflation.

On the other hand, if "demand-pull" inflation should begin at the consumer level, the reverse would take place. Demanding more goods than are currently available, consumers would bid prices up, which would fatten the profit margins of companies that provide those consumer goods. Knowing that these consumer product companies are making very large profits, the suppliers of these goods (producer goods) would soon raise their prices to the consumer products companies to increase their profits. Producers of raw materials would quickly get on the bandwagon and raise their prices to producer goods companies to share in the wealth.

However, history has shown that raw materials prices can be much more volatile than the more broad-based producer and consumer price indexes. Raw material shortages or surpluses, which can occur in specific industries due to specific, short-lived industry conditions, can be misleading with respect to the prices of goods at the national wholesale or retail level. Therefore, although raw material prices should be watched as a signpost, we have included only the producer and consumer price indexes in our list of cyclical, trackable indicators, as shown in Figure 8-24.

Regardless of the type of inflation, disinflation, or deflation that we may experience in a business cycle, the major turning points in inflation can be clearly identified by tracking the

Figure 8-24.

Theoretical Cycle Event	Trackable Indicator Event
Price of goods peak	Producer price inflation peak
	Consumer price inflation peak
Price of goods bottom	Producer price inflation bottom
	Consumer price inflation bottom

12-month rate of change of the producer and consumer price indexes on a monthly basis. Figure 8-25 shows a history of these two indexes.

THE PRIMARY BUSINESS CYCLE

We now have a complete marriage between the theoretical supply, demand, and price business cycle and measurable statistical indicators from a reliable source. We have defined a set of trackable indicators that is directly and logically related to turning points in the theoretical business cycle. The final step is simply to line up all of these trackable indicators against theoretical turning points to develop the complete Primary Business Cycle that investors can monitor on a monthly basis.

This is done in Figure 8-26. The repeating sequence of supply, demand, and price turning points, which was developed in Chapter 7, is shown in the left-hand column. The corresponding trackable indicators from the Commerce Department are shown in the right-hand column, which now represents the complete list of basic components of the Primary Business Cycle. Included in this cycle are the major peaks and bottoms in

Figure 8-25. *Inflation Rate History: Producer and Consumer Price Indexes*

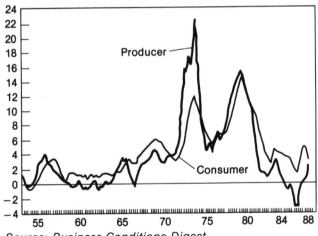

Source: *Business Conditions Digest.*

Figure 8-26. *The Theoretical Business Cycle Versus the Trackable Primary Business Cycle*

Theoretical Cycle Event	Primary Business Cycle Event
1. Recession = Problem	
2. Supply of money bottom	M2 money supply bottom
3. Price of money falls more	All 7 interest rates and velocity of money fall as money supply rises
5a. Demand for goods bottom—Presignals	Stock market bottom Leading indicators bottom C/L ratio bottom
4. Supply of goods peak	Capacity utilization bottom
5b. Demand for goods bottom—Actual	Coincident indicator bottom (begin expansion)
5c. Demand for goods bottom—Postsignals	Official declaration: "Expansion in progress" Lagging indicator bottom
6. Demand for money bottom	Consumer credit ratio bottom
7. Price of goods bottom	Inflation rates for producer goods and consumer goods bottom
8. Price of money bottom	All 7 interest rates and velocity of money bottom
9. Inflation = Problem	
10. Supply of money peak	M2 money supply peak
11. Price of money rises more	All 7 interest rates and velocity of money rise as money supply falls
13a. Demand for goods peak—Presignals	Stock market peak Leading indicator peak C/L ratio peak
12. Supply of goods bottom	Capacity utilization peak
13b. Demand for goods peak—Actual	Coincident indicator peak (begin recession)
13c. Demand for goods peak—Postsignals	Official Declaration: "Recession in progress" Lagging indicator peak
14. Demand for money peak	Consumer credit ratio peak
15. Price of goods peak	Inflation rates for producer goods and consumer goods peak
16. Price of money peak	All 7 interest rates and velocity of money peak

inflation, interest rates, the economy, and the stock market. As shown throughout the text, the cycle is driven entirely by known cause-and-effect relationships.

We can now visually describe this cycle. If a Primary Business Cycle were to unfold *exactly* in accordance with this theory, the Gantt chart of this "ideal" cycle would look like Figure 8-27.

VALIDATION OF THE PRIMARY BUSINESS CYCLE

Our first observation about the Primary Business Cycle chart in Figure 8-27 is that the cycle consists of two distinct

Figure 8-27. *The Ideal Primary Business Cycle*

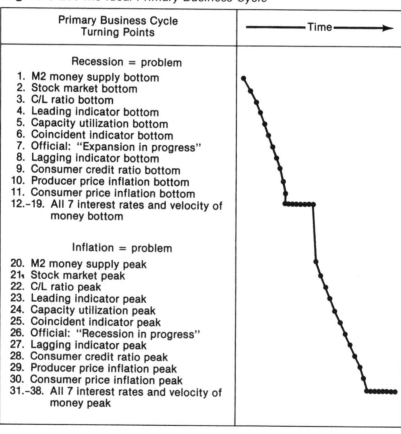

Primary Business Cycle Turning Points	——— Time ———⟶
Recession = problem	
1. M2 money supply bottom	
2. Stock market bottom	
3. C/L ratio bottom	
4. Leading indicator bottom	
5. Capacity utilization bottom	
6. Coincident indicator bottom	
7. Official: "Expansion in progress"	
8. Lagging indicator bottom	
9. Consumer credit ratio bottom	
10. Producer price inflation bottom	
11. Consumer price inflation bottom	
12.–19. All 7 interest rates and velocity of money bottom	
Inflation = problem	
20. M2 money supply peak	
21. Stock market peak	
22. C/L ratio peak	
23. Leading indicator peak	
24. Capacity utilization peak	
25. Coincident indicator peak	
26. Official: "Recession in progress"	
27. Lagging indicator peak	
28. Consumer credit ratio peak	
29. Producer price inflation peak	
30. Consumer price inflation peak	
31.–38. All 7 interest rates and velocity of money peak	

phases: (1) a *bottoming phase* that consists of Events 1–19 of the cycle and (2) a *peaking phase* that consists of Events 20–38. In each phase, a series of indicators reaches turning points in a prescribed sequence.

Theory Versus Commerce Department Analysis

The accuracy of the Primary Business Cycle, which was developed from *theory*, is validated by comparison of its sequence of bottoms and tops with the sequence of turning points defined by the Commerce Department in terms of leading, coincident, and lagging indicators. If theory and history are consistent, the bottoming phase should consist of leading indicators, then coincident indicators, and then lagging indicators—in that order. And the same should be true of the peaking phase of the cyle. Figure 8-28 shows that this is, in fact, true.

History of the Primary Business Cycle

Final validation of the Primary Business Cycle lies in historical evidence. Figure 8-29 shows the actual dates of the major turning points of our trackable indicators for the last 30 years, covering the last five Primary Business Cycles. Although none of the historical cycles follows the ideal cycle precisely, this Gantt chart shows that the turning points occur in a highly reliable sequence that allows us to see our position in the cycle at any point in time.

CASE STUDY OF A TYPICAL PRIMARY BUSINESS CYCLE

To firmly establish the logical sequence of events contained in our business cycle, we can now trace one complete cycle from beginning to end and see the step-by-step progression of causes and effects.

Let's begin the cycle at the bottom of a major economic recession: Unemployment is high; the stock market, inflation, and interest rates have all declined; and all of the economic

Figure 8-28. *Primary Business Cycle Compared with Commerce Department Timing*

Primary Business Cycle Turning Points	Commerce Department Timing Status of Each Indicator		
	At Bottoms	At Peaks	Overall
Recession = problem			
1. M2 money supply bottom	Lead	Lead	Lead
2. Stock market bottom	Lead	Lead	Lead
3. C/L ratio bottom	Lead	Lead	Lead
4. Leading indicator bottom	Lead	Lead	Lead
5. Capacity utilization bottom	Lead	Lead	Lead
6. Coincident indicator bottom	Coincident	Coincident	Coincident
7. Official: "Expansion in progress"	Coincident	Coincident	Coincident
8. Lagging indicator bottom	Lag*	Lag*	Lag*
9. Consumer credit ratio bottom	Lag	Lag	Lag
10. Producer price inflation bottom	Lag	Lag	Lag
11. Consumer price inflation bottom	**		**
12.–19. All 7 interest rates and velocity of money bottom	**		**
	Lag		Lag

Inflation = problem

20. M2 money supply peak	Lead	Lead
21. Stock market peak	Lead	Lead
22. C/L ratio peak	Lead	Lead
23. Leading indicator peak	Lead	Lead
24. Capacity utilization peak	Lead	Lead
25. Coincident indicator peak	Coincident	Coincident
26. Official: "Recession in progress"	Lag*	Lag*
27. Lagging indicator peak	Lag	Lag
28. Consumer credit ratio peak	Lag	Lag
29. Producer price inflation peak	**	**
30. Consumer price inflation peak	**	**
31.–38. All 7 interest rates and velocity of money peak	Either coincident or lag	Lag

* By definition, since it is reported well after the fact.
** No timing status given by the Commerce Department.

Figure 8-29. *History of Primary Business Cycles*

Primary Business Cycle
Turning Points

Recession = problem

1. M2 money supply bottom
2. Stock market bottom
3. C/L ratio bottom
4. Leading indicator bottom
5. Capacity utilization bottom
6. Coincident indicator bottom
7. Official: "Expansion in progress"
8. Lagging indicator bottom
9. Consumer credit ratio bottom
10. Producer price inflation bottom
11. Consumer price inflation bottom
12.–19. All 7 interest rates and
velocity of money bottom

Inflation = problem

20. M2 money supply peak
21. Stock market peak
22. C/L ratio peak
23. Leading indicator peak
24. Capacity utilization peak
25. Coincident indicator peak
26. Official: "Recession in progress"
27. Lagging indicator peak
28. Consumer credit ratio peak
29. Producer price inflation peak
30. Consumer price inflation peak
31.–38. All 7 interest rates and
velocity of money peak

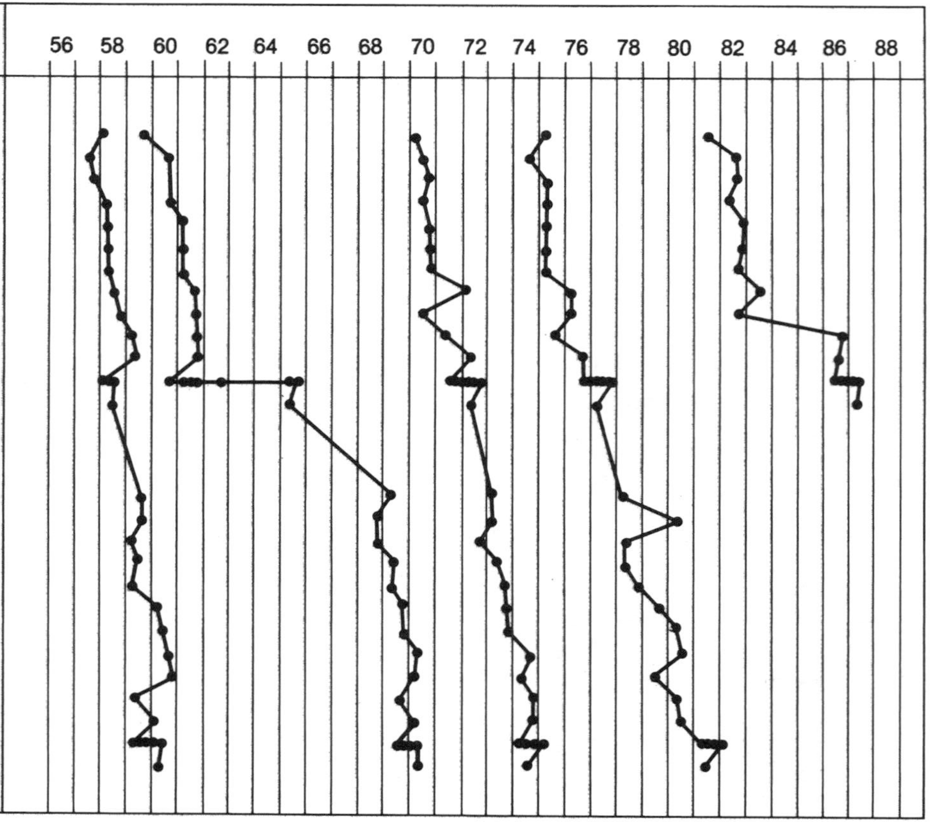

indicators are down. We can now trace the development of the Primary Business Cycle with Figure 8-29.

- *Event 1:* Money supply bottom—Since the current problem is unemployment—not high inflation or interest rates—the Fed increases the money supply to get the economy going again.
- *Event 2:* Stock market bottom—The stock market bottoms out, anticipating the economic recovery driven by the increase in the money supply.
- *Events 3 and 4:* Economic bottom (presignals)—The economic indicators bottom out and begin to rise in sequence, with the C/L ratio and the leading indicators rising first.
- *Event 5:* Capacity utilization bottom—Capacity utilization begins to rise as an increasing number of new orders for manufactured goods are taken and those goods are produced.
- *Event 6:* Economic bottom (actual)—The index of coincident economic indicators bottoms out and rises as actual production, sales, employment, and personal income begin to rise.
- *Events 7 and 8:* Economic bottom (postsignals)—The government officially states that the recession is over and that a period of expansion has begun. Shortly afterward, the index of lagging indicators bottoms out.
- *Event 9:* Consumer credit ratio bottom—Based on the announcement of new economic expansion and renewed consumer confidence, consumers start to borrow more against their income to finance purchases that were deferred during the recession.
- *Events 10 and 11:* Inflation bottom—The producer and consumer price indexes, which had turned down earlier as a result of the recession and tight money, now bottom out and rise steadily as the effects of the money supply increase (Event 1), the economic recovery (Event 6), and increased consumer spending (Event 9) take hold.
- *Events 12–19:* Interest rate bottom—Coupled with a growing economy that needs money for expansion, rising inflation now causes interest rates and the velocity of money to reach lows and start to rise. This bottoming out phase for all eight interest

rate indicators can take only a few months or more than a year to complete; short-term rates usually move up first, followed by long-term rates and the velocity of money. We are now in a little-known but well-defined phase of the business cycle in which the money supply, the stock market, inflation, interest rates, and the economy are all rising together. The economy continues to grow, the money supply is increased to sustain this growth, and inflation and interest rates continue to rise. The stock market moves up in spite of rising interest rates because the focus of attention is now rapid earnings growth instead of higher interest rates.

- *Event 20:* Money supply peak—Eventually, accelerating inflation and interest rates rise to a point at which they become a serious problem—both economically and politically. Thus, the Fed steps in and cuts back the money supply. This reduction of the money supply has several effects on the rest of the business cycle. The Fed's intention in cutting the money supply is to reduce inflation, which it ultimately does. But the initial, short-term effect of tighter money is to raise interest rates even further. At the same time, less money in the system causes a reduction in spending; the seeds of the next recession have now been sown.

- *Event 21:* Stock market high—The stock market now peaks as investors face higher interest rates and foresee lower economic activity due to tighter money.

- *Events 22 and 23:* Economic peak (presignals)—With the cutback in the money supply, all of the economic indicators peak out and begin to decline in their natural sequence as we enter a recession. The C/L ratio and the leading indicators peak out first.

- *Event 24:* Capacity utilization peak—While manufacturing capacity is still expanding due to investments made at the peak of the boom period, new orders for goods begin to decline and the ratio of production to capacity, or capacity utilization, peaks out and begins to fall.

- *Event 25:* Economic peak (actual)—The coincident indicators peak and decline as production, sales, employment, and income begin to fall.

- *Events 26 and 27:* Economic peak (postsignals)—The government announces that we have entered a recession; shortly thereafter, the lagging economic indicators peak out and begin to decline.
- *Event 28:* Consumer credit ratio peak—As consumers reduce their spending due to a lower money supply and higher interest rates, the ratio of consumer borrowing to personal income reaches its cyclical peak.
- *Events 29 and 30:* Inflation peak—The combined effects of the slower economy and the reduced money supply finally have the desired effect of reducing prices at both the producer and consumer levels; both indexes now peak out.
- *Events 31–38:* Interest rate peak—The slower pace of the economy eases the pressure on interest rates. When the financial community finally sees that inflation has been curtailed, the velocity of money and all seven interest rates reach their peaks and begin to decline quite rapidly.
- *Event 1:* Money supply bottom and a new cycle begins—With the economy now in a recession and with inflation, interest rates, and the stock market falling, the problem becomes unemployment again. When the Fed feels that inflation and interest rates are at reasonable or at least manageable levels, the money supply is increased to stimulate the economy and reduce unemployment. Thus, a new cycle begins.

This completes development of the Primary Business Cycle—its structure, movements, and causes. We can now reach some valuable conclusions and insights based on this business cycle foundation.

New Insights from the Primary Business Cycle

THE DOMINANT SEQUENCE

To develop the Primary Business Cycle so that it could be tracked and monitored on a monthly basis, we broke the cycle down into 38 specific events, or turning points. But to capture the essential structure of the business cycle, we can now consolidate those events into five broad, natural categories that reflect the dominant sequence behind each business cycle. This consolidation is given in Figure 9-1, which shows that every Primary Business Cycle is built on the five major bottoms and five major peaks of (1) the money supply, (2) the stock market, (3) the economy, (4) inflation, and (5) interest rates—*in that order.*

In other words, the business cycle can be visualized as a repeating sequence, or flow, of peaks and bottoms of five predominant factors, as shown in Figure 9-2.

MIXED SIGNALS: WHAT THEY REALLY MEAN

As you follow the financial news throughout a business cycle, you very often hear economists, financial analysts, stock pickers, and newscasters announce with dismay that "we are

Figure 9-1. *The Dominant Sequence*

Primary Business Cycle Event (per Figure 8-27)	*Dominant Sequence Event*
1. Money supply bottom	Money supply bottom
2. Stock market bottom	Stock market bottom
3.–9. Economic indicator bottoms	Economy bottom
10.–11. Inflation indicator bottoms	Inflation bottom
12.–19. Interest rate and velocity of money bottoms	Interest rate bottom
20. Money supply peak	Money supply peak
21. Stock market peak	Stock market peak
22.–28. Economic indicator peaks	Economy bottom
29.–30. Inflation indicator peaks	Inflation bottom
31.–38. Interest rate and velocity of money peaks	Interest rate peak

getting mixed economic signals so there is great uncertainty surrounding the stock and bond markets.'' Figure 9-2 shows that these "mixed signals" are only a natural and predictable feature of the business cycle as the five primary components peak at different times. At Point A in Figure 9-2, all five major components are clearly moving up. But as we approach the peak of the business cycle at Point B, the money supply and the stock market are declining, while the economy, inflation, and interest rates are still rising. This is a period of mixed signals. For a brief time at Point C, all five components are declining. Then, at Point D, we see more mixed signals as the money supply and the stock market move up, while the economy is at rock bottom and inflation and interest rates are still declining. Finally, we return to Point A, where everything is rising together.

There are two key points to this analysis:

• The mixed signals that often lead to a great diversity of forecasts from professional analysts and advisers are, in fact, a natural result of a very orderly process in which the five components reach peaks and bottoms in a predictable, sequential pattern.

Figure 9-2. *The Dominant Flow of the Primary Business Cycle*

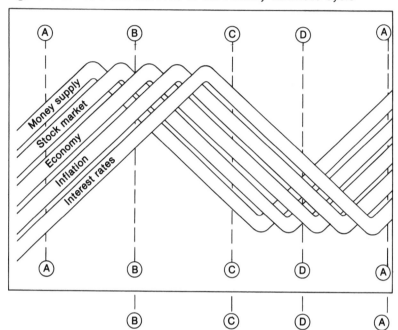

- The mixed signals occur *at the major turning points* of the business cycle and are, therefore, a turning point signal in their own right.

If you see these mixed signals at the end of a period of expansion, you know that the peak has already occurred or is very close at hand; the same principle applies to bottoms. Stated another way, the more discussion there is of "mixed" or "confusing" economic signals, the greater the likelihood that we are at a major financial and economic turning point.

PARTIAL OR MINOR CYCLES

Definition of a Partial Cycle

To explain the phenomenon of partial cycles, we return to the seasonal analogy used in Chapter 2. The sequential transitions from season to season throughout the year are essentially "cast in stone" because of the earth's orbit around the sun and the angle of the north and south poles with respect to the earth's orbit. The forces at work that produce the seasonal changes are defined by absolute laws of physics that are known and inarguably true. Yet every year does not look exactly like the previous one in terms of high and low temperatures or the amount of rainfall. Our attempts to predict these annual variations force us to admit defeat and to rely on the behavior of a groundhog to advise us when spring weather will truly arrive each year.

In addition, aberrations such as hailstorms in June, heat waves in January, and freak storms occur each year. But the most regular of these irregular events that occurs within the fundamental seasonal cycle is the partial seasonal cycle known as Indian summer.

Indian summer generally comes in late October and early November, while the fundamental seasonal forces are moving us toward the cold and snowy days of winter. After a period of cold, windy, wintry days, the season *appears* to change: the wind disappears, the sky turns blue, and the temperature rises noticeably during the days of this one-week to three-week period of time. Then, fairly suddenly, winter begins in earnest. This partial seasonal cycle has several characteristics that are analogous to those of the partial cycles within the Primary Business Cycle:

- It is a *known part of the fundamental cycle:* Observers are not fooled into thinking that winter has come and gone by November.

- It is *not a complete cycle:* The temperature may rise and then fall, but plants do not go through a bloom-and-die cycle, birds do not make an extra migration trip, and leaves do not turn green and then brown again during Indian summer.

- Finally, *the causes are known* and, therefore, do not represent a departure from the seasonal cycle. Instead, they confirm the known forces behind the cycle. In the case of Indian summer, the warm weather is caused by large masses of warm tropical air that move north and then remain stagnant in the northern latitudes for a brief period.

Partial cycles within the Primary Business Cycle follow the same principles and produce the same types of effects. During long periods of economic expansion, when everything is growing or heating up, there are temporary periods in which some, but not all, of the components slow down or cool down for a short time—something like an "Indian winter" but in the business cycle. The money supply turns down slightly, the stock market turns down (in what is traditionally called a technical correction), inflation and interest rates rise somewhat, and, in some cases, the leading economic indicators dip down. But we do not go into a full-fledged recession—this is only a pause in the expansion period.

To illustrate a partial cycle, imagine that the complete Primary Business Cycle had only two components: the leading indicators and the coincident indicators. When both of these indicators peak out together, we have a major turning point or, using our analogy, a change in season. But if only the leading indicators experience a peak and a bottom while the coincident indicators move inexorably upward, we have a partial cycle within a major period of expansion, as shown in Figure 9-3.

The causes of these partial cycles are the same laws that we have described earlier, and the sequence of events in the partial

Figure 9-3. *Illustration of a Partial Cycle*

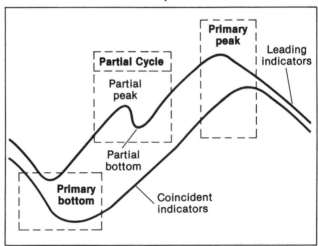

or minor cycles is identical to that in the full Primary Business Cycle. The difference is that the combined actions of businesses, consumers, banks, and the government create a minor course adjustment during a partial cycle, while maintaining the momentum of a major period of expansion. Inflation begins to rise *a little,* so the Fed cuts back on the money supply *a little,* interest rates rise *a little,* the stock market falls *a little,* inventories that have been rising are cut back *a little,* and the economy slows down *a little.* Then inflation moderates; interest rates come back down; and the money supply, the stock market, and the economy resume their upward course.

In other words, the minor cycles represent the correct and appropriate adjustments to the economy and financial markets, which allow the expansion to continue. When these adjustments *are not made,* spending, borrowing, inflation, the money supply, the economy, and the stock market move into a boom phase that is not sustainable and that eventually leads to the inevitable bust that brings the economy back into equilibrium. Because these partial cycles are a *known* part of the business cycle, we can avoid being fooled by them. Also, because they are, by definition, incomplete cycles that involve some but not all of the business cycle components, we can identify them and plan our investments accordingly. We use two historical partial cycles to illustrate how they work.

The Partial Cycle of 1966–1968

Let's imagine that we are back in 1966, tracking the progress of the Primary Business Cycle. The Gantt chart we would be looking at as of early 1966 is shown in Figure 9-4.

The last recession had ended in early 1961, and all of the economic indicators and inflation had bottomed out in 1961. Interest rates did not completely (i.e., all seven interest rates and the velocity of money) bottom out until late in 1965. Thus, by 1966, the business cycle was waiting for the next peaking phase to occur—beginning with Event 20, a money supply peak.

In 1966, the M2 money supply flattened out, but never really declined. The stock market went into a decline in anticipation of higher interest rates and a recession. The leading

Figure 9-4. *Primary Business Cycle Status as of Late 1965*

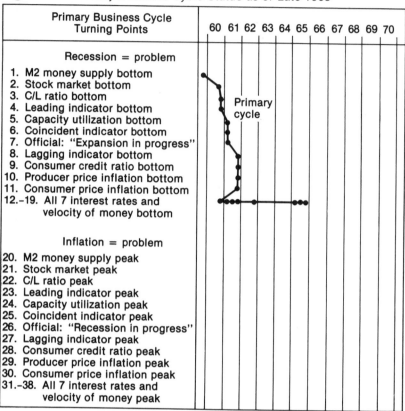

Primary Business Cycle Turning Points	60 61 62 63 64 65 66 67 68 69 70
Recession = problem 1. M2 money supply bottom 2. Stock market bottom 3. C/L ratio bottom 4. Leading indicator bottom 5. Capacity utilization bottom 6. Coincident indicator bottom 7. Official: "Expansion in progress" 8. Lagging indicator bottom 9. Consumer credit ratio bottom 10. Producer price inflation bottom 11. Consumer price inflation bottom 12.-19. All 7 interest rates and velocity of money bottom **Inflation = problem** 20. M2 money supply peak 21. Stock market peak 22. C/L ratio peak 23. Leading indicator peak 24. Capacity utilization peak 25. Coincident indicator peak 26. Official: "Recession in progress" 27. Lagging indicator peak 28. Consumer credit ratio peak 29. Producer price inflation peak 30. Consumer price inflation peak 31.-38. All 7 interest rates and velocity of money peak	Primary cycle

economic indicators, the C/L ratio, and capacity utilization also peaked out and turned down. By the end of the year, inflation, all seven interest rates, and the velocity of money had all peaked out—*but we never went into a recession.* At that point in time, it was clear that we were in only a partial cycle and it was possible to construct the pro forma or anticipated sequence of events that had to follow to complete (1) the partial cycle and (2) the Primary Business Cycle that started in 1960. Figure 9-5 shows the Gantt chart as it would have appeared at the end of 1966.

Since we went through a complete Primary Business Cycle bottoming phase from 1960 to 1965, represented by black circles, we know that a complete peaking phase must occur sometime in the future, represented by white circles. And since the partial

Figure 9-5. *Projected Turning Points Sequence as of Late 1966*

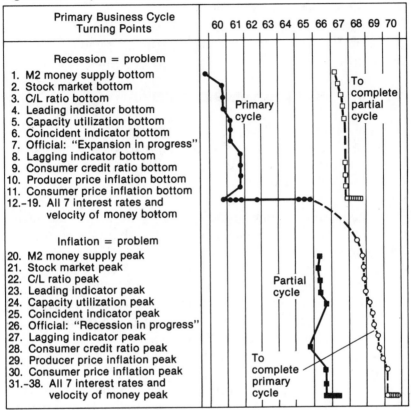

Primary Business Cycle Turning Points	60 61 62 63 64 65 66 67 68 69 70
Recession = problem	
1. M2 money supply bottom	
2. Stock market bottom	
3. C/L ratio bottom	
4. Leading indicator bottom	
5. Capacity utilization bottom	
6. Coincident indicator bottom	
7. Official: "Expansion in progress"	
8. Lagging indicator bottom	
9. Consumer credit ratio bottom	
10. Producer price inflation bottom	
11. Consumer price inflation bottom	
12.–19. All 7 interest rates and velocity of money bottom	
Inflation = problem	
20. M2 money supply peak	
21. Stock market peak	
22. C/L ratio peak	
23. Leading indicator peak	
24. Capacity utilization peak	
25. Coincident indicator peak	
26. Official: "Recession in progress"	
27. Lagging indicator peak	
28. Consumer credit ratio peak	
29. Producer price inflation peak	
30. Consumer price inflation peak	
31.–38. All 7 interest rates and velocity of money peak	

cycle of 1965 and 1966 involved peaks in the money supply, the stock market, the leading economic indicators, consumer credit, inflation, and interest rates, represented by black squares, but not in the economy as a whole, we know that these same indicators must reach their bottoms to complete the partial cycle. One could then have predicted that each component that had just reached a minor peak would soon reach a minor bottom to complete the partial cycle, as shown by white squares.

The practical value of such assessment of the partial cycle can be demonstrated by the stock market. Knowing that the peak of 1966 was only a temporary peak (Event 21, denoted by a black square), investors would have known that as soon as the money supply bottomed out (Event 1, denoted by a white square), the stock market, too, would bottom out (Event 2) and rise until the next major peak.

In fact, this partial cycle did play out almost exactly as shown in Figure 9-5. It was a classic "Indian winter" in one of the longest periods of economic expansion in history.

The Partial Cycle of 1987–1988

The crash of 1987 will go down in history as a day of infamy on Wall Street. It had all of the earmarks of a full-blown, 1929-style depression. Yet within the structure of the Primary Business Cycle, it can be viewed as only a partial cycle within a larger Primary Business Cycle.

Reconstructing the scene of the crime as we did in the previous example, we can see that the bottom of the last recession occurred in 1982. Between 1982 and 1986, we experienced a long period of disinflation that was caused in part by steadily declining oil prices. Inflation rates finally bottomed out in late 1986, interest rates hit bottom in late 1986 and early 1987, and we then waited for the next peaking phase of the Primary Business Cycle, as shown in Figure 9-6.

In January 1987, the M2 money supply again flattened out and the rate of change of M2 declined sharply, which set the stage for at least a partial cycle and a peak in the stock market. However, the economic indicators were all moving steadily upward and inflation was low. Interest rates were in the 7 percent range, but were rising moderately. The stock market was seeing the best of all worlds, with rising corporate earnings and low interest rates. The mounting trade and budget deficits were largely ignored, and the stock market soared to a sorry state of overvaluation (discussed in a later chapter). The stock market peaked in August; by September, it was clear (as we will show in Chapter 16) that the boom was over.

The infamous 508-point drop in the Dow Jones industrials on October 19, 1987, sent panic around the world. Since the S&P 500 Stock Index is a part of the leading economic index, it, too, fell sharply that month. Consumer confidence plummeted, and the world braced itself for a potential financial disaster.

By December 1987, inflation and interest rates had peaked, but the C/L ratio and coincident indicators had failed to turn

Figure 9-6. *Primary Business Cycle Status as of 1986*

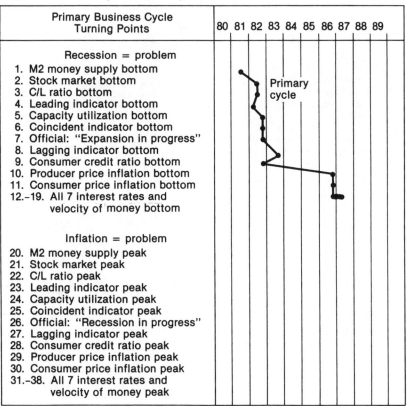

Primary Business Cycle Turning Points	80 81 82 83 84 85 86 87 88 89

Recession = problem
1. M2 money supply bottom
2. Stock market bottom
3. C/L ratio bottom
4. Leading indicator bottom
5. Capacity utilization bottom
6. Coincident indicator bottom
7. Official: "Expansion in progress"
8. Lagging indicator bottom
9. Consumer credit ratio bottom
10. Producer price inflation bottom
11. Consumer price inflation bottom
12.-19. All 7 interest rates and
    velocity of money bottom
 	
Inflation = problem
20. M2 money supply peak
21. Stock market peak
22. C/L ratio peak
23. Leading indicator peak
24. Capacity utilization peak
25. Coincident indicator peak
26. Official: "Recession in progress"
27. Lagging indicator peak
28. Consumer credit ratio peak
29. Producer price inflation peak
30. Consumer price inflation peak
31.-38. All 7 interest rates and
    velocity of money peak
	Primary cycle

down. At that time, it was clear that despite the magnitude of the stock market plunge, we were in only a partial cycle, as shown in Figure 9-7.

The next events in the cycle were, again, predictable. All of the indicators that had reached peaks in the partial cycle would next reach bottoms to complete the partial cycle. We would then wait for the final peaking phase of the Primary Business Cycle, which began in 1981. By May 1988, the partial cycle was completed as projected.

Figure 9-8 shows the Gantt chart for 1980 to May 1988, with completed events denoted by black circles and squares and events remaining to happen represented by white circles.

As of this writing (summer 1988), the next events in the

Figure 9-7. *Primary Business Cycle Status as of December 1987*

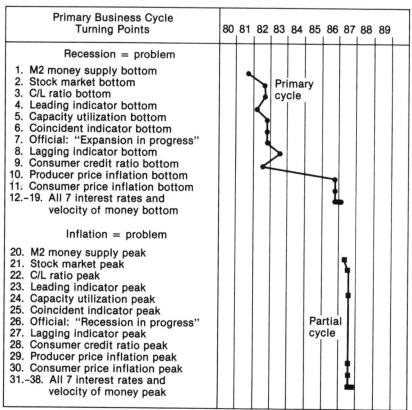

Primary Business Cycle Turning Points	80 81 82 83 84 85 86 87 88 89
Recession = problem	
1. M2 money supply bottom	
2. Stock market bottom	
3. C/L ratio bottom	Primary cycle
4. Leading indicator bottom	
5. Capacity utilization bottom	
6. Coincident indicator bottom	
7. Official: "Expansion in progress"	
8. Lagging indicator bottom	
9. Consumer credit ratio bottom	
10. Producer price inflation bottom	
11. Consumer price inflation bottom	
12.-19. All 7 interest rates and velocity of money bottom	
Inflation = problem	
20. M2 money supply peak	
21. Stock market peak	
22. C/L ratio peak	
23. Leading indicator peak	
24. Capacity utilization peak	
25. Coincident indicator peak	
26. Official: "Recession in progress"	Partial cycle
27. Lagging indicator peak	
28. Consumer credit ratio peak	
29. Producer price inflation peak	
30. Consumer price inflation peak	
31.-38. All 7 interest rates and velocity of money peak	

cycle to take place will be a peak in the M2 money supply (Event 20) and a peak in the stock market (Event 21), which has rebounded from its October 1987 lows. Following those events, the economy will peak out and we will enter a recession of significant magnitude to complete the Primary Business Cycle that began in 1980.

Stock Market Behavior

Although we discuss stock valuation in detail in a later chapter, it is important to highlight here the basic behavioral attributes of the market with respect to both primary and partial business cycles.

Figure 9-8. *Projected Turning Point Sequence as of May 1988*

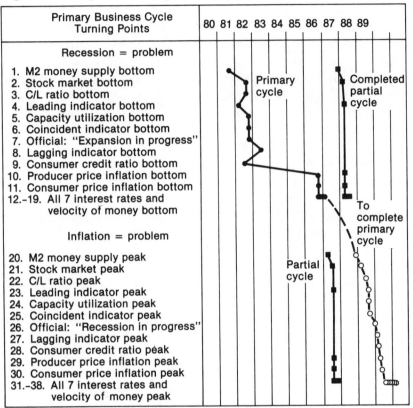

Primary Business Cycle Turning Points	80 81 82 83 84 85 86 87 88 89
Recession = problem	
1. M2 money supply bottom	
2. Stock market bottom	
3. C/L ratio bottom	
4. Leading indicator bottom	
5. Capacity utilization bottom	
6. Coincident indicator bottom	
7. Official: "Expansion in progress"	
8. Lagging indicator bottom	
9. Consumer credit ratio bottom	
10. Producer price inflation bottom	
11. Consumer price inflation bottom	
12.-19. All 7 interest rates and velocity of money bottom	
Inflation = problem	
20. M2 money supply peak	
21. Stock market peak	
22. C/L ratio peak	
23. Leading indicator peak	
24. Capacity utilization peak	
25. Coincident indicator peak	
26. Official: "Recession in progress"	
27. Lagging indicator peak	
28. Consumer credit ratio peak	
29. Producer price inflation peak	
30. Consumer price inflation peak	
31.-38. All 7 interest rates and velocity of money peak	

With or without a basic framework for analysis, millions of investors and investment managers are all looking at the indicators discussed in this book—plus many more, many of which are irrelevant. And since the stock market is essentially a competitive game, the market tends to (1) react to economic and financial events as they occur and (2) anticipate these economic events and their logical aftereffects. Therefore, when the money supply turns down, the market will also turn down in anticipation of higher interest rates *and in anticipation of a possible recession, which will reduce corporate earnings.* If the recession does not develop, the market will rise quickly as investors realize that they overreacted to the money supply reduction.

Mr. Samuelson's quip about the stock market predicting

nine out of the last *five* recessions is true, but does not prove that the market is irrational or inefficient. Mr. Samuelson's concern is the economy, but the concerns of stock market investors are things that *might affect the economy, corporate earnings, and future stock prices*. Therefore, the stock market will react to every partial business cycle, as well as every complete Primary Business Cycle that actually involves a recession, because investors' assessment of the *likelihood of a future recession is an integral part of current stock market valuations*.

Isolated Adjustments

Usually, a partial cycle can be identified as one involving the money supply, the stock market, inflation (or inflation fears), and interest rates, while the economy is unaffected. The worst situation for an investor is the stock market equivalent of a hailstorm in June: Everything is moving up handsomely and then, suddenly, the bottom drops out of the market for no apparent reason.

Such an incident took place in 1962, just after we came out of the 1960–1961 recession. Stocks had climbed to a point of significant overvaluation, with dividend yields falling below 3 percent, and anticipated growth rates of the economy were very high. However, at that time, there was a great deal of world tension due to Fidel Castro's exploits in Cuba, the construction of the Berlin Wall, and resumed nuclear testing in the United States. In the spring of 1962, President Kennedy added more uncertainty by asking for an increase in the federal debt limit and later engaging in a personal confrontation with the U.S. Steel Company over price increases. Finally, when several of the leading indicators turned down and the C/L ratio reached its *false peak* coming out of the 1960–1961 recession, the stock market overreacted and plunged 20 percent in three months. This partial cycle involved only the stock market, the C/L ratio, and the leading indicators.

From the investors' standpoint, three significant points can be made regarding such unpredictable snowfall-in-June type of stock market events:

- They are very rare. The 1962 mini-crash is the only serious decline of this nature in the past 50 years.
- Investors with a long-term perspective would not have been hurt. Since the decline happened at the wrong part of the business cycle, it would have been seen as a short-term decline. In fact, the market recovered quite quickly and then rose steadily to its next peak in 1966.
- For short-term traders, there were visible signs of overvaluation and excessive risk in the stock market at that time. The valuation model and the short-term trading signals presented later in this book would have flashed a clear "sell" signal before this mini-crash.

At the same time, these traders would have quickly known that the decline was to be short-lived, since it was a part of a rapid partial cycle partially caused by the *false* signal in the C/L ratio. With this knowledge, they would have been presented with some handsome buying opportunities by mid-1962.

Conclusions

We've defined a Primary Business Cycle consisting of 38 turning points that are driven by known cause-and-effect relationships. During any lengthy primary cycle, one or more partial cycles that involve some but not all of the 38 turning points may develop. Once a partial cycle begins and is recognized by the absence of turning points in the economic indicators, the next turning points can be predicted to first complete the partial cycle and then return to the prior position in the full Primary Business Cycle. Even a surprise event such as the market mini-crash of 1962 can be seen as a temporary decline when it occurs in the business cycle without the prescribed forerunners or when it is driven by a predictable and *false* signal in the C/L ratio.

Given the structure and historical behavior of primary and partial business cycles, we can now expose to critical scrutiny some well-known but ill-founded investment myths and then develop some true investment insights specifically based on the relationships contained in this business cycle model.

Chapter 10

Worthless Myths, Valuable Relationships, and Knowing the Difference

"It's amazing what a few facts and figures can do to your perspective on things."

—*R. M. Bowker, 1988*

DISPELLING SOME POPULAR MYTHS

The business cycle theory presented herein offers several well-founded and proven methods for investing in stocks, bonds, and gold, all of which will be developed in the next section. But the harsh reality of the investment community is that many investors rely on and fall victim to a multitude of myths, anecdotes, clichés, half-truths, and ill-founded theories about making money in the financial markets. We'd like to put some of these notions to rest at this time and then provide some specific investment insights that are the natural result of the relationships contained in the Primary Business Cycle.

Business Cycle Regularity

We have put the Primary Business Cycle on a time frame of periods of economic expansion and recession and peaks and bottoms of several cyclical indicators. But it is important to point out that nothing in the laws of supply and demand states that these business cycles should last for any specific amount of time. The causes and effects and, thus, the sequence of events are clear, but the time between events can vary by many years.

We make this point to convince investors to be skeptical of any forecasting theory or approach that suggests that things seem to happen every 4 years, 54 years, or 39 weeks. There is simply no factual foundation for these claims. The recession of 1960 lasted one year and was followed by nine years of expansion before the recession of 1970. The recession of 1980 lasted only about 7 months, and the following recovery lasted only one year and was followed by the 1981–1982 recession, which lasted for almost 18 months. That recession was followed by an expansion that lasted more than five years. Yet most people on Wall Street still tell you that the economic cycle is about four years long and is tied to the years of presidential elections. Unfortunately, this simplified view of the economy cannot be supported by the facts.

Figure 10-1 shows the history of economic expansions and contractions from 1854 to the present. The average duration of complete economic cycles (peak to peak) is between 49 and 55 months. The average duration of economic cycles (trough to trough) is nearly the same, averaging between 48 and 56 months for different time periods.

However, a closer look at the table shows that economic cycles have been as short as 18 months (January 1980 to July 1981) and as long as 116 months (April 1960 to December 1969). Therefore, if you had to make a general statement about the length of business cycles, you could accurately state only that *business cycles are about 52 months long—plus or minus 30 to 60 months.* Therefore, history strongly suggests that time cycles and historical average time periods between certain events in the business cycle should not be used as reliable indicators of future economic events.

Of even greater significance is the fact that the elapsed time between events in the business cycle is not an important factor in investment decisions. A full understanding of the sequence of events in the business cycle allows investors to foresee major

Figure 10-1. *Business Cycle Expansions and Contractions in the United States*

Business cycle reference dates		Duration in months			
		Contraction (trough from previous peak)	Expansion (trough to peak)	Cycle Trough from previous trough	Cycle Peak from previous peak
Trough	Peak				
December 1854	June 1857	....	30	....	....
December 1858	October 1860	18	22	48	40
June 1861	April 1865	8	46	30	54
December 1867	June 1869	32	18	78	50
December 1870	October 1873	18	34	36	52
March 1879	March 1882	65	36	99	101
May 1885	March 1887	38	22	74	60
April 1888	July 1890	13	27	35	40
May 1891	January 1893	10	20	37	30
June 1894	December 1895	17	18	37	35
June 1897	June 1899	18	24	36	42
December 1900	September 1902	18	21	42	39
August 1904	May 1907	23	33	44	56
June 1908	January 1910	13	19	46	32
January 1912	January 1913	24	12	43	36
December 1914	August 1918	23	44	35	67
March 1919	January 1920	7	10	51	17
July 1921	May 1923	18	22	28	40
July 1924	October 1926	14	27	36	41
November 1927	August 1929	13	21	40	34
March 1933	May 1937	43	50	64	93
June 1938	February 1945	13	80	63	93
October 1945	November 1948	8	37	88	45
October 1949	July 1953	11	45	48	56
May 1954	August 1957	10	39	55	49
April 1958	April 1960	8	24	47	32
February 1961	December 1969	10	106	34	116
November 1970	November 1973	11	36	117	47
March 1975	January 1980	16	58	52	74
July 1980	July 1981	6	12	64	18
November 1982		16	.....	28	.....
Average, all cycles:					
1854-1982 (30 cycles)		18	33	51	[1]51
1854-1919 (16 cycles)		22	27	48	[2]49
1919-1945 (6 cycles)		18	35	53	53
1945-1982 (6 cycles)		11	45	56	55
Average, peacetime cycles:					
1854-1982 (25 cycles)		19	27	46	[3]46
1854-1919 (14 cycles)		22	24	46	[4]47
1919-1945 (5 cycles)		20	26	46	45
1945-1982 (6 cycles)		11	34	46	44

NOTE: Underscored figures are the wartime expansions (Civil War, World Wars I and II, Korean war, and Vietnam war), the postwar contractions, and the full cycles that include the wartime expansions.

[1] 29 cycles.　　　[2] 15 cycles.　　　[3] 24 cycles.　　　[4] 13 cycles.

Source: National Bureau of Economic Research, Inc.

economic and financial turning points *whenever* they are about to happen because they can identify their causes ahead of time. This is far more reliable than using arbitrary or average time periods as investment guides.

Market-Timing Cycles

Every investor's dream is to have a timing system in his or her pocket. You could enjoy a marvelous state of wealth and peace of mind if you could simply buy stocks every four years, sell them three years later at a huge profit, and buy them back again one year later, after they had declined substantially.

There are two reasons that the real world doesn't operate in this way. First, if everyone knew of a permanent four-year cycle or any other fixed time cycle, who would sell at the bottom when you want to buy and who would buy three years later, at the top, when you want to sell? Second, like the economy, the stock and bond markets do not move in absolute, regular time cycles because there is simply no reason for them to do so. Short of astrology or a phases-of-the-moon theory, which we do not recommend as bases for investment decision making, there is no reason to expect that the increasingly complex and constantly changing economy would be so accommodating of the desires of investors.

The Four-Year Election Cycle. Even if you could present a logical rationale for a rhythmic, repeating time pattern, it should be viewed with skepticism and subjected to long-term historical analysis. One of the most popular and logical time cycles touted by investment advisers is the four-year presidential election cycle.

The reasoning goes like this:

Every four years during the presidential election year, the public is filled with hope for increased prosperity as presidential candidates flood the airwaves with their plans, programs, and dreams for America's future. Lower taxes, more jobs, higher pay, social justice, world peace, a war on crime and drugs, and greater economic growth are constantly paraded before the

American public for almost a full year. As a result, people's confidence in the future rises and they all buy stocks.

But then, after the election, the reality that some of these dreams may not be so easily attained—or worse, that they might cost money—slowly sinks in. Confidence wanes and stocks go down. In addition, any unpopular economic policies or adjustments are enacted in the early years of the new administration so that the world will look good again in four years—at reelection time. Midway between the elections, the market bottoms out on the bet that the government will try to make things better by the next election and then rises until the next election actually occurs. The market peaks again, and the cycle repeats itself.

This is a logical story that many people believe. And to confirm this logic, a proponent of the theory has "hard evidence" to prove it: a chart of the stock market between 1968 and 1982. During this time period, the stock market reached peaks during the election years of 1968, 1972, 1976, and 1980 and bottomed out about two years after each peak in 1970, 1974, 1978, and 1982. Surely, this is proof positive that to get rich, all you have to do is buy stocks in 1986, 1990, 1994, and 1998 and then sell them in 1988, 1992, 1996, and 2000. What could be easier?

However, before you bet the ranch on this approach, it's instructive to take a longer-term view of history. We've had elections in this country for over 200 years, so perhaps the results of a 14-year slice of time should not be accepted as everlasting truth.

We can test this theory more clearly by going back a few more decades and comparing actual market peaks with those that the presidential election cycle theory would have predicted. The results are shown in Figure 10-2.

As seen in Figure 10-2, the brief period from 1968 to 1980 was 100 percent accurate. However, over the long haul, the method was accurate less than 50 percent of the time. An investor could match this performance by flipping a coin.

Cycles, Cycles, Everywhere. A wonderful book was published in 1971, entitled *Cycles: The Mysterious Forces That*

Figure 10-2. *Four-Year Presidential Cycle Theory Peaks Versus Actual Stock Market Peaks*

Predicted Peak Based on Presidential Election Years	Was There a Major Stock Market Peak in This Year?		Batting Average
1928	No		
1932	No		
1936	Yes		
1940	No		
1944	No		7 right
1948	No		8 wrong
1952	Yes		
1956	Yes		Accuracy
1960	No		= 47%
1964	No		
1968	Yes	Claimed	
1972	Yes	proof	
1976	Yes	of	
1980	Yes	validity	
1984	No		

Trigger Events. This book and its supplement, the *Catalog of Cycles,* provide a virtual encyclopedia of things that go up and down on a regular basis all around the world. Since the stock market offers so much opportunity for profit with a cyclical betting system, the research on stock market cycles has been exhaustive. The relentless search for periodic cycles has consumed enormous amounts of time and effort by many students of the financial markets. The result is a massive catalog of "proven" stock market cycles identified by dozens of research analysts and detailed in *Cycles.* Figure 10-3 contains a list of some—but not all—of these "statistically proven" time cycles for the stock market.

It is now clear that some "statistically valid" time cycle can be found to explain any two or three successive peaks in the stock market. In fact, any two market peaks that are between three months and 89 years apart can be "explained" by a statistically proven cycle. But since this can only be done after the fact, this catalog of "proven" cycles has very little practical

Figure 10-3. *Time Cycles for Industrial Stock Prices*

Length of Time from Peak to Peak		
2.97 months	1.10 years	5.56 years
3.77 months	1.20 years	5.91 years
3.95 months	1.48 years	6.07 years
5.10 months	1.80 years	6.86 years
5.90 months	1.90 years	7.40 years
6.50 months	2.10 years	8.00 years
7.50 months	2.30 years	9.20 years
7.80 months	2.60 years	9.60 years
8.30 months	2.80 years	10.65 years
9.90 months	3.06 years	11.30 years
10.70 months	3.19 years	13.10 years
11.60 months	3.39 years	17.80 years
12.00 months	3.74 years	18.20 years
	3.94 years	19.10 years
	4.02 years	23.20 years
	4.31 years	25.80 years
	4.40 years	37.50 years
	4.88 years	45.00 years
		54.00 years
		56.00 years
		89.50 years

Source: *Catalog of Cycles* (Foundation of the Study of Cycles, 1964).

value. However, investors should note that the next time that an analyst writes an article or appears on television with a "clear, cyclical explanation" of why the market just went up or down, that cyclical evidence should be taken with a grain of salt.

The important point is that unless the investor is prepared to believe that a set of external forces somehow governs the behavior of millions of individual investors and institutions around the world, that investor should avoid the pitfalls of believing in regular time cycles in the financial markets. Whether an analyst's stock market advice is based on the Kondratieff wave theory, the Elliott wave theory, a phases-of-the-moon theory (there really is one), or any other time cycle theory, we would advise investors to ask two questions before accepting that advice as valid:

- Is there a logical cause-and-effect relationship behind the proposed cycle?
- Has the proposed cycle been proven over a *long-term* period of history?

Clichés for Fun and Profit

The Clichés of Life. You can probably remember many of the pearls of wisdom that were bestowed on you as a child. These clear, simple one-liners that appeared to make so much sense at the time—imparted to you by an older and, obviously, wiser person in whom you had trust and confidence—can make a lasting impression on a young mind. "Look before you leap," "Don't count your chickens before they hatch," "A penny saved is a penny earned!" How easy life must be with simple rules like these to guide the way. But as we grow older, we hear more clichés and platitudes, and life begins to get confusing. By the time we reach adulthood, we have heard hundreds of such sayings that relate to every aspect of our lives. There is even a book on the market today entitled *The Dictionary of Clichés*, which has over 2,000 entries of tried and true statements representing the collective wisdom of the ages.

However, a closer look at these clichés, anecdotes, and platitudes reveals that these wonderful ideas about how one should behave are, in many cases, completely contradictory and mutually exclusive. In any given situation, you might proceed slowly and carefully, in accordance with the time-tested principle that "haste makes waste"—only to discover that you made a mistake because you failed to follow the equally timeless principle that "he who hesitates is lost."

In Figure 10-4, some popular clichés are listed in the first column. The second column lists popular clichés that represent the exact opposite point of view.

This list goes on and on.

The unfortunate truth of the matter is that once you have a long list of proverbs and clichés that have all been true on at least one occasion, you can present yourself as extremely wise and well informed simply by drawing out whatever cliché fits the situation of the moment. No matter what mistakes people make,

Figure 10-4. *Conflicting Truths*

Truths—Side 1	Truths—Flip Side
Haste makes waste	He who hesitates is lost
Look before you leap	The early bird gets the worm
Better safe than sorry	No guts—no glory
It's better to give than to receive	Charity begins at home
Two heads are better than one	Too many cooks spoil the stew
Spare the rod and spoil the child	You'll catch more flies with honey than with vinegar
Beware of Greeks bearing gifts	Don't look a gift horse in the mouth
Patience is a virtue	Time waits for no man
Don't put all your eggs in one basket	Don't keep too many irons in the fire, stick to your knitting
A thing of beauty is a joy forever	Beauty is only skin deep
Love thy neighbor as thyself	I'm not my brother's keeper
The meek shall inherit the earth	The squeaky wheel gets the grease

you can show them that, in hindsight, they clearly should have "looked before they leaped" or remembered that "the early bird gets the worm"—depending on the mistake.

The Clichés of Wall Street. The investment community is riddled with clichés—particularly clichés about the stock market. You hear them everyday—whenever someone wants to explain why the market did what it did yesterday or whenever some expert or technical analyst explains why he or she was expecting the market's recent behavior.

Cliché 1: *The market dropped because investors were worried about something or other.*

Flip side: *The market rose because everyone knows that the market climbs a wall of worry.*

Cliché 2: *The market foresaw higher interest rates, so it went down.*

Flip side: *The market saw higher interest rates as a sign of a strengthening economy, so it went up.*

Cliché 3: *The bond market fell because the stock market fell.*

Flip side: *The decline in the stock market was caused by falling bond prices.*

Cliché 4: *Higher interest rates caused the dollar to strengthen as foreign investors bought bonds.*

Flip side: *Higher interest rates caused the dollar to weaken as foreign investors worried about a recession.*

Cliché 5: *Don't fight the momentum of the market—go with the flow.*

Flip side: *The market is always wrong—be a contrarian.*

Cliché 6: *The market ignored the earnings reports and focused on interest rates.*

Flip side: *The market ignored the higher interest rates and focused on earnings reports.*

> **Cliché 7:** *The investor psychology is driving this market.*
>
> **Flip side 1:** *This is now a "technical" market.*
>
> **Flip side 2:** *The market is being driven by news events.*
>
> **Flip side 3:** *The market is returning to fundamentals now.*

> **Cliché 8:** *The market is declining in **anticipation** of a recession.*
>
> **Flip side 1:** *The current recession is driving stock prices down.*
>
> **Flip side 2:** *The market often goes up in recessions because interest rates are lower.*

> **Cliché 9:** *People are keeping money in cash, which is very bearish.*
>
> **Flip side:** *There is so much cash on the sidelines now, that it's very bullish.*

If you want to play amusing games along these lines, make two columns on a sheet of paper. Label one column "what happened" and the second column "why it happened." Then, everyday, jot down the explanations for yesterday's stock market action on your paper. After a month or so, check all of the "experts'" daily explanations of why the market went up or down. You will be astounded at the inconsistency of these investment "experts."

The point of this analysis of clichés is to illustrate that to a large extent Wall Street "wisdom" is very similar to the wisdom of the clichés that we are told as children. Each cliché may apply to a given day or a given situation, but none holds as a general guideline for long-term investing. The professional investment industry has generated enough one-liners to convince the investing public that they know what they're talking about, although they have simply drawn out appropriate Wall Street clichés of the day. In this author's opinion, informed investors should not fall victim to the belief that (1) these Wall Street anecdotes are inherently true or (2) the people who use them necessarily have a solid understanding of the dynamics of the financial markets.

SOME VALUABLE RELATIONSHIPS

The Truth About Interest Rates and the Stock Market

One of the most widely accepted clichés on Wall Street deals with the relationship between stock prices and interest rates: When interest rates go down, the stock market goes up, and when interest rates go up, the stock market goes down. Unfortunately, history shows otherwise. In fact, since 1920, this broad, categorical statement has been true only 55 percent of the time.

The relationship between interest rates and the stock market is seriously misunderstood based on the historical evidence at hand. The old "truth" about interest rates and stock prices always going in opposite directions is a classic example of this misunderstanding. The following analysis of interest rate turning points and stock market turning points is intended to provide a more clear and accurate set of relationships between interest rates and stock prices.

As outlined earlier, the Primary Business Cycle tracks seven specific interest rates:

• The federal funds rate
• The 91-day T-bill rate

- The prime rate
- The corporate bond rate
- The long-term T-bond rate
- The municipal bond rate
- The FHA mortgage rate

By our definitions, a top or bottom in interest rates occurs only when *all seven* rates have clearly reached turning points. The following analysis describes the specific historical relationships between:

- Interest rate peaks and stock market bottoms
- Interest rate bottoms and stock market peaks

Interest Rate Peaks and Stock Market Bottoms. Figure 10-5 shows the historical relationship between interest rate peaks and stock market bottoms since 1948. The first column shows the month in which the first of the seven interest rates

Figure 10-5.

	Interest Rate Tops			Next Stock Market Bottom	
					No. of
	First Interest Rate	Last Interest Rate	Months from First		Months After Last Interest
Cycle	Top	Top	to Last	Date	Rate Top
1	10/48	6/49	8	6/49	0
2	6/53	2/54	8	9/53	−5
3	6/57	12/57	6	12/57	0
4	9/59	7/60	10	10/60	3
5	8/66	12/66	4	10/66	−2
6	8/69	6/70	10	6/70	0
7	7/74	12/74	5	12/74	0
8	3/80	4/80	1	4/80	0
9	5/81	1/82	8	7/82	6
10	5/84	8/84	3	7/84	−1
		Average = 6.3		Average = 0.1	

reached a peak. The second column shows the month in which the last of the seven rates reached a peak. The third column shows the number of months that it took for all seven rates to reach peaks. The "peaking" period ranged from 1 to 10 months and *averaged 6.3 months over all ten primary and partial cycles.*

The fourth column shows the date of the next stock market bottom following the interest rate peaking period, and the last column shows the number of months that elapsed from the last interest rate top to the next stock market bottom. The elapsed time ranged from –5 months (the stock market bottomed 5 months before the last interest rate peak) to 6 months, with an average of 0.1 month.

Based on these data, we can conclude that:

- Interest rates peak over a relatively short period of time (average = 6.3 months).
- Stock market bottoms do, in fact, occur very near the date on which the last of the seven interest rates reaches its peak.

Interest Rate Bottoms and Stock Market Peaks. Figure 10-6 examines the relationship between interest rate bottoms and stock market peaks; here we see a *very different picture.* The time span required for all seven interest rates to bottom out ranges from 3 months to 59 months and averages 15.1 months. Furthermore, *the stock market does not peak during the bottoming-out period of interest rates,* but reaches the next peak between 2 and 27 months later, averaging 10.1 months.

Therefore, history clearly shows that:

- Interest rates bottom out over a long period of time (average = 15.1 months).
- The next stock market peak occurs *well after* the date of the last interest rate bottom.

As a point of interest, this relationship extends all the way back to 1910, including the crash of 1929. Interest rates bottomed out in 1928, well before the stock market peak in September 1929.

Figure 10-6.

| | Interest Rate Bottoms | | | Next Stock Market Top | |
| | | | | Date | No. of Months After Last Interest Rate Bottom |
Cycle	First Interest Rate Bottom	Last Interest Rate Bottom	Months from First to Last		
1	7/49	2/51	19	1/53	23
2	3/54	7/55	16	7/56	12
3	1/58	8/58	7	7/59	11
4	12/60	11/65	59	1/66	2
5	1/67	10/67	9	12/68	14
6	10/71	11/72	13	1/73	2
7	12/76	11/77	11	2/80	27
8	5/80	8/80	3	11/80	3
9	10/82	7/83	9	10/83	3
10	11/86	4/87	5	8/87	4
			Average = 15.1		Average = 10.1

This means that in every business cycle, a major stock market top should not be expected until *well after* all seven interest rates have clearly bottomed out. This also means that in every business cycle, there is a period in which interest rates and the stock market are *both* rising together. Following is a "road map" of these relationships.

The Road Map of Stock Prices and Interest Rates. A complete, lifetime investment system could be built on just the relationship described here, which shows why many investors make major timing errors by relying on basic "truths" that are, in fact, only half true.

Figure 10-7 shows the typical timing of stock market and interest rate turning points of *every major business cycle since 1910*. The top line is the path of our seven interest rates. The bottom line is the path of the stock market. What happens at each phase in the cycle is as follows:

• In Phase A, all seven interest rates are rising toward a peak.

Figure 10-7. *The Road Map of Stock Prices and Interest Rates*

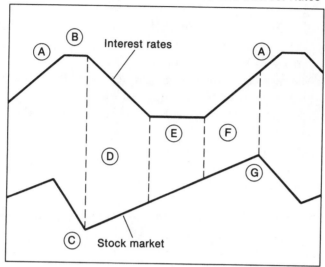

- In Phase B, all seven interest rates peak out together. It takes an average of *six months* for all seven rates to peak and turn down.
- At Point C, the stock market reaches a *major bottom* just as the last of the seven interest rates peaks out.
- During Phase D, interest rates all decline and the stock market rises sharply, confirming the first half of the old cliché.
- In Phase E, all seven interest rates reach bottom together. However, this is a much longer process. *It takes an average of 15 months for all seven rates to bottom out. And during this time, the stock market continues to rise.*
- In Phase F, interest rates and the stock market *both rise together.* In other words, *the part of the cliché that says that the stock market always goes down when interest rates go up is false.*
- At Point G, *well after all seven interest rates have bottomed out, the stock market reaches its next major peak.* This happens just *before* interest rates rise to their next major peak.
- *We now return to Phase A, where all seven interest rates rise to their next peak and stock prices decline.*

We can clearly see this phenomenon in the same business cycle Gantt chart that we've used throughout the book. Figure 10-8 is exactly the same as Figure 8-29, but with all dots removed from the chart except for those denoting turning points for interest rates and the stock market.

Following the arrows, you can see that the stock market peaks appear well after the last interest rate bottoms and that the stock market bottoms occur very close to the last of the interest rate peaks.

Using these relationships in conjunction with those described earlier, we can develop a stock market investment strategy that requires only two decisions:

• When (1) we are *in* a recession and (2) interest rates peak out and head down while (3) the M2 money supply turns up (because the Fed now wants to end the recession)—buy stocks.

• When (1) we are in a period of expansion and (2) inflation and interest rates begin to move up—hold stocks until the M2 money supply turns down (because the Fed wants to stop inflation)—and then sell stocks.

We will tie these two rules into a complete portfolio management system in a later chapter.

Inflation and Interest Rates

Inflation. The two broadest measures of inflation that are recorded and tracked on a monthly basis are the producer price index and the consumer price index. While the Commerce Department reports these figures each month, it is necessary to calculate the 12-month percentage change in these indexes to arrive at an annual *rate of inflation* at the producer or consumer level.

As you would expect, these two annual inflation rates tend to move up and down together, but an examination of these inflation rates over the last 35 years reveals two other characteristics that are not widely discussed:

Figure 10-8. *Interest Rate and Stock Market Turning Points*

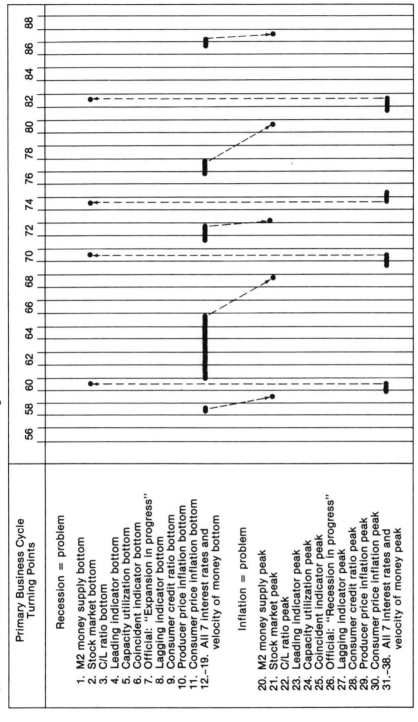

Primary Business Cycle
Turning Points

Recession = problem

1. M2 money supply bottom
2. Stock market bottom
3. C/L ratio bottom
4. Leading indicator bottom
5. Capacity utilization bottom
6. Coincident indicator bottom
7. Official: "Expansion in progress"
8. Lagging indicator bottom
9. Consumer credit ratio bottom
10. Producer price inflation bottom
11. Consumer price inflation bottom
12.–19. All 7 interest rates and
        velocity of money bottom

Inflation = problem

20. M2 money supply peak
21. Stock market peak
22. C/L ratio peak
23. Leading indicator peak
24. Capacity utilization peak
25. Coincident indicator peak
26. Official: "Recession in progress"
27. Lagging indicator peak
28. Consumer credit ratio peak
29. Producer price inflation peak
30. Consumer price inflation peak
31.–38. All 7 interest rates and
        velocity of money peak

- The producer inflation rate tends to reach peaks and bottoms before the consumer inflation rate does.
- The producer inflation rate is more volatile than the consumer inflation rate.

Historical data for these two inflation rates are shown in Figure 10-9.

Inflation's Clear Linkage to Interest Rates. The question of volatility may not seem important from an investor's point of view, since you cannot buy or sell an inflation rate. But the history of these two inflation rates show how the movements of inflation are related to movements in interest rates—which is very significant to investors.

In Figure 10-9, we can see that from 1952 until about 1970, the producer and consumer inflation rates track together very closely. But during the early 1960s and later in 1967, the producer inflation rate actually turned negative while the consumer inflation rate remained positive at all times. The same phenomenon occurred in 1985 and 1986. Since interest rates are always positive, this suggests that the consumer inflation rate may be more closely tied to interest rates than the producer inflation rate is.

Figure 10-9. *Producer and Consumer Inflation Rates: 1953–1988*

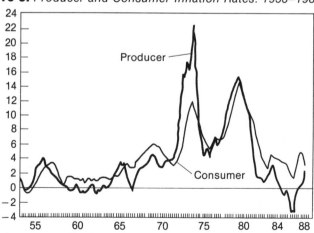

Source of raw data: *Business Conditions Digest.*

Another significant difference between these two rates provides a strong clue as to how inflation is related to interest rates. Figure 10-9 shows that the 35-year historical peak in the producer inflation rate occurred in 1974—at over 22 percent—while the second big peak, in 1980, only reached 15 percent. This is not the case with the consumer inflation rate, which reached 12.2 percent in 1974 but reached its 35-year peak in 1980—at over 14 percent.

If we compare the annual consumer inflation rate with the short-term T-bill interest rate, as shown in Figure 10-10, we can make two observations:

- The relationship between inflation and interest rates that was defined in Chapter 7 is clearly true. The turning points of consumer inflation and T-bill rates are very closely correlated over the entire 35-year time period.
- The T-bill rates follow the consumer inflation pattern of hitting one major peak in 1974 but reaching a higher 35-year peak in 1980.

This strong linkage between the consumer inflation rate and the T-bill rate can be translated into an investment strategy for gold and bonds that is based on clear and decisive turning points.

Figure 10-10. *Consumer Inflation Rate Versus Treasury Bill Rate*

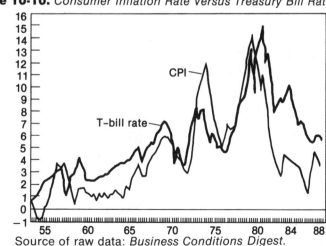

Source of raw data: *Business Conditions Digest.*

If we remember that long-term interest rates *follow* short-term interest rates, such as the T-bill rate, only two rules are needed:

• When both the consumer inflation rate and the T-bill rate turn down, investors can be confident that they are seeing a decisive peak in inflation and interest rates. Therefore, at that time, investors should sell gold, which moves in the same direction as inflation, and should prepare to buy bonds, which will start to move up when long-term interest rates soon follow the T-bill rate down.

• When both consumer inflation and T-bill rates turn up, investors can count on a decisive upturn in inflation and interest rates. Therefore, investors should buy gold and prepare to sell bonds when long-term rates soon follow the T-bill rate up.

It is clear from Figure 10-10 that at any point in the business cycle, investors' portfolios may contain some investments in gold or bonds but, except for the very brief period between the inflation and interest rate turning points, not both at the same time. We discuss the fundamentals of gold and bond markets and see how they fit into a complete portfolio management system in Chapter 18.

An Intriguing Observation on the Money Supply

An Amazing Correlation. Figure 10-11 is a rather fascinating chart. The two lines in the upper part of the chart are the same as those in Figure 10-10: the consumer inflation rate and the T-bill rate. The third line, the lower of the three, consists of bold, sweeping, up and down movements that reach clearly defined peaks and bottoms at almost exactly the same time as the peaks and bottoms in inflation and interest rates. If an investor wanted to play only the inflation cycle (with gold) or only the interest rate cycle (with bonds), this third indicator would provide a very strong confirmation of the peaks and bottoms in inflation and interest rates.

But what is this third indicator? It is the 12-month percentage change of the M2 money supply—*inverted*. That is, the highest points on the M2 line are the bottoms and the lowest

Figure 10-11. *Inflation, Interest Rates, and the Annual Percentage Change in M2—Inverted*

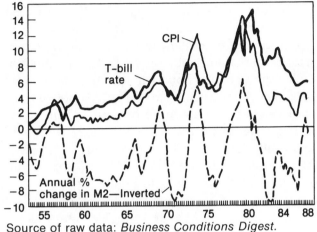

Source of raw data: *Business Conditions Digest.*

points on the chart are really the peaks. In Figure 10-11, the scale of the 12-month percentage change in M2 is the same as the left-hand side of the chart, but with the opposite sign.

What's Behind It? This chart really shows that while inflation and interest rates are moving from their lows to their highs (e.g., 1976 to 1980), the annual percentage change in M2 is actually declining from its high to its low. On the surface, this is illogical. Although more money in the system should increase inflation, this chart shows that inflation goes up when the *change* in M2 goes down, and vice versa. This apparent logical conflict can be resolved by looking at (1) some automatic mathematical phenomena that happen in the business cycle and (2) the behavior of the Fed.

To explain this relationship, let's first set up the known timing relationships between the money supply, inflation, and interest rates. We know that the money supply peaks out *before* the beginning of a recession; then the recession begins; and then, later, during the recession, inflation and interest rates peak at nearly the same time, with inflation peaking first. The same relationships hold at the bottom of the cycle. The money supply bottoms out first during the recession, followed by the end of the

recession and then the bottoms in inflation and interest rates.
This sequence of events is displayed in Figure 10-12.

But now look at the line in Figure 10-12 that is labeled the
"% change in M2." In an earlier section, we discussed that the
annual rate of change of an indicator would tend to reach turning
points before the actual indicator itself. This is another case of
that expected mathematical phenomenon. As seen on this chart,
the line marked "% change in M2" reaches bottom just before
the M2 money supply does in the recession. But by bottoming
out here, this percentage change in M2 bottom coincides with
the peaks in inflation and interest rates. This explains why the
percentage changes in M2 bottoms occur at the same time as the
inflation and interest rate peaks in Figure 10-11.

However, as we come out of the recession, something
unusual happens. We would expect the percentage change in M2
to rise and then peak out prior to the next recession. Instead, the
percentage change in M2 peaks out much earlier, soon after the
first recession ends. The reason for this is that at the bottom of a
recession, the Fed increases the money supply *very rapidly* to
stimulate spending and consumption. Thus, as we come out of
the recession, the money supply is increasing *and* the rate of

Figure 10-12. *M2 Timing Relationships*

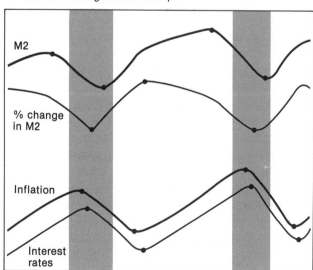

increase of the money supply is *very high*. Later, the actual money supply continues to grow, but at a slower rate. Therefore, the rate of change of M2 peaks out and declines shortly after the end of the recession, which happens to be exactly when inflation and interest rates naturally bottom out.

We can now conclude that the rate of change in M2 can be used as a confirming indicator of inflation and interest rate turning points, remembering the inverse relationships:

• When the annual percentage change in M2 bottoms out, we are at inflation and interest rate peaks.

• When the annual percentage change in M2 peaks out, we are at inflation and interest rate bottoms.

Since this indicator has both a logical foundation and a strong track record as a confirming indicator, we add the peak and the bottom of the annual percentage change in M2 to our list of 38 trackable indicators in the final business cycle—bringing the complete cycle to a total of 40 events.

Part III

OUTSIDE INFLUENCES ON THE BUSINESS CYCLE

"There has never been a perfect government because men have passions; and if they did not have passions, there would be no need for government."

—*Voltaire,* Politique et legislation: Idées républicaines,
18th century

As we have defined the Primary Business Cycle, it is a closed system of economic and financial forces and inter-relationships. It comprises the natural causes and effects that take place in the domestic U.S. economy and the normal response of the Fed to prevailing economic situations.

However, three other major influences on the Primary Business Cycle are outside of the business cycle itself. These independent external influences, which run on their own time-table and are driven by external forces, are:

- The effects of the government's fiscal policy (tax laws and spending programs)
- The effects of U.S. dollar exchange rates relative to foreign currencies
- The effects of outside political, military, or economic events that can happen at any time

In all cases, an unanticipated event or situation could develop anytime during a normal business cycle. Even though these events might not be predictable, the *effects* of these events on the business cycle can be predicted with relative certainty—at least in terms of direction and magnitude.

For example, a major tax increase would obviously take money out of consumers' hands and slow down the economy. A major decline in the international value of the U.S. dollar would—at least temporarily—strengthen our economy by making our exports more price-competitive. A sudden increase in oil prices, such as those of the 1970s, would obviously have a serious effect on inflation and then interest rates.

The next three chapters address each of these areas separately to allow investors to react quickly to such changes by understanding fundamental effects that they have on the business cycle and the financial markets.

Chapter 11

The Cyclical Effects of Government Policies

TAXES AND SPENDING

Theoretically, there are two components of fiscal policy: federal tax policy and federal spending policy. But history shows that only one of these components—tax policy—ever changes significantly over the years or the decades. As opposed to being cyclical or dictated by prevailing economic situations, spending policy appears to be more like a commandment than a policy option, as follows: "The government shall spend as much as it can at all times." This tendency to spend is the direct result of our political system, in which politicians win their offices by promising to do things for their constituents. But doing things costs money, so Congress has a built-in bias toward spending money. This propensity to spend through good times and bad is evidenced by Figure 11-1.

This chart shows federal government expenditures since 1962. While there are occasional, microscopic, one-quarter declines over the years, the total level of federal expenditures just goes up and up, regardless of the economic situation.

We can conclude from this evidence that, in total, government spending is not cyclical. Over a span of several business cycles, government spending levels will not exert any dominant

Figure 11-1. *Federal Government Expenditures*

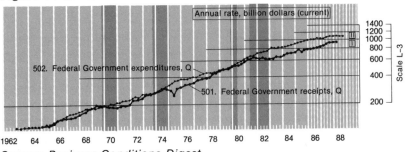

Source: *Business Conditions Digest.*

cyclical influence on any of the key components of the Primary Business Cycle.

On the other hand, the federal government's tax revenues are quite cyclical because they are tied directly to the annual wealth of the nation. Given no change in the tax laws or rates over a period of years, annual tax revenues would equal the average tax rate times the total taxable income of all individuals, businesses, and other taxable institutions. In concept, we could define annual tax revenues as the average tax rate times the GNP:

Tax Revenues = GNP × Tax Rate

Given this concept, it's easy to see that if the tax rate doesn't change, the government's tax revenues will increase when the GNP goes up and decrease when the GNP goes down. Figure 11-2 shows what happens. As we go through a business cycle, the economy rises, falls, and rises again—and tax revenues rise and fall with the economy. Meanwhile, government spending just goes up in a straight line.

THE FEDERAL BUDGET SURPLUS OR DEFICIT

Given the ups and downs of tax revenues and consistent increases in government spending, the budget balance, which is

Figure 11-2. *The GNP, Tax Revenues, and Spending over a Business Cycle*

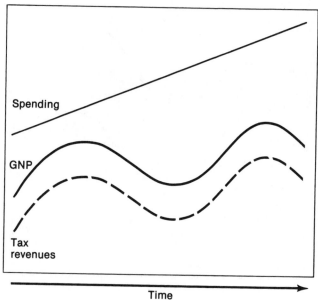

Time

the difference between the government's tax revenues and the government's annual spending, must also be cyclical. If we lived in a world in which the government tried to live on a balanced budget, over a business cycle, a surplus would develop when the economy went up and a deficit would appear when the economy went down (as tax revenues fell short of our constantly increasing spending levels). This hypothetical situation is illustrated in Figure 11-3.

However, the real world of politics shows that this cyclical shift from surplus to deficit to surplus again is simply not achievable. First, if the government ran a significant budget surplus for an extended period of time, the public would be outraged because the government would obviously be taking away too much in taxes. There would be an outcry for tax reduction, and the surplus would disappear. Second, the government couldn't possibly sit on a budget surplus—a pile of extra money—when so many senators and congressmen have so many constituents who want this money spent. Instead of

Figure 11-3. *The Budget Balance in an Ideal World*

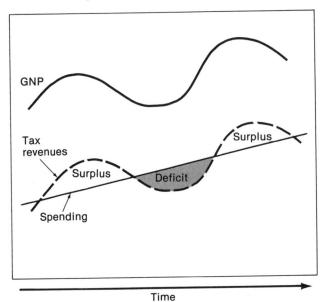

running a surplus during good times, the government chooses to spend it on increased government spending programs.

With these political realities contributing to the virtual elimination of a sustainable budget surplus, the budget balance effectively takes on the shape displayed in Figure 11-4.

During good times, tax revenues approach or even equal the federal spending level; during recessions, tax revenues fall and a deficit occurs. This would be the normal, politically pragmatic picture of the budget balance without any tax policy changes on the part of the government.

NORMAL TAX EFFECTS ON THE BUSINESS CYCLE

Under normal historical circumstances, federal tax and spending policies are outside of the business cycle since they can be changed by Congress at any time. But whenever the investor hears of a substantial change in tax or spending policy, he can place those government actions into one of two categories: expansive or recessive.

Figure 11-4. *The Budget Balance in the Real World*

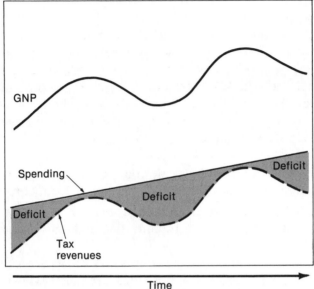

A government-mandated program to either *decrease taxes* or *increase spending* is an *expansive* program, designed to *stimulate* the economy by putting more money into the hands of the consuming public. These expansive actions have the same directional effect as an increase in the money supply. Similarly, any government action to *increase taxes* or *decrease spending* is a *recessive* program, designed to *slow down* the economy. Accordingly, such actions have the same constraining economic effect as a decrease in the money supply.

No matter where we happen to be in the business cycle, an *expansive* government action normally tends to stimulate the economy, and a *recessive* action normally slows the economy. Accordingly, the stock market responds favorably to expansive tax policy changes and negatively to recessive policy actions.

TAX POLICY OPTIONS

Given a normal budget cycle between zero or a small surplus and a deficit, we can examine the implications of a

change in federal tax policy. Theoretically and, again, just
theoretically, tax policy could be used as a tool to control the
economy, just as the money supply can be used by the Fed to
influence economic growth. But if the monetary policy of the
Fed is a fly swatter, tax policy is a sledgehammer. Tax laws take
a long time to develop and make their way through both Houses
of Congress and the White House. And once they have been put
into effect, they influence all aspects of the economy and remain
in effect until another round of tax legislation can be passed.

At any time, Congress may choose to:

- Increase taxes to slow down the economy if it was growing too
  fast, taking potential spending money away from consumers
- Decrease taxes to stimulate the economy during a recession by
  leaving more spendable income in the hands of consumers

The second option, decreasing taxes in a recession, was
one of the most attractive political features of Keynesian economics, which legitimized the government's power to run a
planned deficit during slow economic times. The accepted and
well-publicized theory held that tax rate cuts would allow people
to spend more money, ignite economic growth, and increase
GNP to the point at which the higher GNP multiplied by the
lower tax rate would eventually produce *more* total revenues
and close the deficit. Figure 11-5 shows how this would work—
at least in theory.

Now, suppose you are in charge of the fiscal policy of the
United States. You are armed with the ability to run deep federal
deficits under the umbrella of a highly regarded, well-accepted
body of economic wisdom—specifically, Keynesian economics.
You know that regardless of political rhetoric, you will spend as
much as you can up to the limit authorized by law. With this
background, you now have two fundamental policy options:

Policy 1—Spend and tax: Begin with the knowledge
that spending will rise, so plan on increasing tax revenues to
meet federal spending requirements.

Figure 11-5. *The GNP and Tax Revenues: Illustration*

	Situation	GNP	Effective Tax Rate	Total Tax Revenues	Total Spending	Deficit	Tax Revenue and Budget Deficit Impact
	Before recession	$3,000	26.6%	$800	$820	$ 20	
	During recession (GNP falls, no change in tax rate)	2,600	26.6	693	830	137	Revenues fall and the deficit increases
	Government lowers tax rate and the GNP rises a little	2,700	23	621	840	219	Revenues initially fall further and the deficit increases more
	Lower taxes stimulate more economic growth	3,600	23	828	850	22	Revenues increase and the deficit is reduced

Time

Republicans have perennially accused the Democrats of following this policy. Under this policy, spending increases and taxes increase more or less proportionately. The economy grows, but not too rapidly because the tax burden is high. While government spending programs are always welcomed by their recipients, the taxpaying public does not appreciate the increasing burden of higher and higher taxes. If you think that you will have trouble selling the public on spend-and-tax policies, you have still another "legitimate" option:

Policy 2—Spend and borrow: Begin with the knowledge that spending will rise, but instead of raising the tax rate to finance this spending, you cut the tax rate, increase the budget deficit, and assume that the economy will grow faster. The higher taxable income base is supposed to offset the lower tax rate, and tax revenues will increase to finance increased spending, and close the budget deficit.

This is a much more politically popular approach to fiscal policy—everyone supports lower tax rates. It is also the essence of the highly touted Reaganomics. During the 1981–1982 recession, Congress and the White House joined forces to cut tax rates to grow the economy out of the recession. According to theory, lower tax rates, an increased supply of money from the Fed, and a rapidly growing economy would generate additional tax revenues to close the budget deficit, which was approaching $100 billion.

But, alas, something went wrong. By 1986, following four years of solid economic growth, the budget deficit had increased to $220 billion. At the time, many economists believed that the Reagan tax cuts were simply too much—that even a very high sustained rate of economic growth would not be enough to offset the tax revenues that would be lost from cutting the tax rate so much. History now suggests that they were right.

Now, in 1988, a slight reduction in the annual growth rate of government spending has allowed the budget deficit to fall to about $150 billion. Some believe that this proves the viability of the spend-and-borrow approach. But behind the scenes, we have quietly created a very serious long-term financial problem for which there is no fiscal policy solution.

TURNING A SOLUTION INTO A PROBLEM

Returning to Keynesian theory for a moment, the idea of using fiscal policy to control the economy got us where we are today. A recession developed, and a cut in the effective tax rate helped to end the recession and bring about an unusually long period of steady growth. Running a short-term budget deficit was part of the *solution* to the economic *problem* of a recession. But now, the deficit hasn't gone away as we near the end of this economic boom. And now the *deficit* itself is *part of the problem*—both economically and politically.

At the moment, while the economy is still growing, the problem is only serious as opposed to critical. It is serious because the amount of debt that the government is amassing has three financial effects on the economy. First, the government, as a big borrower of money, is exerting a constant and increasing amount of upward pressure on interest rates. Second, the government must service this debt by paying an increasing amount of interest on its bonds, which leaves less in the coffers for other government programs. Third, because our interest rates have been relatively attractive on a worldwide basis, more and more foreign money is buying our government bonds. This means that we are becoming increasingly indebted to foreign nations.

At the moment, none of these problems is earth-shattering—as long as the economy is still growing and the tax base is still increasing. But like any individual, corporation, or government that continues to go deeper and deeper in debt and justifies this increased debt by assuming continuing, uninterrupted economic growth, we are setting ourselves up for a fall—and quite a serious one at that. Let's look at the recent record. Figure 11-6 shows the federal government's budget surplus or deficit since 1962.

Figure 11-6. *Federal Government Budget Surplus or Deficit*

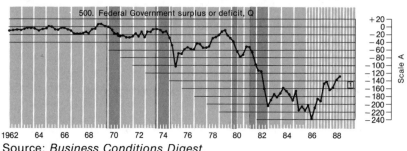

Source: *Business Conditions Digest.*

Before the 1970 recession, the federal budget actually had a surplus of $4.3 billion. As that recession unfolded, we went from a $4.3 billion surplus to a $23.6 billion deficit. Higher government spending and lower tax revenues brought about by the recession caused a *$27.9 billion* deterioration in the budget deficit.

Going into the 1974 recession, the deficit was only $1.8 billion; however, by the end of the recession in 1975, it was over $100 billion. The total impact of that recession on the budget deficit was *$98.3 billion.*

In 1979, prior to the back-to-back recessions of 1980 and 1981–1982, the budget deficit was $6.0 billion. But after those recessions, the deficit rose to $202.6 billion. Those recessions triggered an increase of *$196.6 billion* in the deficit.

Now, as we come to the end of the current period of expansion, it is very likely that we could *begin* the next recession with a deficit of $150 billion. The key question is where it will be at the end of the next recession. $250 billion? $350 billion? Higher? The question cannot be answered numerically, but in a recession, the amount of the budget deficit would clearly be much higher than it is today.

This brings us to the potential crisis that is looming ahead of us. That crisis is defined by the fact that (1) we are nearing the end of a prolonged economic expansion and are heading toward a normal cyclical recession and (2) no monetary or fiscal policy options are available to the government to either prevent or control this recession. As we approach this economic peak, the economy is now growing, inflation is rising, and interest rates are steadily moving up. Recently, the prime rate reached 10 percent. With no federal policy actions, the normal forces of economic growth will cause inflation and interest rates to rise to the point at which economic activity falls and we will slide into a recession.

Monetary policy cannot prevent this from happening. An *increase* in the money supply would now only fuel inflation, which would drive interest rates up more, which would then trigger the recession. A *decrease* in the money supply would immediately drive interest rates up and lead us to the recession. Thus, the next recession, either as a normal cyclical event or as the result of any change in monetary policy, is unavoidable.

But once we enter the next recession, we will be in an unprecedented financial situation. First, the new Gramm-Rudman Act mandates that the budget deficit be reduced by increased taxes, reduced spending, or both. Based on the historical evidence at hand, if we begin a recession with a $150 billion deficit, the reduced tax revenues from that recession could drive the deficit to $250 billion or $300 billion. Now, however, the government cannot cut taxes or raise spending to pull us out of the recession because that would raise the deficit even higher. Any action to cut the deficit—raising taxes or cutting spending—will take even more money away from consumers and make the recession worse.

We can only conclude that if a recession begins with the deficit anywhere near its current level, we will be in a catch-22 situation in which any government fiscal action will either deepen the recession or increase the deficit, which will raise interest rates and worsen the recession, in addition to being in direct conflict with the Gramm-Rudman Act.

NO EASY WAY OUT

In summary, the spend-and-borrow policies of the 1980s have generated an unprecedented period of economic growth, but have also created a budget deficit that is dangerously high if we should enter a recession in the near future. History has shown that running a temporary deficit can cure a recession.

And bringing an end to a recession can cure a temporary budget deficit. But combined with a recession, the current excessive deficit creates an intolerable situation in which any fiscal action at all will either lengthen and deepen the recession or significantly increase the deficit—which, in turn, will lengthen and deepen the recession. The old cure has become a problem, and fiscal policy offers no other cure for the combined problems of an excessive deficit and a recession.

This problem cannot be avoided unless the deficit can be reduced *before* the next cyclical recession develops as a result of the normal business cycle. Considering the current rate of economic expansion, our current position in the business cycle, and the current rate of deficit reduction, this now appears to be very unlikely. How Congress and the White House will react to a combined recession/deficit problem in anyone's guess. Inflate our way out of it? Absolve some of the debts? Repeal Gramm-Rudman? The answer is not clearly predictable.

However, there is one historical clue as to which way Congress and the administration might lean in a fiscal crisis. History shows that the statutory debt limit set by Congress and the actual level of government borrowing are virtually identical. There is no doubt that every dollar that *can* be borrowed *will* be borrowed.

However, there is another way to interpret this historical pattern. That interpretation holds that whenever there is an obvious need to borrow more money, the statutory debt limit is raised to legalize the increase in debt that cannot be otherwise controlled. Either way, the combined factors of historical debt and debt ceilings and political reality suggest that the Gramm-Rudman Act may not survive in its current state. If the going gets rough, an increase in debt and in the budget deficit is still easier to sell than a deep recession or a fiscal crisis. Of course, the problem is that solving a debt problem with more debt is not a viable long-term solution. It can only defer and exacerbate the inevitable fiscal crisis.

From an investor's point of view, the logical actions to take to prepare for this scenario are quite clear. The portfolio actions specifically recommended to be taken at this time are spelled out in detail in Chapter 18. However, a summary of those actions here is that investors should think defensively, maximize liquidity, avoid and eliminate personal debt, and generate recession-proof income. These actions will insulate investors from the next recession and the government's response to it, whatever it may be. They will also allow investors to preserve liquidity for some incredible buying opportunities as the next bottoming phase of the business cycle develops.

Chapter 12

The Cyclical Effects of Exchange Rates

Foreign exchange is a complex matter to explain. Many large textbooks have been devoted entirely to this subject. For our purposes, we deal only with the aspects of foreign exchange that affect the business cycle in predictable ways and that can be directly translated into profitable investment actions.

TERMINOLOGY

Basic Definitions

The subject of exchange rates is inherently confusing. This confusion stems from the fact that an exchange rate is not an absolute number like an interest rate, a commodity price, and a stock value, which are measured in terms of dollars or percentages.

An exchange rate measures the *relative value* of one country's currency versus another country's currency. Therefore, there is never a single answer to the question, "What's the value of the dollar today?" Instead, there are always multiple answers. Today, the dollar is worth 136 Japanese yen, but is also worth 1.855 German deutsche marks, 1.55 Swiss francs, 1,382 Italian lire, and 2,270 Mexican pesos.

To add to the confusion, exchange rates can be—and frequently are—expressed in two opposite ways. If the dollar happened to be equivalent to exactly 2 German deutsche marks on a given day, you might read in one paper that the exchange rate was 2 deutsche marks per dollar and in another paper that the exchange rate was 0.5 dollars per German deutsche mark. These statements are both correct, but it becomes difficult to think about a dollar exchange rate compared with 30 or 40 different currencies, especially when each exchange rate is expressed in two different reciprocal ways. Figure 12-1 shows a table provided in the *Wall Street Journal* everyday, which tracks the dollar exchange rates—both ways—against all of the major international currencies. The "U.S. $ equiv." columns refer to dollars per other currency (e.g., dollars per yen), and the "currency per U.S. $" columns refer to other currencies per dollar (e.g., yen per dollar) as of September 6, 1988.

To track exchange rate trends and to understand the implications of changes in various exchange rates, we first have to settle on a single definition of an exchange rate. The best definition to use as a basis for thinking about an exchange rate is the other currency per dollar. From now on, we'll think about 136 yen per dollar as opposed to 0.0073 dollars per yen, and the exchange rate between the dollar and the German deutsche mark will be 1.855 deutsche marks per dollar instead of 0.539 dollars per deutsche mark. As we show in the next section, this definition is consistent with the words that are used to describe exchange rate movements.

Exchange Rate Movements

Another way to say 136 yen per dollar is to say that you can buy 136 yen for one dollar. But suppose that you flew to Japan next week, went to a bank to exchange your dollars for Japanese yen, and were then told that the exchange rate had changed and that you could now only buy 128 yen for one dollar. Since you could not now buy as many yen with your dollar as you could last week, your dollar would have *declined* in value during that week.

To report the change in the dollar/yen exchange rate from

Figure 12-1. *Foreign Exchange Rates*

FOREIGN EXCHANGE

Tuesday, September 6, 1988
The New York foreign exchange selling rates below apply to trading among banks in amounts of $1 million and more, as quoted at 3 p.m. Eastern time by Bankers Trust Co. Retail transactions provide fewer units of foreign currency per dollar.

Country	U.S. $ equiv. Tues.	U.S. $ equiv. Fri.	Currency per U.S. $ Tues.	Currency per U.S. $ Fri.
Argentina (Austral) ...	.06978	.08361	14.33	11.96
Australia (Dollar)	.8050	.7975	1.2422	1.2539
Austria (Schilling)	.07722	.07672	12.95	13.035
Bahrain (Dinar)	2.6532	2.6525	.3769	.377
Belgium (Franc)				
Commercial rate	.02589	.02571	38.63	38.89
Financial rate	.02548	.02535	39.24	39.45
Brazil (Cruzado)	.003315	.003375	301.70	296.30
Britain (Pound)	1.7030	1.6840	.5872	.5938
30-Day Forward	1.6980	1.6788	.5889	.5957
90-Day Forward	1.6880	1.6680	.5924	.5995
180-Day Forward	1.6760	1.6553	.5967	.6041
Canada (Dollar)	.8103	.8091	1.2340	1.2360
30-Day Forward	.8093	.8080	1.2357	1.2377
90-Day Forward	.8068	.8053	1.2395	1.2417
180-Day Forward	.8035	.8023	1.2445	1.2468
Chile (Official rate) ...	.004065	.004053	246.00	246.76
China (Yuan)	.2693	.2687	3.7127	3.7221
Colombia (Peso)	.003223	.003223	310.28	310.28
Denmark (Krone)	.1411	.1404	7.0850	7.1200
Ecuador (Sucre)				
Official rate	.004008	.004008	249.50	249.50
Floating rate	.001852	.001852	540.00	540.00
Finland (Markka)	.2286	.2270	4.3750	4.4050
France (Franc)	.1594	.1586	6.2725	6.3050
30-Day Forward	.1595	.1587	6.2700	6.3015
90-Day Forward	.1596	.1588	6.2675	6.2970
180-Day Forward	.1596	.1589	6.2660	6.2915
Greece (Drachma)	.006689	.00667	149.50	150.00
Hong Kong (Dollar) ...	.1280	.1281	7.8115	7.8060
India (Rupee)	.06906	.06930	14.48	14.43
Indonesia (Rupiah)	.0005896	.0005903	1696.00	1694.00
Ireland (Punt)	1.4515	1.4430	.6889	.6930
Israel (Shekel)	.6094	.6094	1.6410	1.6410
Italy (Lira)	.000726	.0007233	1377.00	1382.50
Japan (Yen)	.007413	.007353	134.90	136.00
30-Day Forward	.007435	.007373	134.50	135.63
90-Day Forward	.007478	.007417	133.72	134.83
180-Day Forward	.007547	.007485	132.50	133.60
Jordan (Dinar)	2.6759	2.6455	.3737	.378
Kuwait (Dinar)	3.5045	3.5100	.2853	.2849
Lebanon (Pound)	.002513	.002729	398.00	366.50
Malaysia (Ringgit)	.3762	.3742	2.6580	2.6720
Malta (Lira)	2.9093	2.9093	.3437	.3437
Mexico (Peso)				
Floating rate	.000435	.0004405	2300.00	2270.00
Netherland(Guilder) .	.4808	.4773	2.0800	2.0950
New Zealand (Dollar) ..	.6225	.6025	1.6064	1.6598
Norway (Krone)	.1462	.1454	6.8400	6.8775
Pakistan (Rupee)	.05435	.05509	18.40	18.15
Peru (Inti)	.003697	.0303	270.49	33.00
Philippines (Peso)	.04764	.04766	20.99	20.98
Portugal (Escudo)	.006557	.006483	152.50	154.25
Saudi Arabia (Riyal) ..	.2667	.2666	3.7500	3.7505
Singapore (Dollar)	.4904	.4888	2.0390	2.0460
South Africa (Rand)				
Commercial rate	.4143	.4098	2.4140	2.4400
Financial rate	.2688	.2728	3.7200	3.6650
South Korea (Won)	.001386	.001386	721.30	721.70
Spain (Peseta)	.008143	.008100	122.80	123.45
Sweden (Krona)	.1567	.1555	6.3800	6.4325
Switzerland (Franc) ..	.6441	.6418	1.5525	1.5580
30-Day Forward	.6470	.6442	1.5455	1.5524
90-Day Forward	.6496	.6494	1.5395	1.5400
180-Day Forward	.6598	.6568	1.5155	1.5225
Taiwan (Dollar)	.03472	.03475	28.80	28.78
Thailand (Baht)	.03913	.03923	25.55	25.49
Turkey (Lira)	.000623	.0006497	1606.00	1535.10
United Arab(Dirham) ..	.2723	.2724	3.672	3.671
Uruguay (New Peso)				
Financial	.002632	.002632	380.00	380.00
Venezuela (Bolivar)				
Official rate	.1333	.1333	7.50	7.50
Floating rate	.02778	.02778	36.00	36.00
W. Germany (Mark) ..	.5427	.5391	1.8425	1.8550
30-Day Forward	.5444	.5406	1.8368	1.8498
90-Day Forward	.5474	.5437	1.8267	1.8394
180-Day Forward	.5519	.5481	1.8117	1.8245

Source: *Wall Street Journal* (September 7, 1988).

136 yen per dollar to 128 yen per dollar, the news media would use several possible phrases:

- The dollar *fell* from 136 to 128 yen last week.
- The dollar *declined* against the yen last week.
- The dollar *weakened* against the yen last week.

And if the dollar *declined* against the yen, the yen obviously *rose* against the dollar. From the Japanese standpoint, the old exchange rate of 136 yen per dollar was equal to 0.00735 dollars per yen. And when the exchange rate changed to 128 yen per dollar, it also changed to 0.00781 dollars per yen—which is an increase in dollars per yen. Thus, at the same time that you would hear that the dollar *fell, declined, or weakened* against the yen, you might also hear that the yen *rose, advanced, or strengthened* against the dollar.

The trick to keeping it all straight is twofold:

- Remember that the number of dollars per yen is always the reciprocal of the number of yen per dollar, and vice versa.

$$\frac{1}{\text{Yen per Dollar}} = \frac{\text{Dollars per Yen}}{}$$

$$\frac{1}{136 \left(\dfrac{\text{Yen}}{\text{Dollar}} \right)} = 0.00735 \left(\frac{\text{Dollars}}{\text{Yen}} \right)$$

- Always use or convert exchange rates to yen per dollar to avoid confusion.

In this way, you know that if the yen fell, the dollar rose, and if the yen strengthened, the dollar weakened. And in each case, the description of what happened to the dollar naturally corresponds to the numbers used in the yen per dollar exchange rate (if the dollar *rises,* the number of yen per dollar *rises,* and vice versa).

Figure 12-2 tracks the numbers and descriptions of a series of exchange rate changes over a hypothetical cycle.

If we hear that the yen per dollar exchange rate fell from 132 to 128, we know that the dollar weakened—one dollar can now buy only 128 yen instead of 132 yen. But if we hear that the dollar per yen exchange rate rose from 0.00757 to 0.00781, we could divide 1.0 by 0.00757 to get 132 yen per dollar, divide 1.0 by 0.00781 to get 128 yen per dollar, and then reach the same conclusion: The dollar weakened from 132 to 128 yen per dollar.

Figure 12-3 shows a table, which we will build on throughout this chapter, that shows the relationship between exchange rate changes and the words and numbers used to describe these changes. This table applies to any foreign currency exchange rate, but we use the Japanese yen as an example throughout this chapter.

Figure 12-2. *A Hypothetical Cycle in Exchange Rates*

	Dollars per Yen	Yen per Dollar	What Happened to the Dollar	What Happened to the Yen
Day 1	0.00735	136		
Day 2	0.00757	132	Weakened, declined, or fell	Strengthened, advanced, or rose
Day 3	0.00781	128	Weakened, declined, or fell	Strengthened, advanced, or rose
Day 4	0.00763	131	Strengthened, advanced, or rose	Weakened, declined, or fell
Day 5	0.00746	134	Strengthened, advanced, or rose	Weakened, declined, or fell

Figure 12-3. *Exchange Rate Terms and Relationships*

If the dollar:	Strengthens, advances, or rises	Weakens, declines, or falls
Then the Japanese yen must:	Weaken, decline, or fall	Strengthen, advance, or rise
Which means that:	Yen per dollar increases	Yen per dollar decreases
	Dollars per yen decreases	Dollars per yen increases

FUNDAMENTAL CAUSES OF EXCHANGE RATE CHANGES

What causes the dollar, the yen, the deutsche mark, or any other currency to rise or fall in value compared with other currencies? The answer goes back to the absolute basics of the price of any good: supply and demand.

Supply

The supply of dollars can be equated to the supply of money as defined in the business cycle. If the supply of U.S. money were to decline, the value of U.S. money would tend to go up for foreign buyers. This means that the number of Japanese yen per dollar would rise, and the dollar would be said to strengthen against the yen.

On the other hand, suppose that the government decided to inflate seriously the amount of available U.S. money. As a result of this overabundance of money, large-scale inflation would necessarily cheapen the value of the U.S. dollar abroad. This happened to the currency of Mexico and other large debtor nations, which seriously overinflated their currencies.

An example can illustrate this type of situation more clearly. Suppose that you are a Mexican official with a one billion lire debt to repay to Italy. When you borrowed the one billion Italian lire, they were worth exactly one billion Mexican pesos. In other words, the exchange rate between Mexico and Italy was one peso per lira, or one lira per peso.

But since then, the Mexican economy has declined severely and, as a result, you now do not have one billion pesos to repay Italy. But someone has a great idea: Simply inflate the Mexican money supply, print the extra one billion pesos, and use that newly created money to pay off the debt to Italy. Terrific idea. But, alas, the financial world is smarter than that.

Taking this example to an extreme, if the total amount of goods and services produced by Mexico remained the same but the government simply doubled the amount of Mexican money, the extra pesos are effectively counterfeit money and each peso would be worth only half as much as it was before. In this case, the peso would weaken; in terms of pesos per lira, the exchange rate would double to 2.0 pesos per lira, and the lira per peso exchange rate would drop in half to 0.5 lire per peso. To pay one billion lire to Italy, Mexico would now have to produce two billion pesos. Thus, the inflation exercise would be futile, and the change in the exchange rate (the decline of the peso) would be the great equalizer in settling this international debt. This principle is behind what is known as the purchasing power parity theory of exchange rates. This theory holds that if one country inflates its currency faster than other countries do, exchange rates will eventually reflect the cheaper value of the most inflated currency until each currency has the same real purchasing power.

We can conclude that if a nation's *money supply is increased,* that *currency will weaken* on the international market. And if the *supply is decreased,* the *currency will tend to strengthen* internationally.

Demand

The demand for dollars or any other currency is directly related to the demand for things that can be bought with that currency. While there is a cadre of professional currency traders and speculators and national banks that intermittently buy and sell currencies to try to increase or decrease a particular exchange rate, it is the international financial transactions requiring a currency exchange that drive the world's exchange rates. When IBM sells a computer to Germany, it wants to be paid in U.S. dollars. When Honda sells a car in America, it wants to be paid in Japanese yen. So in every international transaction, the buyer's currency must eventually be converted to the seller's currency to pay for the purchased product.

It stands to reason that if a lot of foreign buyers want American products, they have to buy a lot of U.S. dollars with their currencies to pay for those products. Thus, when worldwide demand for U.S. products goes up, demand for U.S. dollars also goes up—and vice versa.

But foreigners buy more than U.S. products from America. They also buy stocks, bonds, real estate, factories, and entire U.S. businesses. At the same time, U.S. citizens and corporations are buying the same things in foreign countries. At any point in time, the exchange rate between the United States and any other country will change depending on which country is buying more from the other country. If Japan buys more American things than the United States buys from Japan, the net demand for dollars will increase and the dollar will strengthen. If we buy more from them, the yen will strengthen and the dollar will weaken.

Extending this principle to the whole world, we can say that:

- If the *rest of the world* wants an *increasing amount of whatever the United States has or produces,* demand for the dollar will increase and the *dollar will rise* (strengthen).

- If the *rest of the world* wants a *decreasing amount of U.S. things,* demand for dollars will decrease and the *dollar will fall* (weaken).

- If the *United States* wants an *increasing amount of foreign goods,* U.S. demand for foreign currencies will rise, the foreign currencies will strengthen, and the U.S. *dollar will weaken.*

- If the *United States* wants a *decreasing amount of foreign goods,* U.S. demand for foreign currencies will fall, the foreign currency will weaken, and the *dollar will strengthen.*

Exchange Rate Cycles: The International Equalizer

While international exchange rates tend to be cyclical, exchange rates operate outside of the U.S. business cycle and run on their own cyclical timetables. Since the dollar exchange rate is a measure of the *relative* attractiveness of the dollar and some other currency, it is not tied directly to the U.S. business cycle. In fact, it can be viewed as a link between the U.S. business cycle and the business cycles of other countries.

Suppose that the U.S. economy and financial markets were systematically moving through the 40 turning points that we described in our Primary Business Cycle. And suppose that the Japanese economy and financial markets were going through the same 40 events in their business cycle—in lockstep with our business cycle. As our economy grew, their economy grew. As our imports and exports grew, theirs grew at the same rate. As our money supply and inflation rate climbed, their money supply and inflation rate climbed. As our interest rates rose, their interest rates rose—all at exactly the same rates. In this scenario, the dollar-to-yen exchange rate would not change because there would be no change in the relative currency supply or the relative demand for each country's goods, services, or investment securities.

Therefore, we can see that a major change in the exchange rate occurs only *as the result of a major change in one country's business cycle compared with that of the United States.* For example, if U.S. interest rates rose faster than Japan's, U.S. bonds would be more attractive than Japanese bonds and Japanese investors would flock to the U.S. bond market— driving up the value of the dollar. And this new foreign demand for U.S. bonds would push bond prices up, which would then drive U.S. interest rates down until they reached equilibrium with Japanese interest rates. In this way, the exchange rate again serves as an equalizer to eventually bring temporary imbalances in national interest rates back into balance.

The same self-correcting mechanism takes place in the trade deficit arena. If the United States becomes uncompetitive in world markets and cannot export as much as it imports, a large trade deficit results. At the same time, the fact that

Americans are buying more Japanese goods and that the Japanese are buying fewer American goods causes the yen to strengthen and the dollar to decline. However, as we show in the next section, the lower dollar reduces the effective price of U.S. goods in Japan and raises the effective price of Japanese goods in the United States. As a result, the lower effective U.S. prices in Japan cause the Japanese to buy more U.S. products and higher effective prices for Japanese goods cause Americans to buy fewer Japanese goods. When this happens, the U.S. trade balance improves; at the same time, the U.S. dollar strengthens because there is more Japanese demand for U.S. goods and less U.S. demand for Japanese goods. So, we come full circle and, again, the exchange rate has acted as a self-correcting mechanism that keeps world trade in equilibrium.

We can say three things about the dollar exchange rate cycle:

- It is driven by supply, demand, and the *differences* between the U.S. business cycle and those of other countries.
- It tends to equalize these international differences and serve as a stabilizing force in the world economy.
- Although it is not directly tied to any single country's business cycle, an exchange rate movement of any significance affects each country's business cycle in defined and predictable ways.

THE EFFECTS OF EXCHANGE RATE MOVEMENTS

To trace the effects of a change in exchange rates, we use a set of examples involving the United States and Japan. These examples focus on the two main arenas of international transactions: (1) goods and services, which affect the trade balance, and (2) the financial markets.

Trade Balance Effects

In international business transactions, it is easiest to think about an exchange rate as a toll or a second price of the product being bought. Consider, Mr. Ito, a Japanese buyer of an IBM personal computer. He is looking at the price that he has to pay for that computer. That price (yen per computer) is going to be the product of two other prices: the yen per dollar exchange rate and the dollars per computer price that is set by IBM. The buyer's price equation is shown in Figure 12-4.

Figure 12-4 shows clearly all of the factors that influence the foreign demand for U.S.-made IBM personal computers. The Japanese buyer's *price* per personal computer *will go up* if *either* IBM's *selling price goes up or* the *yen per dollar exchange rate goes up* (i.e., the dollar strengthens). The price that the Japanese buyer has to pay *will go down* if *either IBM's selling price goes down or* the *yen per dollar exchange rate goes down* (i.e., the dollar weakens).

If IBM's price to the U.S. market is constant, foreign demand for their personal computer will vary depending on the exchange rate. And the swings in demand that will result from exchange rate shifts are very predictable:

> **Effect 1:** *If the dollar strengthens (yen per dollar increases), the price to foreign buyers will go **up** and, as a result, **foreign demand for this U.S. product will go down** and IBM will sell fewer personal computers in Japan.*

Figure 12-4.

Japanese Buyer's Price for a Computer (Yen per Computer)		Exchange Rate (Yen per Dollar)		IBM's U.S. Price (Dollars per Computer)
$\dfrac{\text{Yen}}{\text{computer}}$	$=$	$\dfrac{\text{Yen}}{\text{dollar}}$	$\times$	$\dfrac{\text{dollars}}{\text{computer}}$
$\dfrac{390{,}000 \text{ yen}}{\text{computer}}$	$=$	$\dfrac{130 \text{ yen}}{\text{dollar}}$	$\times$	$\dfrac{\$3{,}000}{\text{computer}}$

> **Effect 2:** *If the dollar weakens (yen per dollar decreases), the foreign price will go down and, accordingly, foreign demand for this U.S. product will go up and IBM will sell more personal computers in Japan.*

Let's now look at the flip side of the exchange rate situation by examining the point of view of a U.S. buyer of a Japanese car. The U.S. buyer's price of a Toyota (dollars per Toyota) will be the product of (1) the exchange rate in terms of dollars per yen and (2) the Toyota's sticker price in yen per Toyota. The U.S. buyer's equation is shown in Figure 12-5.

Figure 12-5 now shows that *the U.S. buyer's price* for a Toyota *will go up* if either Toyota's price per car goes up or the dollar per yen exchange rate goes up (i.e., the yen per dollar exchange rate goes down, which means that *the dollar weakens*).

Similarly, *the U.S. buyer's price goes down* if either the Toyota price per car declines or if the dollar per yen exchange rate goes down (i.e., the yen per dollar exchange rate goes up, which means that *the dollar strengthens*).

So, if Toyota's price doesn't change, the demand for Toyotas will also vary in a predictable way, depending on the exchange rate.

Figure 12-5.

U.S. Buyer's Price for a Toyota (Dollars per Car)		Exchange Rate (Dollars per Yen)		Toyota's Japanese Price (Yen per Car)
$\dfrac{\text{Dollars}}{\text{Toyota}}$	=	$\dfrac{\text{Dollars}}{\text{yen}}$	$\times$	$\dfrac{\text{yen}}{\text{Toyota}}$
$\dfrac{\$9{,}000}{\text{Toyota}}$	=	$\dfrac{\$0.007692}{\text{yen}}$	$\times$	$\dfrac{1{,}170{,}047 \text{ yen}}{\text{Toyota}}$

Effect 3: *If the dollar strengthens, the U.S. buyer's price will go down, the U.S. demand for Toyotas will go up, and Toyota will sell more cars in the United States.*

Effect 4: *If the dollar weakens, the U.S. buyer's price will go up, U.S. demand for Toyotas will go down, and Toyota will sell fewer cars in the United States.*

We can now combine these four demand effects to see how a change in exchange rates affects the U.S. balance of trade. The trade balance between any two countries is defined as the difference between each country's exports to and imports from the other country. If the United States exported $10 billion worth of U.S. products to Japan and imported $8 billion of Japanese products into the United States, the U.S. trade balance would be reported as a *positive $2 billion*. In other words, we would have received $2 billion more for our exports than we paid for our imports. At the same time, since Japan sent less to the United States than it received, the Japanese trade balance would be a *negative $2 billion.*

Combining Effects 1 and 3, we can see that *if the dollar strengthens* (yen per dollar increases), *foreign demand for U.S. products will decline* and the *U.S. demand for Japanese products will increase.* This obviously means that the *U.S. balance of trade will decline*, as fewer U.S. goods are sold and exported to the Japanese and more Japanese goods are imported and bought in America.

Combining Effects 2 and 4, *if the dollar weakens* (yen per dollar decreases), *foreign demand for U.S. products will increase* and the *U.S. demand for foreign products will decrease. The U.S. balance of trade will increase*, as more U.S. goods are exported and sold in Japan and fewer Japanese goods are imported and bought in the United States.

Given these relationships, we can now add the exchange rate and international trade relationships to our exchange rate table in Figure 12-6.

We can now see that a weaker dollar stimulates U.S. exports, constrains foreign imports, and improves our balance of

Figure 12-6. *Exchange Rate Effects on Trade*

If the dollar:	Strengthens, advances, or rises	Weakens, declines, or falls
Then the Japanese yen must:	Weaken, decline, or fall	Strengthen, advance, or rise
Which means that:	Yen per dollar increases Dollars per yen decreases	Yen per dollar decreases Dollars per yen increases
And the effects of the change are:	Price of U.S. goods to Japanese buyer increases So, Japanese demand for U.S. goods decreases So, the United States exports less to Japan *and* Price of Japanese goods to U.S. buyer decreases So, U.S. demand for Japanese goods increases So, the United States imports more from Japan *so* More imports from Japan and fewer exports to Japan cause the U.S. trade balance to fall	Price of U.S. goods to Japanese buyer decreases So, Japanese demand for U.S. goods increases So, the United States exports more to Japan *and* Price of Japanese goods to U.S. buyer increases So, U.S. demand for Japanese goods decreases So, the United States imports less from Japan *so* More exports to Japan and fewer imports from Japan cause the U.S. trade balance to rise

trade. But the change in the balance of trade that results from a declining dollar is not immediate. In fact, it takes about one year for the change in the trade balance to catch up with the change in the exchange rate. Figure 12-7 shows the trade balance compared with the international value of the dollar plotted one year later (or lagged by one year). The dollar index is inverted because a weaker, or lower, dollar correlates with an increase in the balance of trade. It is very clear from this historical evidence that a cyclical change in the dollar exchange rate causes a proportional change in the balance of trade one year later.

We can now ask a fascinating question: "Which is better—a strong currency or a weak currency?"

Obviously, every country wants a strong currency because it shows that worldwide demand for the country's goods and services is strong and that the world has confidence in the future of the country's economy and currency. But just as obviously, every country wants a positive balance of trade, created by exporting more goods than it imports. A country's positive trade balance is identical to a company's positive cash flow. If a country continually imports more than it exports, it must pay more for its imports than it receives from its exports. And that is the path to a national version of a corporate bankruptcy. A positive trade balance means that the country takes in more

Figure 12-7. *The Dollar and the Balance of Trade*

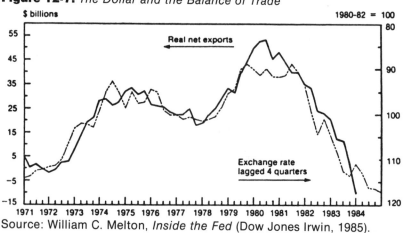

Source: William C. Melton, *Inside the Fed* (Dow Jones Irwin, 1985).

money than it pays out to other countries and has a positive cash flow to use for its own internal development.

And how could a country improve its trade balance? Figure 12-6 shows that by allowing the dollar to *weaken,* the U.S. balance of trade will improve. And so it is with any other country. Therefore, a national policy to *weaken* a country's currency would improve its trade balance.

So, the answer to the question, "Which is better—a strong currency or a weak currency?," is, "It depends on the current state of the country's economy and its trade balance and national goals at the time."

Business Cycle Effects

To interpret the impact of an exchange rate movement on the business cycle and the financial markets, remember that the exchange rate cycle is completely separate from the U.S. business cycle. To picture this situation conceptually, Line A in Figure 12-8 might represent the U.S. economic cycle, with Line B representing the value of the dollar.

At any point in time, the trend in exchange rates might be

Figure 12-8. *The Business Cycle and the Exchange Rate: Illustration*

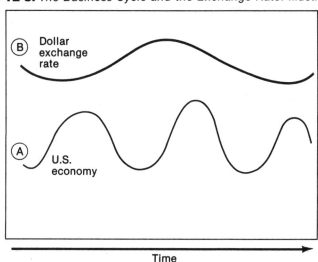

working with or against the ups and downs of the U.S. business cycle.

We already know that a major decline in the dollar has a positive long-term effect on the U.S. economy and the U.S. trade balance. But a declining dollar also triggers other effects in the U.S. business cycle. Figure 12-9 shows the initial implications of a decline in the dollar that causes the U.S. trade balance to improve.

As more goods produced in the United States are targeted for foreign sales and foreign imports to the United States decline, *fewer goods* become available to the U.S. consumer. If industry is operating anywhere near capacity, the new demands from foreign buyers, coupled with fewer foreign imports, can cause shortages in the United States. The natural result of this is *inflationary pressure*. In addition, the increased inflow of foreign money into U.S. banks has the same effect as a money supply increase by the Fed: *inflationary pressure*. Therefore, a large decline in the value of the dollar is *inherently inflationary*.

Since inflation is a key driver of interest rates, any large decrease in the dollar will push interest rates up because of the new inflationary pressure. We can now extend our list of the implications of a change in the dollar exchange rates:

- A declining dollar will put *upward pressure* on:
  —The U.S. economy
  —The U.S. balance of trade
  —U.S. inflation
  —U.S. interest rates
- A rising dollar will have the opposite effect and will put *downward pressure* on:

Figure 12-9. *Initial Effects of a Declining Dollar*

United States	Japan
More U.S. goods ——————————————————→	
←—————————————— Fewer Japanese goods	
Less U.S. money ——————————————→	
←———————————————— More Japanese money	

—The U.S. economy
—The U.S. balance of trade
—U.S. inflation
—U.S. interest rates

Financial Market Effects

One of the other confusing aspects of exchange rates is the multitude of effects that a rising or falling dollar may have on different parts of the economy. We've just seen that a weaker dollar might be reported by a news commentator as either bad news (because it will raise inflation and interest rates) or good news (because it will improve the economy and the balance of trade).

In addition to this confusion, an investor is also subjected to several other mixed opinions of the implications of a weaker currency. A declining dollar is often blamed for declining stock and bond prices and credited for rising gold prices. But on other days, a declining dollar boosts stock prices because higher exports and an improved trade balance are foreseen.

To clarify some of this, we repeat the fact that foreigners buy more than goods and services from the United States. They also buy Treasury bonds and U.S. stocks and make significant investments in U.S. business and real estate. When it comes to foreign investments in the United States or U.S. investments in foreign countries, exchange rates and predicted future exchange rates can significantly alter the attractiveness of international investments. Let's begin with a U.S. T-bond illustration.

Bond Market Effects. Suppose that our Japanese investor, Mr. Ito, wants to buy a U.S. T-bond because U.S. interest rates are higher than Japanese rates at the moment. At the time of purchase, this investor's equation is as shown in Figure 12-10. The price he will pay for the bond (yen per bond) is the U.S. price of the bond (dollars per bond) times the prevailing exchange rate (in yen per dollar).

In this case, Mr. Ito pays 1,300,000 yen, converts it to $10,000 at 130 yen per dollar, and buys a $10,000 T-bond at par. Now suppose that this is an 8 percent T-bond that matures in

Figure 12-10.

Japanese Buyer's Price for a Bond (Yen per Bond)	=	Exchange Rate (Yen per Dollar)	×	U.S. Bond Price (Dollars per Bond)
$\dfrac{\text{Yen}}{\text{bond}}$	=	$\dfrac{\text{Yen}}{\text{dollar}}$	×	$\dfrac{\text{dollars}}{\text{bond}}$
$\dfrac{\text{1,300,000 yen}}{\text{bond}}$	=	$\dfrac{\text{130 yen}}{\text{dollar}}$	×	$\dfrac{\$10,000}{\text{bond}}$

five years. If the bond is held to maturity, he will receive $800 per year and then receive his $10,000 back, earning an annual profit of 8 percent on his investment—at least, that is what he will make if the exchange rates don't change at all.

But what if they do? He paid 1,300,000 yen to buy the $10,000 bond at 130 yen per dollar. The U.S. government will pay out annual interest of $800 per year. Then, in five years, the U.S. government will pay back the $10,000 principal, but Mr. Ito will receive the equivalent of $10,000 after conversion back to yen at the exchange rate prevailing in five years. Some quick calculations show us what happens to his investment if the dollar/yen exchange rate changes in either direction.

Just looking at the $10,000 repayment of principal on the bond, if the dollar were to strengthen to 150 yen per dollar in five years, Mr. Ito would receive $10,000 times 150 yen per dollar, or 1,500,000 yen—20,000 yen more than he paid for the bond at par. But if the dollar were to weaken to 110 yen per dollar in five years, he would receive 1,100,000 yen for the investment—20,000 yen less than was paid for the bond.

With no change in the exchange rate, the foreign investor's return is 8 percent per year, derived from the $800 per year interest payment and the return of $10,000 converted back at 130 yen per dollar. With the dollar steadily strengthening to 150 yen over five years, the investor will earn 11.15 percent per year.

Figure 12-11. *Foreign Returns on T-Bonds with Different Exchange Rate Trends*

	In Dollars	Stable Exchange Rate		Weaker Dollar		Stronger Dollar	
		Yen/Dollar	Yen	Yen/Dollar	Yen	Yen/Dollar	Yen
Investment	10,000	130	1,300,000	130	1,300,000	130	1,300,000
Returns							
Year 1 interest	800	130	104,000	126	100,800	134	107,200
Year 2 interest	800	130	104,000	122	97,600	138	110,400
Year 3 interest	800	130	104,000	118	94,400	142	113,600
Year 4 interest	800	130	104,000	110	88,000	150	120,000
Year 5 repayment of principal	10,000	130	1,300,000	110	1,110,000	150	1,500,000
Compound rate of return on investment	8%	8%		4.47%		11.15%	

But with the dollar weakening to 110 yen in five years, the investor will earn only a compound rate of return of 4.47 percent per year. This is quite a difference in financial outcomes for a risk-free investment in a U.S. T-bond. Figure 12-11 shows the difference between cash flows to the Japanese investor under the different exchange rate trends.

From the viewpoint of the foreign investor, the conclusion is clear. U.S. bonds are much more attractive when the *outlook* for the dollar is strengthening and the *anticipated* exchange rate (in yen per dollar) is higher in the future than it is at the time. Conversely, an *outlook* for a *weaker dollar quickly erodes the potential foreign profits* from a T-bond, even if the actual interest rate on the bond is quite high. Therefore, any events that lead investors to conclude that the dollar will weaken in the future will cause foreign investors to sell their U.S. bonds— which will push U.S. bond prices down and U.S. interest rates up.

Thus, the *short-term effects* of a declining dollar are *negative,* as foreign investors sell their U.S. bonds to avoid the erosion of profits that a declining dollar exchange rate may bring. But the *long-term effects* are *also negative.* Since the declining dollar portends an increase in U.S. economic activity, inflation, and interest rates, downward pressure on bond prices is sustained over the period of the declining dollar.

Obviously, a rising dollar would have the opposite effects. The U.S. economy would tend to slow down, inflation would be reduced, and interest rate pressure would subside, which would cause bond prices to rise.

Stock Market Effects. The effects of a declining dollar on the stock market are more complex: The *short-term effects* are clearly *negative.* The foreign sales of bonds, which push up interest rates, adversely affect stock prices. In addition, the foreign sales of stocks, resulting from fears of rising inflation and interest rates, add more downward pressure to stock prices. A rising dollar creates the opposite scenario, which is bullish for stocks in the short run.

Clearly, the *long-term implications* of an expanding economy and more U.S. exports to foreign countries are *good* for corporate sales and earnings. But the expanding economy carries with it higher inflation and interest rates. As we show in Chapter 16, stock prices are directly related to expected growth rates and inversely related to interest rates. Therefore, the combined effects of higher growth and higher interest rates tend to offset each other, essentially neutralizing the long-term impact on the stock market over a complete exchange rate cycle.

At different times in the business cycle, the stock market responds differently to news concerning earnings growth and interest rates. Coming out of a recession—just after the stock market has bottomed out and while interest rates are low—the potential future earnings growth from a decline in the dollar might outweigh the negative implications of higher inflation and interest rates, and the market might move up at news of a declining dollar. But toward the end of an economic expansion, when inflation and interest rates are already rising, a sudden decline in the dollar will be perceived as very bad news for inflation and interest rates, and stocks will decline. This was one of the key factors that contributed to the crash of October 1987.

Gold Market Effects. As opposed to the stock market, the gold market reactions to changes in U.S. dollar exchange rates are clearly defined. A weaker dollar, which is inherently inflationary, is bullish for gold and gold stocks. A stronger dollar will depress gold and gold stock prices as inflationary fears are reduced.

The relationship between the dollar and gold is clearer than the exchange rate between the dollar and other foreign currencies. As we stated earlier, the exchange rate is the result of changes in the U.S. economy and financial markets *compared* with those of other countries. Therefore, a change in the exchange rate might result from a change in the situation of either country.

However, the amount of available gold in the world at any time is essentially constant. Thus, a weakening in the dollar, usually caused by inflation of the dollar, automatically forces the price of gold to rise in terms of dollars since we would then have more dollars and the same amount of gold in the world. Similarly, a reduction in the U.S. money supply would decrease the price of gold in terms of dollars. We discuss the gold/dollar relationship in more detail in Chapter 17, but the bottom line is that a weaker dollar is bullish for gold and that a stronger dollar is bearish for gold.

Summary of Market Effects. We can now summarize the short-term and long-term effects of a significant change in exchange rates in Figure 12-12.

In addition, we can now see two sets of rules concerning our three playable investment markets—stocks, bonds, and gold—as we move through each Primary Business Cycle:

Exchange rate rules—Set 1: No matter where we are in the business cycle:

- A *decline in the dollar* will put *downward pressure on* both *stocks and bonds* (because it puts upward pressure on interest rates) and *upward pressure on gold* (because a decline in the dollar is inflationary).

- An *increase in the dollar* will put *upward pressure on stocks and bonds* and *downward pressure on gold.*

Exchange rate rules—Set 2: If we are at or near a major turning point for stocks, bonds, or gold and an increase or

Figure 12-12. *Summary of Market Effects of Exchange Rate Changes*

	If the Dollar Strengthens, Advances, or Rises	If the Dollar Weakens, Declines, or Falls
In the short term	Bond prices rise Stock prices rise Gold prices fall	Bond prices fall Stock prices fall Gold prices rise
Over the long term	Bond prices rise Gold prices fall Stock prices are largely unaffected, as lower growth is offset by lower interest rates	Bond prices fall Gold prices rise Stock prices are largely unaffected, as higher growth is offset by higher interest rates

Figure 12-13. *Summary of Exchange Rate Effects*

If the dollar:	Strengthens, advances, or rises	Weakens, declines, or falls
Then the Japanese yen must:	Weaken, decline, or fall	Strengthen, advance, or rise
Which means that:	Yen per dollar increases	Yen per dollar decreases
	Dollars per yen decreases	Dollars per yen increases
The short-term implications are:	No change in the U.S. economy	No change in the U.S. economy
	No change in the trade balance	No change in the trade balance
	U.S. inflation falls	U.S. inflation rises
	U.S. interest rates fall	U.S. interest rates rise
	Bond prices rise	Bond prices fall
	Stock prices rise	Stock prices fall
	Gold prices fall	Gold prices rise
The long-term implications are:	The U.S. economy slows	The U.S. economy grows
	The U.S. trade balance deteriorates	The U.S. trade balance improves
	U.S. inflation falls	U.S. inflation rises
	U.S. interest rates fall	U.S. interest rates rise
	Bond prices rise	Bond prices fall
	Gold prices fall	Gold prices rise
	No major impact on the stock market, as lower economic growth is offset by lower interest rates	No major impact on the stock market, as higher economic growth is offset by higher interest rates

decrease in the dollar also occurs, that shift in the exchange rate can trigger the pending turning point in stocks, bonds, or gold. Specifically:

• If we are near a stock market peak, a decline in the dollar will trigger the stock market peak and send stocks lower.

- If we are near a stock market bottom, an increase in the dollar will trigger that bottom and push stocks higher.
- If we are near an interest rate bottom (which would be a bond market peak), a decline in the dollar will cause bond prices to peak out and decline as interest rates rise.
- If we are near an interest rate peak (a bond market bottom), an increase in the dollar will cause bond prices to bottom out and rise as interest rates fall.
- If we are near an inflation (and gold price) bottom, a decline in the dollar will cause gold prices to bottom out and begin to rise.
- If we are near an inflation (and gold price) peak, an increase in the dollar will cause gold prices to peak out and decline.

This completes our discussion of foreign exchange rates with respect to the business cycle and the basic investment decisions that should be made if the value of the dollar reverses direction or makes a significant movement in either direction. Figure 12-13 summarizes all of the economic, business cycle, and investment effects that result from a change in the dollar exchange rate.

Chapter 13

The Predictable Effects of Unpredictable Outside Events

TWO MIND-SETS ARE BETTER THAN ONE

Recently, a television comedy show included a satire on news broadcasting. A comedian played the role of a national news network anchorman, and one of his news announcements was: "Good morning. Today, the Soviet Union launched a barrage of nuclear missiles on every nation in the free world. Tune in at 6:00 p.m. for Wall Street's reaction to the pending end of the world."

The point of this not-so-funny joke is that, short of the end of the world, almost every major event has some kind of economic consequence. From an investment standpoint, it's important to put isolated military, political, meteorological, or sociological events into proper perspective. Whenever an investor sees or hears a dramatic event on the news, he or she should immediately ask six questions:

- Does this change the supply of goods?
- Does this change the demand for goods?
- Does this change the price of goods?
- Does this change the supply of money?

• Does this change the demand for money?
• Does this change the price of money?

If the answer is yes, an investment decision may be necessary. Figure 13-1 lists some real and hypothetical "events" that would have predictable economic consequences and could happen without notice at any time.

This list illustrates an important message. The hopes, dreams, and values around which we all live—those of peace,

Figure 13-1.

Noneconomic Event	Economic Implications
OPEC establishes an oil embargo against the United States	Supply of oil to the United States declines Price of oil rises
There is a sudden freeze in Florida	Orange crops are damaged Supply of oranges declines Price of oranges rises
Alcoholic beverages are legally prohibited by the government	Supply of legal booze falls to zero However, demand for booze remains constant Demand for illegal booze rises Price of illegal booze rises
Conventional war breaks out	Demand (by the government) for military hardware rises Defense stocks rise
Worldwide peace breaks out	Defense stocks plummet
Drought hits the Midwest	Supply of wheat, corn, and soybeans declines All grain prices rise
The government taxes something	The consumer's price for the product rises Demand for the product falls Stocks of companies making that product decline

Noneconomic Event	Economic Implications
The government subsidizes something	The producer's cost of making the product declines Supply of the product rises Price of the product falls
An earthquake breaks off the California coastline, which sinks	Stocks of companies with operations on the sunken land fall Price of real estate on the new shoreline rises
Water pollution grows dramatically worse	Demand for purified water increases Price for purified water increases
The ozone layer is eaten away by fluorocarbons	Ultraviolet rays saturate the earth Sales of sunglasses and sunscreen lotion rise Skin cancer rises Stocks of drug companies working on skin cancer medications rise
Forest fires sweep the western states	Timber prices rise

stability, security, moral and ethical standards, and fair play—are important to us as human beings, but must be viewed in an entirely different light in the world of investments. Very often, what is good for us as human beings is bad news from an investment standpoint, and vice versa. Shortages of anything are going to be bad for those who need items that they can no longer get. But shortages mean higher prices for that item, and those who can foresee those shortages have an opportunity to capitalize on them. Conversely, surpluses mean that everyone can get as much as they want of things. However, as an investor, you don't want to hold the stock of a company that makes a product when five new competitors enter the market and create a vast surplus of that product.

Therefore, investors must deal with outside events with two different and separate mind-sets. First, you have to react to an event as a human being in a "human mind-set"; then analyze that event in a cold, objective, and pragmatic "investor mind-set" to see if you are exposed to potential loss or have an opportunity for potential gain.

OUTSIDE EVENTS AND THE BUSINESS CYCLE

As we've pointed out on several occasions, the backbone of the business cycle is a series of *known* cause-and-effect relationships between the supply, demand, and price of goods and money. We also noted earlier that the timing between economic peaks or bottoms—or stock market peaks or bottoms—is *not regular,* as so many people want to believe.

The most remarkable fact about this business cycle is that the basic sequence of events has remained the same over decades of changes in our economy and throughout periods of major "outside events." Although these outside events *do not change the sequence* of turning points, they *can change the timing*.

For example, an economic expansion under controlled inflation could be cut short by another oil crisis if it drove oil prices back to $30 per barrel, drove inflation and interest rates to 20 percent, and triggered a recession. This is a classic illustration of a business cycle that would follow the prescribed sequence of events, but whose timing would be affected by an outside event.

Only the principle of cause and effect could generate a business cycle sequence that has been maintained for such a long time period in the face of the many domestic events, new trends, technological developments, foreign escapades, natural disasters, and political crises that we have experienced in this century. A few of the key events that have changed our world in the last 80 years are included in Figure 13-2.

Figure 13-2. *Highlights of Events and Changes in the Twentieth Century*

Invention of telephone
Invention of car
Invention of airplane
World War I
Depression
New Deal
World War II
Atomic bomb
Korean War
Space exploration
Bay of Pigs
Kennedy assassination
Vietnam
Civil rights movement
Watergate
Computer revolution
1973 Mideast crisis
1979 Mideast crisis
20 percent interest rates
Terrorism
Reaganomics
Invasion of Granada
U.S. escort policy in the Persian Gulf

However, despite all these changes, the fundamental cause-and-effect relationships within the business cycle have held up, which brings us to the next key point: An investor cannot exclude news events from an analysis of the world's financial markets. Even though the technical stock market analysts of the world exclude all such news events on general principle, it is clear that any outside event that could alter the supply and demand factors in the business cycle must be evaluated. Investors must examine these outside events with an understanding that they will not alter the sequence, but may accelerate or delay the timing of events within the business cycle.

NON-EVENTS

The other category of outside events is that of non-events. For the purpose of investment strategy, these can be defined as events that get newspaper headlines, but *do not* fundamentally alter any supply or demand relationships in the business cycle.

For the most part, those events temporarily change the "investor psychology" of the day and often lead to technical rallies or declines in the stock, bond, or commodities markets. Recognition that these events do not change any fundamentals—even though the markets react to them—can offer tremendous opportunities to investors.

For example, suppose that we are in an economic and stock market upswing when an event occurs that undermines investor confidence, but does not change any fundamentals. News of the event causes the stock market to fall swiftly, and all of the market analysts point to deteriorating investor confidence as the reason for the decline. An investor who recognizes that no fundamentals have changed and that we are still in a growing stage of the business cycle, now has a terrific buying opportunity at effectively discounted stock market prices.

What kinds of events receive big headlines, but have no real, fundamental effect on the business cycle? Some examples are:

- Most Washington, D.C., scandals
- Most Wall Street insider trading news
- Most nonmilitary foreign incidents, such as:
  —Plane crashes
  —Chemical plant explosions
  —Kidnappings and bomb threats
  —Drug problems with Nicaragua
- All political rhetoric that does not, *in fact,* translate into a new Fed monetary policy or specific legislation that affects supply, demand, or prices
- Most isolated industry "events," such as a downturn in the beer industry or a television Writer's Guild strike
- Specific takeover speculation and rumors

Figure 13-3. *Reacting to News Events*

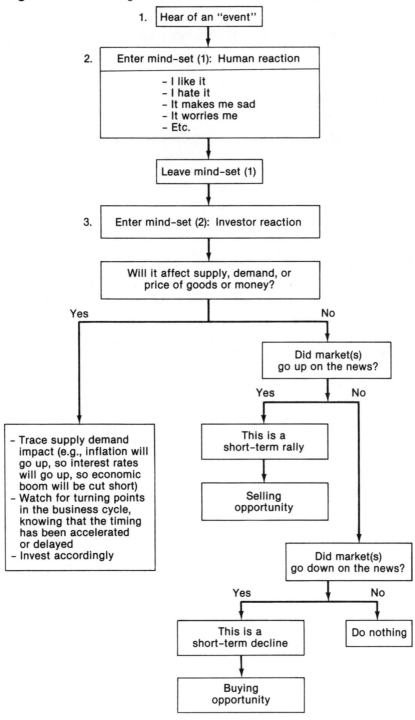

- Most internal civil incidents in foreign countries (car bombings in Ireland, assassinations in the Philippines, etc.)

CONCLUSIONS

Unpredictable outside events are a part of life on earth. Since they are unpredictable, an investor can only assess them properly. Proper assessment involves four steps:

- Pay attention to these news events.
- Take the appropriate amount of time to react as a human being to these events.
- Then move into an investor mind-set to assess them in terms of business cycle analysis and portfolio management.
- Determine whether the events truly affect the fundamentals of supply and demand. If they do, you can foresee how the timing of the turning points in the business cycle will be affected and act accordingly. If not, you may have a short-term trading opportunity if the market has overreacted to events that will not, in fact, affect the fundamentals within the business cycle.

This thought process is diagrammed in Figure 13-3.

Part IV

INVESTING IN THE BUSINESS CYCLE

The Primary Business Cycle has been defined as having 40 events, or turning points, and we showed earlier that the "big picture" of the business cycle could be described by tracking the broad movements of only five major indicators:

- The money supply
- The stock market
- The economy
- Inflation
- Interest rates

Viewed in this light, the cyclical movements of only three of these indicators—the stock market, inflation, and interest rates—can be translated directly into a long-term investment strategy.

The money supply and the economy are critical influences on the other three indicators, but obviously cannot be "played" directly in a market. As we now show, inflation, along with some other factors, can be analyzed to produce buy and sell signals for gold, silver, and other hard assets that are inflation sensitive. Of course, interest rates move in direct opposition to long-term bond prices and, therefore, can generate buy and sell signals for bonds.

The stock market is clearly the most complex of all basic forms of investment, in that stock prices are influenced by a large number of both real and perceived events and trends. At the other extreme is the investment known as cash. In reality, this is not pure cash, but a package of highly secure, very liquid, short-term lending instruments that are acquired by money market funds. Or an investor who keeps money in short-term T-bills and continues to roll them over upon maturity is also said to be invested in cash. The return on investment for cash will rise or fall with short-term borrowing rates and, unlike bonds, will earn more as interest rates rise and less as interest rates fall.

These, then, are the four mainstays of investment portfolios for corporations, pension funds, or individual investors:

• Stocks
• Long-term bonds
• Gold or other hard assets
• Cash

Of course, many other forms of investment are available to almost everyone today: real estate, convertible bonds, warrants, options, and commodity futures, to name just a few. But each of these has some inherent disadvantages and risks that can easily be avoided without giving up any profit opportunities. To examine the characteristics of different kinds of investments, we define an ideal portfolio of investments for an individual investor. We assume that the investor has a full-time job and, therefore, cannot devote hours and hours to investment research. We'll further assume that the investor wants to (1) maximize the annual profits from his investments, but (2) preserve the value of his investment funds by avoiding excessive risks. Based on the known cyclical nature of the economy and the financial markets, we assume that the investor also wants liquidity and the flexibility to get into or out of any investment on short notice without subjecting himself to a loss.

By themselves, these simple criteria reduce the complete list of investment vehicles to a very small number. *Real estate* is not liquid on short notice (e.g., a few days). *Options, commodities,* and *futures* are highly volatile and risky, can involve the loss of the entire bet made by the investor, and often involve the use of borrowed, or margined, money. While buying on margin can substantially increase your return on an investment if you are right, it can lead to financial ruin if you are wrong. Thousands of investors who had highly leveraged margin plays in the stock market on October 19, 1987, will attest to this fact. As *convertible securities* are hybrid forms of stocks and bonds and we know that the stock market and interest rates do not move in corresponding cyclical patterns, these hybrids are often caught in a cross-current of positive and negative trends and produce no net gain. *Hard assets,* such as rare coins and stamps, jewels, art, antiques, and even baseball cards, require that one have the expertise to evaluate their authenticity and value—which would require years of study and research.

This brings us back to our four basic investments of stocks, bonds, gold, and cash. Appropriate buy and sell signals for these four investments (1) can be observed by studying only the business cycle, (2) can be managed to avoid margin buying and high-risk speculation, (3) allow rapid (one-day) changes in a portfolio, and (4) do not require specific expertise to evaluate the authenticity of a purchased security.

In the next four chapters, we discuss the specifics of investing in cash, bonds, stocks, and gold with respect to the Primary Business Cycle. Then we tie these four investments into several alternative approaches for managing a complete business cycle–timed portfolio that will significantly outperform the market over the long run.

Chapter 14

Investing in Cash:
Easy Money at No Risk

CASH: THE RISKLESS INVESTMENT

The term "investing in cash" is not used very often in investment literature, and cash is generally treated as idle money. But, in fact, cash is one key component of the ideal portfolio and, as such, must be treated with the same respect as the other components. An investor who puts money into cash is generally investing in either a short-term money market fund or in government T-bills with short maturities. These investments in cash provide investors with several specific and distinctive performance characteristics, as shown in Figure 14-1.

Types of Cash Investment

The purest form of a cash investment is plain old U.S. dollar bills. And although some pure, liquid cash dollar bills may be a good hedge against a banking crisis, they earn no interest at all and are obviously not a good form of investment in a managed portfolio.

Banking certificates of deposit are popular savings vehicles,

Figure 14-1. *Performance Characteristics of Cash Investments*

An investment in cash:

Provides maximum liquidity.

Provides maximum safety.

Earns the short-term money market or T-bill rate of return.

Essentially offers a guaranteed profit.

Provides a hedge against possible downturns in other parts of an investor's portfolio.

Provides higher returns when interest rates go up. Since money is invested at today's rate and is then reinvested at next week's rate, and then the following week's rate, and so on, the cash investment essentially rides the short-term interest rate trend both up and down throughout the business cycle.

Minimizes investment risk.

---

but we do not recommend them as a part of an investor's portfolio. Their rates are slightly higher than those of money market funds or T-bills, but they do not offer easy access or liquidity. Also, they must be bought with a specific time to maturity at a fixed rate. An investor who buys a one-year certificate of deposit at 7 percent could not get at that money during the year without paying a penalty; if rates should rise during the year, the investor would receive only the locked-in 7 percent interest payment. In addition, to move money for a short period of time from an account with a stockbroker or a mutual fund to a bank under separate management adds complexity and difficulty to the management of a total portfolio.

There are two practical ways to invest in cash as a part of an overall portfolio management system:

- By switching money from stocks, bonds, or gold into a money market fund as a part of a total money management system through a mutual fund or a stock brokerage firm

- By switching money from stocks, bonds, or gold into U.S. T-bills under a similar money management system

Money Market Funds

Investing in money market funds is extremely easy. Virtually every brokerage firm and mutual fund family has a cash, or money market, fund that can be used for regular investment accounts, IRA accounts, or Keogh accounts.

The typical cash, or money market, fund contains investments in several types of short-term debt securities:

- U.S. government securities
- Bank obligations
- Commercial paper
- Obligations of foreign banks
- Repurchase agreements
- Other investments approved by the managers of the fund

The average maturity of these financial instruments is usually 120 days or less, and the fund managers are generally restricted to buying low-risk, highly secure short-term debt instruments. These investments would have to be considered more risky than government-backed T-bills, but since they are so short term in duration, the added risk is very low.

Also, more than two dozen tax-exempt money market funds are now available to high-income investors. As these funds invest only in low-risk, tax-exempt bonds that are very short in maturity, they are quite safe, as well as liquid. Depending on the investor's tax bracket, these funds could generate a higher after-tax yield than the normal, taxable money market funds.

An investor who is working through a broker pays a brokerage commission when buying or selling stocks or bonds. However, there is no transaction cost for moving money into or out of cash, or money market, funds. If the investor is working with a mutual fund family, there may be a fee for switching money between stock or bond funds and the money market fund, but this fee is usually negligible and is a small price to pay for the ability to move even large sums of money into and out of cash on short (one-day) notice as we move through the business cycle. Either way, money market funds or brokerage firm cash management accounts are attractive and secure ways to invest in cash when it is prudent to do so.

Treasury Bills

Investors who want their money in the most secure investment in the world at a decent rate of return have an opportunity to buy T-bills on the open market. This can be done either by switching money to a T-bill fund with a mutual fund company, or by purchasing T-bills from any stock brokerage firm. The brokerage commission, which is paid when the T-bill is purchased, amounts to *$25 per purchase* regardless of the size of the purchase. Therefore, the total commission on $10,000 of T-bills is about 0.25 percent or ¼ of 1 percent, and the commission on $100,000 of T-bills is a very low 0.025 percent.

T-bills are somewhat unique in that they are discounted at the time of purchase. With most bonds, an investor might buy a 6 percent $10,000 bond, receive interest payments of $600 per year, and then get the $10,000 principal back. But T-bills are offered at a discount from their face value, just as Series EE savings bonds are sold. A typical T-bill with a $10,000 maturity value might be offered at a price of $9,500. The investor pays the discounted amount ($9,500), waits a few months until the T-bill matures, and then collects the $10,000 face value amount— earning interest of $500 in this example.

Flexibility. T-bills are offered on the open market from one week to one year in maturity; an investor can buy T-bills that mature in one month, three months, 37 weeks, or a full year, at his option. The minimum amount of a T-bill purchase is $10,000 face value.

To see the prevailing interest rates on T-bills, one has only to look in the back of any *Wall Street Journal*. A typical schedule of T-bill maturity dates and interest rates is shown in Figure 14-2.

The first column shows the date when the T-bill matures. The second and third columns show the bid and ask figures for the discount on the T-bill. And the fourth column shows the

Figure 14-2. *T-Bill Offerings*

U.S. Treas. Bills Mat. date	Bid	Asked	Yield Discount	U.S. Treas. Bills Mat. date	Bid	Asked	Yield Discount
-1988-				5-12	6.11	6.04	6.26
1-21	5.94	5.67	5.77	5-19	6.10	6.03	6.26
1-28	5.66	5.39	5.49	5-26	6.10	6.03	6.27
2-4	5.76	5.64	5.75	6-2	6.18	6.11	6.36
2-11	5.44	5.32	5.43	6-9	6.24	6.17	6.43
2-18	5.56	5.44	5.56	6-16	6.23	6.16	6.43
2-25	5.54	5.42	5.54	6-23	6.26	6.19	6.47
3-3	5.74	5.67	5.81	6-30	6.23	6.16	6.45
3-10	5.83	5.76	5.91	7-7	6.31	6.24	6.54
3-17	5.83	5.76	5.91	7-88	6.30	6.26	6.57
3-24	5.91	5.84	6.00	8-4	6.44	6.37	6.70
3-31	5.84	5.77	5.94	9-1	6.50	6.43	6.77
4-7	5.88	5.81	5.99	9-29	6.57	6.50	6.86
4-14	5.84	5.80	5.98	10-27	6.63	6.56	6.95
4-21	5.87	5.80	5.99	11-25	6.68	6.61	7.03
4-28	5.98	5.91	6.11	12-22	6.67	6.63	7.08
5-5	6.00	5.93	6.14				

Source: *Wall Street Journal* (January 15, 1988).

effective annualized yield of the T-bill. For example, the first entry for January 21, 1988, shows that the buyers want the T-bill at a 5.94 percent discount from $10,000 and that the sellers want a 5.67 percent discount from the $10,000 price. Since a 5.94 percent discount is more than a 5.67 percent discount, the buyers want a lower price and the sellers want a higher price, which is typical of all financial transactions.

Doing the Numbers. T-bills are guaranteed by the government, extremely liquid, and simple to buy and sell from a broker. The hardest part of investing in T-bills is correctly doing the arithmetic to figure out the price of the bill and the effective annual rate of return that it will pay. The arithmetic is a little complex because T-bills mature every single week, so we're dealing with fractions of a year, as well as the concept of buying the T-bill at a discounted price.

For example, what discounted price should an investor pay to receive $10,000 in six months and get an annualized rate of return of 10 percent? Or if the discount of a $10,000 T-bill that matures in three months is 5.75 percent, what would investors have to pay for the T-bill and what effective annual rate of return (or yield) would they receive?

A couple of examples are the easiest way to illustrate the required calculations. In each case, three steps are required to get all the answers.

Example 1: Principal amount = $10,000
              Discount = 6.0%
              Time to maturity = 180 days

• *Step 1:* Calculate the interest that will be made on this investment by multiplying the discount rate by the principal amount, and then multiply that amount by the fraction of a year that the bill has left to maturity.

$$
\text{Interest} = \text{Discount \%} \times \text{Principal} \times \frac{180}{360}
$$

$$
\text{Interest} = \quad 0.06 \quad \times \quad \$10,000 \quad \times \quad 0.50
$$

$$
\text{Interest} = \quad \$300
$$

• *Step 2:* Calculate the price of the T-bill by subtracting the interest from the face value of the bill.

$$
\text{Discounted Price} = \text{Face Amount} - \text{Interest}
$$

$$
\text{Discounted Price} = \quad \$10,000 \quad - \quad \$300
$$

$$
\text{Discounted Price} = \quad \$9,700
$$

• *Step 3:* Figure the annualized yield of this investment by using the following formula, which computes the return on investment and factors in the length of time to get an annualized yield.

$$\text{Annualized Yield} = \frac{\text{Interest}}{\text{Price}} \times \frac{360}{\text{N}}$$

where N = the number of days remaining until the T-bill matures

$$\text{Annualized Yield} = \frac{\$300}{\$9,700} \times \frac{360}{180}$$

$$\text{Annualized Yield} = 0.03093 \times 2 = 0.06185 \text{ or } 6.185\%$$

Example 2: Principal amount = $10,000
Discount = 5.0%
Time to maturity = 90 days

• *Step 1:* Calculate the interest to be received in 90 days.

$$\text{Interest} = \text{Discount} \times \text{Principal} \times \frac{90}{360}$$

$$\text{Interest} = 0.05 \times \$10,000 \times 0.25 = \$125$$

• *Step 2:* Calculate the price to be paid.

$$\text{Price} = \text{Principal} - \text{Interest}$$

$$\text{Price} = \$10,000 - \$125 = \$9,875$$

• *Step 3:* Calculate the annualized rate of return or yield.

$$\text{Annualized Yield} = \frac{\$125}{\$9,875} \times \frac{360}{90}$$

$$\text{Annualized Yield} = 0.01266 \times 4 = 5.06\%$$

Looking at Figure 14-2, which gives the annualized yield on any given day, an investor might want to know how much a $10,000 T-bill might cost for different lengths of time. To do this, you only have to perform the first two steps, as shown in the following example:

Example: What will the price of a February 11 T-bill be given the numbers in Figure 14-2?
   If bought at the asking price: Principal amount = $10,000
                                  Asked discount = 5.32%
                                  Time to maturity = 28 days

• *Step 1:*

$$\text{Interest} = \text{Discount \%} \times \text{Principal} \times \frac{\text{Days}}{360}$$

$$\text{Interest} = 5.32\% \times \$10,000 \times \frac{28}{360} = \$41.38$$

• *Step 2:*

$$\text{Price} = \text{Principal} - \text{Interest}$$

$$\text{Price} = \$10,000 - \$41.38 = \$9,958.62$$

If bought at the bid price: Principal amount and time to maturity are the same as above
Bid discount = 5.44%

• *Step 1:*

$$\text{Interest} = 5.44\% \times \$10,000 \times \frac{28}{360} = \$42.31$$

• *Step 2:*

$$\text{Price} = \$10,000 - \$42.31 = \$9,957.69$$

On January 15, 1988, the one-month T-bill maturing 28 days later would cost the investor between $9,957.69 and $9,958.62.

The T-Bill Worksheet. Figure 14-3 is a worksheet for figuring out the prices and yields for T-bills.
Of course, a broker can always do this on the phone and save investors the time and trouble of this arithmetic exercise, but it is helpful for investors to speak the same language as their brokers when moving money into and out of T-bills throughout the business cycle.

Conclusions. The point of this discussion on cash investments is to emphasize the fact that cash is not just idle money. It is the anchor of stability of all portfolios, has its own performance traits, and should be viewed as an equal opportunity investment in managing a portfolio—one that is often the most attractive investment at specific points in the business cycle. If,

Figure 14-3. *T-Bill Worksheet*

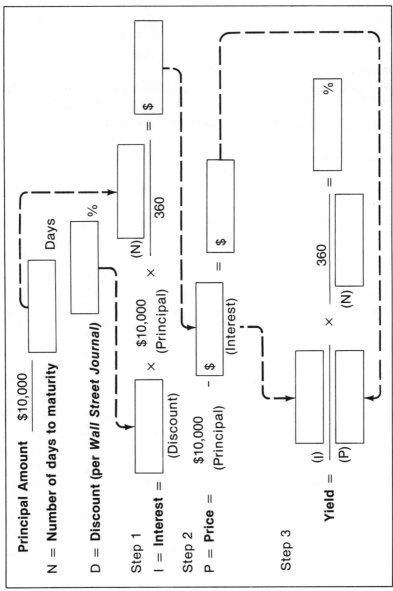

Principal Amount $\underline{\$10,000}$

N = **Number of days to maturity** _____ Days

D = **Discount (per Wall Street Journal)** _____ %

Step 1

I = **Interest** = _____ × $\$10,000$ × $\dfrac{\text{_____ (N)}}{360}$ = $\$\text{_____}$
        (Discount)   (Principal)

Step 2

P = **Price** = $\$10,000$ − $\$\text{_____}$ = $\$\text{_____}$
        (Principal)   (Interest)

Step 3

Yield = $\dfrac{\text{_____ (I)}}{\text{_____ (P)}}$ × $\dfrac{360}{\text{_____ (N)}}$ = _____ %

during a business cycle, an investor exits the stock market at its peak and moves those funds into cash, he or she might earn 7 percent from a portfolio during the next year while the market drops 25 percent—a 32 percent difference in the value of the portfolio at the end of the year. It must be remembered that the bedrock objective of managing a portfolio of securities is to have one's money invested in the right place at the right time, and there are times in every business cycle in which the only investment that will generate a positive return is some form of cash investment.

MOVING INTO THE RISK ZONE

The Concept of Risk

One of the key characteristics of cash investments is the avoidance of "investment risk," which is more than just a phrase that deals with the avoidance of the perils of the financial markets. Within the context of investments, the term "risk" can be defined as a measure of "the variability of the possible outcomes" of an investment. Any investment that has a wide range of possible financial results is said to be high risk, while investments with a narrow, more secure set of possible financial outcomes are said to be low risk. The most common substitute for the word "risk" in the investment world is the word "volatility."

In terms of managing a portfolio, this concept is clarified by examination of the possible one-year profits on several types of investments. In any given year, past history shows that gold could easily rise or fall by 75 percent, stocks could rise or fall by 50 percent, and bonds could rise or fall by 30 percent or more. On the other hand, cash and T-bills have a much more limited set of outcomes. If the current short-term interest rate is 6 percent and it rises to 8 percent in a year, the investor's annual return might be 7 percent for the year as a whole. If interest rates begin at 6 percent and fall to 4 percent during the year, the investor's return for that year might be 5 percent on average. The range of

Figure 14-4. *Variability of Outcomes for Stocks, Bonds, Gold, and Cash: Illustration*

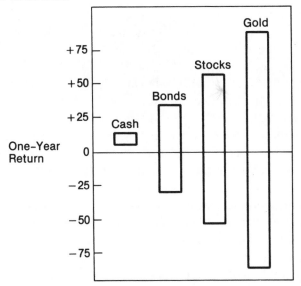

possible outcomes in this example is a return of 5 percent to 7 percent. The risk involved in the four kinds of basic investments is illustrated in Figure 14-4.

Figure 14-4 shows that cash investments are fundamentally different from all the other forms of investment in two specific ways:

- The highest possible return from cash is lower than the highest possible returns on all the others.
- The lowest possible return from cash is not only higher than that of the other investments, but cash is the only form of investment in which the worst possible outcome is *still positive*.

Thus, although you can't make a huge return on investments in cash, you can't lose money in cash unless the whole country folds up and collapses. Therefore, cash is the lowest-risk and the lowest-reward component of an investment portfolio.

Risk Versus Reward

The concepts of risk and reward are clarified in a financial theory known as the "capital asset pricing model." Although the full model is somewhat complex at the detail level, the essence of the model is quite simple: Risk and reward are inextricably linked together in the financial markets. Low-risk investments provide low returns; an investor who wants a higher return has to take a higher risk. In other words, there's no free lunch in the investment game. Figure 14-5 graphically shows this relationship. Risk, or the variability of outcomes, is measured on the horizontal scale, and reward, as measured by an annual return on investment percentage, is shown on the vertical scale.

Figure 14-5 shows that the first point on the chart, T-bills, generates a low return, but with essentially no risk. Money market funds are slightly riskier because they are not restricted to government securities. T-bonds are a little higher on the curve because they are longer-term bonds and, in any single year, their price could rise or fall significantly if interest rates change during that time. (However, there is no risk or variability in the return on a T-bond if it is held to maturity.)

Figure 14-5. *Risk and Reward: Illustration*

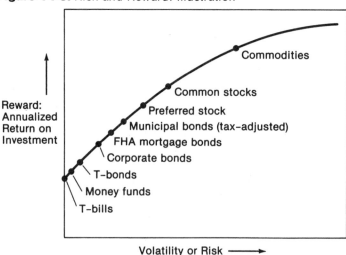

As we move up the curve, each investment has an increasing risk based on historical volatility; as the risk increases, the potential return increases as well. As we move away from guaranteed T-bonds to corporate bonds, which are not guaranteed, the risk goes up. Thus, the interest rate that these bonds offer must be higher than the T-bond rate. And as we move from bonds, which are legal debts, to preferred and common stocks, which are ownership certificates in businesses, the risk goes up even more; so the total return demanded by investors is higher still. At the end of the curve, we have commodities, which are extremely volatile but offer huge potential returns (and/or losses) to investors and speculators.

Having established cash as the anchor of our four-part portfolio, we can now examine the other three investment components in order of increasing risks and rewards: first bonds, then stocks, and, finally, gold.

Chapter 15

Investing in Bonds: Timing Is Everything

Many kinds of bonds are available to investors. Bonds are issued by the U.S. government, government agencies, states, munici-palities, and corporations. As shown in Figure 14-5, some broad truths can be stated about bonds. Short-term bonds are less risky and usually pay lower interest than long-term bonds do. Government bonds, which are backed by the government's ability to tax and to print money, are generally the least risky and, accordingly, the lowest-yielding bonds. State bonds are more risky because state governments are more limited in their ability to tax and cannot print money. Municipal bonds are issued on a tax-free basis to attract investors, but the risk is even higher because any municipality can run into serious local financial problems (remember the New York City crisis a few years ago?).

From an investment standpoint, only three fundamental principles need to be understood about bonds:

- The *return*, or interest rate, that a bond yields is *directly related to the risk* associated with the bond issue.
- The *interest rates* on bonds of all risk categories tend to *move up and down together*, reaching turning points at the same time.

- The *price* of a bond is *inversely* related to the prevailing interest rate paid on bonds in the same risk category and time to maturity.

RISKS AND REWARDS FOR BONDS

In Figure 14-5, we showed that certain kinds of bonds carry a higher risk than others. This principle can be demonstrated by showing the market interest rate structure for four types of long-term bonds over the same time period. Figure 15-1 shows the market yields, or interest rates, for municipal bonds, Treasury bonds, corporate bonds, and FHA mortgage bonds from January 1986 to June 1988.

Other than municipal bonds, which are discussed separately, T-bonds are the safest and consistently pay the lowest yield. Corporate bonds, which are riskier because they are not guaranteed, have to pay a higher yield to attract investors. FHA mortgage bonds are higher-risk bonds because they are backed by individuals instead of corporations. They are also longer term than most others—usually 30 years—and command a higher rate for the extra time of the loan.

The municipal bond rate appears to be lower than all the others in Figure 15-1. But this is because it is an after-tax rate. To see what municipal bonds would yield on a pretax basis, which would be comparable to the other three rates, let's assume that the average investor's tax rate is 36 percent. The investor's after-tax interest income would be 64 percent of the pretax interest income. Thus, if the after-tax interest equals the pretax interest *times* 64 percent, the pretax interest must equal the after-tax interest *divided by* 64 percent:

$$\text{Pretax Rate} \times 0.64 = \text{After-Tax Rate}$$

or

$$\text{Pretax Rate} = \frac{\text{After-Tax Rate}}{0.64}$$

Figure 15-1. *Long-Term Interest Rate Structure*

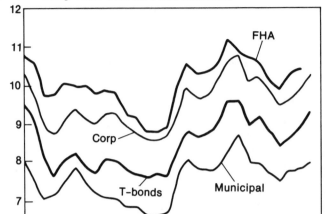

Source: *Business Conditions Digest.*

In January 1986, the after-tax municipal rate was 8.0 percent, so the comparable pretax rate would be 8.0 ÷ 0.64, or 12.5 percent—significantly higher than the FHA rate. In January 1987, the pretax municipal rate was down to 6.5 percent, so the tax-adjusted rate was 6.5 percent ÷ 0.64, or 10.15 percent—still higher than the other rates. This higher, tax-adjusted rate illustrates the "higher risk–higher reward" principle and reflects the risks involved in debt securities that are issued by local municipalities that may or may not have the tax base, the business support, or the overall financial wherewithal to pay their debt to bondholders.

Figure 15-1 also illustrates the second point about interest rates. The movements of all four interest rates clearly demonstrate the tendency to move up and down together, thus maintaining the interest rate differential between the bonds in different risk categories. Anything that causes a movement in one bond interest rate will quickly move the other interest rates in the same direction.

BOND PRICES AND INTEREST RATES

Why are bond prices and interest rates inversely related? Some investors know that bond prices and interest rates always move in opposite directions, but do not know exactly why. Others know that the relationship is true and understand the basics behind it, but have never worked out the mathematics to prove it. Still others are completely conversant with the discounted cash flow and present value calculations necessary to link an interest rate to a bond price. In this chapter, we address the question on a fundamental level and allow the reader to refer to an appendix for a more detailed analysis of bond evaluations.

While bonds can have maturities from 1 year to over 30 years, we can capture the basic relationship between bond prices and interest rates by using a one-year, single interest payment bond as an example. Suppose that on January 1, the prevailing interest rate on one-year Treasury bonds was 10 percent and an investor purchased a newly issued, one-year, $10,000 par value government bond with a 10 percent coupon rate (meaning that a $1,000 interest payment would be paid at the end of one year).

On January 1, the annual rate of return (known as the yield to maturity when dealing with bonds) can be calculated quite simply. The investment is the $10,000 principal amount of the bond. The return is the $1,000 interest payment plus the repayment of the $10,000 principal—a total of $11,000. Since $11,000 is 110 percent of $10,000, the investor made a 10 percent profit on this one-year bond investment.

But now let's suppose that on the next day, the prevailing interest rate picture changed significantly and all interest rates for government bonds plummeted to 6 percent. The government now issues some new $10,000 bonds with a 6 percent coupon rate, and some other investors buy them for $10,000 each. These new bond buyers will receive $600 in interest (6 percent of $10,000) plus the $10,000 repayment of principal—a total return of $10,600. And since $10,600 is 106 percent of the $10,000 cost of the bond, these investors earn only 6 percent for their trouble.

But they are still happy to get this 6 percent because that is the market interest rate that prevails on that day.

But now we have a problem. We have two groups of bonds on the market. One pays a 10 percent coupon rate and the other pays a 6 percent coupon rate. They both have principal amounts of $10,000 and mature in one year. However, the first issue will pay every bondholder a total of $11,000 in one year ($10,000 principal plus $1,000 interest), and the second issue will pay every bondholder $10,600 ($10,000 principal plus $600 interest). Both sets of bonds are actively traded on the market, and anyone can buy either bond at the market price.

But what is the correct market price for these bonds on the second day? Since the prevailing interest rate is 6 percent, the second group of bonds with a 6 percent coupon rate will still sell at a price of $10,000 because those bonds will generate a return of $10,600 for a return on investment of 6 percent—which is exactly the going interest rate.

However, the first group of bonds will generate a total return of $11,000 ($10,000 principal plus $1,000 interest). So the question becomes: At what bond price will a return of $11,000 equate to a return on investment of 6 percent, which is the prevailing interest rate for all T-bonds? Stated another way, "$11,000 is 106 percent of what?" Dividing $11,000 by 1.06 gives us the correct bond price of $10,377.36. In other words, the market price of this issue of T-bonds rose from $10,000 when it was issued to $10,377.36 because the market interest rate fell from 10 percent to 6 percent.

And why shouldn't it rise? If investors can buy a piece of paper that will produce $10,600 for a price of $10,000, why shouldn't they pay more for a similar piece of paper that will produce $11,000 in the same time and with the same degree of risk? By the same token, if interest rates had risen between days 1 and 2 of our example, the price of the T-bonds would have fallen proportionately.

The relationship can be seen in an equation that links the prevailing interest rate to a one-year bond with a fixed coupon rate:

$$\text{Bond Price} = \frac{\text{Principal} + \text{Coupon Interest Payment}}{1 + \text{Prevailing Interest Rate}}$$

Examples 1, 2, and 3 show what happens to an 8 percent T-bond when the prevailing interest rates move from 6 percent to 8 percent to 10 percent—using the bond price equation.

Example 1: Prevailing market interest rate = 6%
$$\text{Bond Price} = \frac{\$10,000 + \$800}{1 + 0.06} = \frac{\$10,800}{1.06} = \$10,188.68$$

Example 2: Prevailing market interest rate = 8%
$$\text{Bond Price} = \frac{\$10,000 + \$800}{1 + 0.08} = \frac{\$10,800}{1.08} = \$10,000.00$$

Example 3: Prevailing market interest rate = 10%
$$\text{Bond Price} = \frac{\$10,000 + \$800}{1 + 0.10} = \frac{\$10,800}{1.10} = \$9,818.18$$

HOW AND WHEN TO BUY BONDS

Although these examples deal only with one-year bonds, they illustrate the key cause-and-effect relationships between all interest rates and bond prices: *When market interest rates go down, all bond prices go up, and when interest rates go up, all bond prices go down.* Not only that, but bond prices will move up or down with absolute mathematical precision based on known bond price and interest rate formulas.

Since bond prices and interest rates always move in opposite directions, *it is clear that long-term bonds should be bought at interest rate peaks and sold at interest rate bottoms as we progress through each business cycle.* Playing the interest rate cycle through long-term bonds can be extremely profitable, especially when you consider that the investment is made in the safest form of security available.

In our one-year-to-maturity example, the price of a $10,000 bond rose by $377.36 when interest rates fell from 10 percent to 6 percent. This was only a 3.7 percent increase in price as the result of a 4 percent decline in interest rates. This price change was small because there was only one year from the time of purchase to maturity. Long-term bonds are much more volatile and will exhibit *very* significant price changes whenever interest rates change.

For example, an investor who purchased a new 20-year T-bond for $10,000 in 1981, when the T-bond rate was 14 percent, would have seen this very secure investment appreciate to $13,400 in the next *12 months* as interest rates fell to 10 percent. And if he or she had held it until 1986, when interest rates fell further to less than 8 percent, the bond would have appreciated to $15,200. This is a handsome profit for an investment in an essentially risk-free security.

The general rule for making bond investments is that *the longer the time to maturity, the more volatile the bond will be when interest rates change.* Therefore, when we approach an interest rate peak in the business cycle, the longest bonds on the market will appreciate the most when interest rates fall. So an investor who chooses to invest in individual bonds should look for those with at least a 20-year maturity to maximize the profits from a significant decline in interest rates.

Although our bond price equation for a 1-year bond with one interest payment is fairly straightforward, the equation and required calculations for a 20-year bond with semiannual interest payments are much more complex. To calculate the effect that a change in prevailing interest rates would have on the price of a bond, it is necessary to use the present value and discounted cash flow techniques mentioned earlier.

But the analysis of bond prices, interest rate changes, and potential profits can be made quite simple and efficient by using some precalculated charts that show the price of bonds for any possible combination of years to maturity, coupon rates, and prevailing interest rates. Appendix D of this book is a self-contained, copyrighted system of instructions and yield-to-maturity charts that can be used to quickly assess bond prices and potential profits without complex formulas or lengthy interest rate tables. Investors interested specifically in playing the bond market or obtaining a more detailed understanding of the dynamics of bond prices and interest rates are referred to that appendix.

However, investors do not have to deal with individual bonds to reap the benefits of interest rate cycles. Numerous bond mutual funds buy a wide variety of bonds at different maturity dates and different levels of risks. Tax-exempt bond funds are also available to individual investors in high tax brackets.

Any of these bond-related investments provide investors with a way to generate consistent long-term profits by tracking the business cycle and investing at interest rate peaks and exiting at interest rate bottoms. Our recommended approach to bond investments is to capitalize on the diversity and flexibility that are offered by the mutual fund families, which allow investors to move money into and out of bond funds as dictated by the business cycle. These investment switches can be made on a timely basis at virtually no cost to the investor. The specifics of this investment approach are discussed in Chapter 18 as a part of our complete investment management system.

Chapter 16

Investing in Stocks: Recognizing the Major Tops and Bottoms

THE LINKAGE BETWEEN BONDS AND STOCKS

Many investors directly associate the words "investments" and "stocks." They believe that stocks are what you invest in when you are an investor. We hope that the previous few chapters of this book have shown the reader that both the concept and the practical art of investing need to be viewed in a broader context. The business cycle offers investment opportunities in stocks, bonds, gold, and cash, which can all be either exploited or avoided at different times in the business cycle. In addition, each of these four forms of investment possesses its own set of risk and reward characteristics.

Since we live in a constantly changing world, we need to recognize a critical fact about investments throughout each business cycle: *There are no absolutes!* Albert Einstein's theory of the universe applies equally to the world of investments. Everything is relative at any given point in time. Is a 10 percent return on investment good? In 1980 and 1981, it wasn't, because inflation was nearly double that rate. Is $120 a good price for IBM stock? Is an 8 percent dividend yield from a blue chip company good? Is gold undervalued at $400 an ounce? The answer to all of these questions is the same: "Relative to what?"

There are dozens of ways in which people can invest money—either for long-term investment purposes or short-term profits (or losses). People can now invest in common stocks; preferred stocks; corporate bonds; convertible stocks or bonds; rights; warrants; options; mutual funds; futures; precious metals; T-bills, T-bonds, or Treasury notes; or many kinds of real estate.

But while a select group of arbitrageurs and speculators may play the futures and options markets and others may speculate in oil wells or diamond mines, the vast majority of money that is invested in financial assets is invested in either stocks or bonds. For governments, corporations, and wealthy investors with millions of dollars (or deutsche marks or yen) to invest, the other markets, including gold, are either too small, too thinly traded, or too risky for these huge sums of money. Pension fund managers, who now control billions of dollars, concentrate their investments in stocks, bonds, and cash. And since these money managers are competing for funds to manage, they run their funds aggressively—with cash the haven of last resort when stocks and bonds are perceived as bad investments. Therefore, one of the most critical factors in the investment decision-making process is the *relative attractiveness* of stocks versus bonds. We can make the first comparison by examining the structure of the total return to the investor from both bonds and stocks.

The Total Return on a Bond

As stated in the last chapter, a government bond is considered the safest investment in the world. Because it is a bond, it carries a fixed rate of return. Because it is a debt owed to the bondholder by the U.S. government, it is backed by the full faith and credit of the U.S. government. And since the government has the power to raise taxes and to print currency, the full repayment of a government bond is virtually guaranteed.

When you buy a T-bond for $10,000 that matures in five years with an 8 percent coupon rate, you will receive $800 per year for five years and you will receive your $10,000 principal at the end of the five-year period. Your effective annual rate of return, or yield to maturity, for this investment will be exactly 8 percent.

The cash flows from an investment in a bond can be visualized by itemizing each element of the investment and its returns on a time chart. Figure 16-1 shows the cash flows for a $10,000 bond with a coupon rate of 8 percent that matures in five years. The cash investment is shown by the arrow pointing up *into* the bond line, and the cash returns are shown by the arrows pointing up *out of* the bond line.

Since investors can buy T-bonds for any maturity date that fits their needs and the rate of return can be precalculated ahead of time, the T-bond investment can be considered the base investment at no risk, against which any other investment can be compared and evaluated.

The Total Return on a Stock

While stocks are the primary alternative to bonds in the world's markets, the financial characteristics of stocks are different from those of bonds in several fundamental ways. Instead of paying out a guaranteed interest payment, stocks pay out dividends, which are not guaranteed. The interest from a bond is secure and is a fixed amount, whereas a stock's dividend can either grow over the years or be reduced during business downturns. Instead of having a defined repayment of principal in

Figure 16-1. *Cash Flows for a T-Bond*

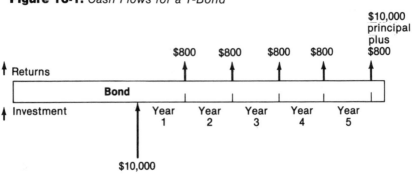

Annual yield–to–maturity (rate of return) = 8%

Figure 16-2. *Cash Flows for a Stock*

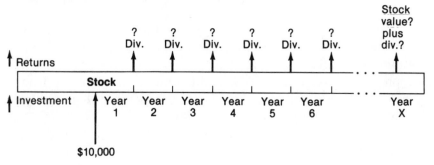

five years, the stock investor can collect only the market value of the stock at some point in the future. And instead of being backed by the full faith and credit of the United States, stocks are backed only by the market's current perception of their value. Finally, of course, stock-issuing companies cannot print money as the government can.

Therefore, the cash flow chart for a stock is dramatically different from that of a T-bond, as shown in Figure 16-2.

The $10,000 cost of the stock is fixed, but nothing else can be counted on with certainty. The dividends could increase each year, and the stock could be worth $20,000 in five years. On the other hand, the company's dividends could be cut and the value of the stock could be reduced to $5,000 in five years. In addition, it is possible that the company itself could do quite well but that the stock price could fall due to external economic conditions. For example, from the beginning of 1973 to the end of 1974 (during a severe recession), the earnings of Bristol-Myers grew by more than 20 percent per year and the dividend payout grew by 10 percent per year, but the stock price fell by more than 50 percent in the two-year period as overall interest rates soared into double digits.

So, the investment question becomes one of trying to measure the *relative* risks and rewards of stocks versus bonds when only the risk of the bond (zero, if held to maturity), the return of the bond (the fixed coupon interest), and the price of the stock are known.

The Relative Return Equation

In the cash flow charts for bonds and stocks, one thing is very clear. The return on stocks is much more uncertain than the return on bonds. Therefore, based on the risk/reward curve in Figure 14-5, investors will demand a higher total return from stocks than they will from bonds—to compensate them for the higher risk that they take in buying stocks.

How much more will investors want? Just as there is a fairly stable interest rate difference between various kinds of bonds, as shown in Figure 15-1, history shows us that investors have established a fairly stable difference between the total return on stocks and the total return on bonds. Over the past several decades, the total return on stocks has exceeded the long-term T-bond return by about 5 percent per year.

This extra 5 percent return on investment is known as the "risk premium" that stocks must provide to entice investors to buy stocks instead of long-term T-bonds. Stated mathematically, the return on stocks must be equal to the return on T-bonds *plus* a *risk* premium of 5 percent, as shown in Figure 16-3.

Thus, if long-term T-bonds are yielding 8 percent, investors need to believe that a stock investment will provide a total return of 13 percent to make the investment in stocks. This total stock return of 13 percent can come from only two sources: dividends and stock price appreciation. From a return-on-investment standpoint, this means that the return on stocks will equal the dividend yield (dividends ÷ stock price paid) plus the expected percentage gain (or growth rate) of the stock price (price increase ÷ stock price paid). This relationship is shown mathematically in Figure 16-4.

By combining Figures 16-3 and 16-4, we can now create Figure 16-5, the "relative return equation," which holds true at all times throughout the business cycle.

Figure 16-3.

Return on Stocks	=	Return on T-Bonds	+	Risk Premium
RS	=	RT	+	rp

Figure 16-4.

Return on Stocks	=	Dividend Yield	+	Expected Growth (%) of Stock Price
RS	=	$\dfrac{d}{p}$	+	G

where d = annual dividends paid per share
G = expected annual growth rate in stock price per share
p = price per share paid by the buyer

This concept can be clarified with some examples. Suppose that the prevailing yield to maturity of one-year T-bonds is 8 percent and that investors want an extra 5 percent for risking their money in any kind of stocks—a total stock return of 13 percent. This 13 percent return could be realized if an investor bought:

- A utility stock with a 7 percent dividend yield that rose in price by 6 percent in the next year
- A consumer product stock with a 5 percent dividend yield that rose by 8 percent in the next year
- A high tech stock with a modest 3 percent dividend yield that rose by 10 percent in the next year
- A new issue with no dividend yield that rose by 13 percent in the next year

These examples are illustrated in Figure 16-6 using the relative return equation.

Figure 16-5. *The Relative Return Equation*

Return on T-Bonds	+	Stock Risk Premium	=	Total Return on Stocks	=	Stock Dividend Yield	+	Expected Growth (%) of Stock Price
RT	+	rp	=	RS	=	$\dfrac{d}{p}$	+	G

Figure 16-6. Examples of the Relative Return Equation

	Return on T-Bonds	+	Stock Risk Premium	=	Total Return on Stocks	=	Stock Dividend Yield	+	Expected Growth (%) of Stock Price
	R_T	+	r_p	=	R_S	=	$\dfrac{d}{p}$	+	G
Utility stock	8%	+	5%	=	13%	=	7%	+	6%
Consumer product stock	8%	+	5%	=	13%	=	5%	+	8%
High tech stock	8%	+	5%	=	13%	=	3%	+	10%
New issue stock	8%	+	5%	=	13%	=	0%	+	13%

Reading the chart *in words* highlights the real meaning of the relative return equation. In the example of high tech stock, this chart says, from left to right, "Given an 8 percent T-bond rate, I need to make 5 percent more, or 13 percent in total, in stocks to feel that stocks are worth the risk. And with stocks giving a 3 percent dividend yield, I have to believe that the stock price will appreciate by 10 percent to give me my 13 percent total return."

However, there is one problem with Figure 16-6 as it now appears. We can see some significant differences in the risk involved in the four illustrations that we used. The utility stock pays a 7 percent dividend, which means that more than half of the investor's required 13 percent return is fairly stable and reliable. Only 6 percent of the required 13 percent return must come from stock price appreciation, which is more uncertain. In other words, this is a *relatively low-risk stock investment*.

On the other hand, the new issue stock pays no dividend, so the entire 13 percent return that the investor seeks must come from stock price appreciation. And since the price of this stock could be affected by its own performance, the performance of the company's industry, or the performance of the stock market as a whole—which could, in turn, be affected by the money supply, inflation, interest rates, the economy as a whole, or several other factors—this is a *relatively high-risk stock investment*.

Therefore, the risk premiums for the utility stock and the new issue stock should not be the same. The risk premium for the new issue stock should be higher than that of the utility stock to compensate for the added risk—the higher degree of uncertainty of the financial outcome of the investment. Based on historical evidence, we can adjust risk premiums upward for higher-risk stocks and downward for lower-risk stocks.

Our historical analysis has shown that the relationship between stock dividend yields and stock risk premiums shown in Figure 16-7 can be used as an effective guide.

Figure 16-8 shows the same four examples with these adjusted risk premiums.

With an 8 percent T-bond rate, an investor considering a utility stock that pays a 7 percent dividend need believe only that

Figure 16-7. *The Yield-Risk Table*

	y	rp	
	If the Stock Dividend Yield Is	*Then the Stock Risk Premium Is*	
	0%	15%	
	1	13	
Lower	2	11	Higher
Dividend	3	9	Risk
Yield	4	7	Premium
	5	5	
Higher	6	3	Lower
Dividend	7	1	Risk
Yield	8	−1	Premium
	9	−3	
	10	−5	

the price of the stock will grow by 2 percent per year to justify buying the stock. And under the same conditions, the same investor would have to believe that a new issue of stock with no dividends will grow by 23 percent per year to deserve the investment.

Lessons from the Relative Return Equation

The relative return equation carries with it some very valuable lessons:

• It is the universal conceptual approach to evaluating all investments. You begin with a base case investment with a known degree of risk and reward, you add a risk premium to adjust for the added risk of another investment, and finally you estimate the potential rewards of the other investment to see if they meet or exceed your risk-adjusted return on investment needs.

• It is the only framework that allows the same kind of analysis to be performed regardless of the amount of money involved. Is $5,000 a good profit from an investment? It's a terrific profit if you only invested $1,000 to get it, but it's a poor profit on an

Figure 16-8. *Revised Examples of the Relative Return Equation*

	Return on T-Bonds	+	Stock Risk Premium	=	Total Return on Stocks	=	Stock Dividend Yield	+	Expected Growth (%) of Stock Price
	RT	+	rp	=	RS	=	$\frac{d}{p}$	+	g
Utility stock	8%	+	1%	=	9%	=	7%	+	2%
Consumer product stock	8%	+	5%	=	13%	=	5%	+	8%
High tech stock	8%	+	9%	=	17%	=	3%	+	14%
New issue stock	8%	+	15%	=	23%	=	0%	+	23%

investment of $500,000. Putting all possible investments on a percentage return on investment basis allows a fair comparison to be made, regardless of the actual dollar amounts involved.

- This equation *must always be in balance*. A change in any one variable must change one or more of the others.

- Most important, *it is the stock price that changes and adjusts itself to keep the relative return equation in balance.* In other words, *a relationship between the returns drives the prices of stocks* over a business cycle.

This last point may seem a bit obscure, but we insist that it is the only correct way to look at the relative attractiveness of investments and the determination of stock prices. Most stock market valuation models end up with an equation that says, "Stock price equals this plus that plus this divided by that." But this is not the correct approach.

For example, we could rearrange the terms of the relative return equation to say that stock price equals . . . , and the equation would then look like this:

$$p = \frac{d}{RT + rp - g}$$

This says that a stock's price equals its dividend payment divided by the Treasury bond rate plus the risk premium minus the stock's expected growth rate. This equation reduces further to a familiar equation that comes from a "future stream of dividends" theory of stock price valuation:

$$p = \frac{d}{k_e - g}$$

where k_e = the sum of the T-bond rate and the risk premium.

Despite wide acceptance of this model, it has some serious flaws. One of the most widely discussed issues concerns the calculated stock price if the stock does not pay any dividends. If $d = 0$, the price of the stock equals zero as per this equation. But we know that this isn't true. Many stocks begin at $10 per share, grow to $100 per share, split, and grow some more without ever paying any dividends. Thus, this equation does not realistically explain stock price behavior.

But the logical problem disappears by simply maintaining the concept and the form of the relative return equation:

$$
\begin{array}{ccc}
& \text{Stock} & \text{Total} \\
\text{Return on } + & \text{Risk} & = \text{Return on} \\
\text{T-Bonds} & \text{Premium} & \text{Stocks} \\
\\
& \text{Stock} & \text{Expected Growth} \\
& = \text{Dividend } + & (\%) \text{ of Stock} \\
& \text{Yield} & \text{Price}
\end{array}
$$

Here it is easy to see that if the stock dividend yield is zero, the total return on stocks must come entirely from the expected growth rate in the stock price, which, in principle, will mirror the expected growth rate of the company's earnings and cash flow.

By using the relative return equation, as shown in Figure 16-6, we can keep the correct perspective on all components of the equation and see that *stock prices will change as the result of changes in other components* to keep the equation in balance. Let's look at a few examples.

Base case: We'll analyze stock market behavior by using a single hypothetical stock that has earnings of $10 per share, pays out 40 percent of its earnings in dividends for an annual dividend of $4 per share, is currently selling at ten times annual earnings (or $100 per share), and has an expected growth rate of 11 percent per year based on the analyses of most Wall Street analysts. The risk premium on this stock is 7 percent, and the current T-bond rate is 8.0 percent.

The starting point for our analysis in terms of the relative return equation is shown in Figure 16-9.

Figure 16-9. Stock Price Behavior: Base Case

Return on T-Bonds		Stock Risk Premium		Total Return on Stocks		Stock Dividend Yield		Expected Growth (%) of Stock Price
RT	+	rp	=	RS	=	$\dfrac{d}{p}$	+	G
8%	+	7%	=	15%	=	$\dfrac{\$4}{\$100}$	+	11%
or								
8%	+	7%	=	15%	=	4%	+	11%

230

Looking at Figure 16-9 and remembering that the relative return equation *must always be in balance,* we can see several things. To keep the equation in balance, the stock price must change if:

- The T-bond rate changes.
- The stock's risk premium changes.
- The market's expected growth rate of the company's stock price changes.
- The company's annual dividend changes.

We now examine the impact of each of these cases on the stock's price.

Example 1—Interest rates rise: What if interest rates rise across the board because inflation is beginning to rise? In this case, let's say that interest rates rise from 8 percent to 9 percent. Given a 9 percent risk-free rate and a 7 percent risk premium, the stock must generate a 16 percent total return to be competitive with bonds. If our hypothetical company's dividend payout and its earnings growth rate outlook do not change, what will happen to its stock price? To generate a total return of 16 percent with an earnings growth rate of 11 percent, the yield must rise to 5 percent to make the yield plus the growth rate equal 16 percent. And since the dividend of $4 hasn't changed, the stock price must now drop to $80 to give a yield of 5 percent.

Example 1 shows that a 1 percent increase in interest rates will trigger a 20 percent decline in the price of this stock if nothing else changes. (See Figure 16-10.)

Example 2—Risk premium rises: An individual company's risk premium might change under several circumstances. If a new set of uncertainties should arise, such as an electric utility with nuclear facilities or a manufacturing company with new environmental liability risks, the company's risk premium would rise. Or even if the company's earnings and dividends remained the same but the company was going deeply into debt to finance operations, the risk premium might rise.

Figure 16-10. *Interest Rates Rise by 1 Percent: Example 1*

	Return on T-Bonds	+	Stock Risk Premium	=	Total Return on Stocks	=	Stock Dividend Yield	+	Expected Growth (%) of Stock Price
	RT	+	rp	=	RS	=	$\dfrac{d}{p}$	+	G
Base case	8%	+	7%	=	15%	=	$\dfrac{\$4}{\$100}$	+	11%
	or								
	8%	+	7%	=	15%	=	4%	+	11%
Example 1	9%	+	7%	=	16%	=	5%	+	11%
	or								
	9%	+	7%	=	16%	=	$\dfrac{\$4}{\$80}$	+	11%

New price = $80

The result of an isolated 1 percent increase in the risk premium would be the same as an increase in the T-bond rate. The total stock return would rise from 15 percent (8 percent + 7 percent) to 16 percent (8 percent + 8 percent), and the stock price would drop to $80 per share.

Example 2 shows that a 1 percent increase in the risk premium would also trigger a 20 percent decline in the stock price. (See Figure 16-11.)

Example 3—The growth rate expectation is cut: Suppose now that the collective analytical wisdom of Wall Street decides that this company's earnings growth rate will be only 10 percent instead of 11 percent. Since the total return on the stock must be 15 percent to make people buy the stock instead of bonds, the yield must rise to 5 percent so that the 10 percent growth rate plus the 5 percent dividend yield will total the required 15 percent. But if the dividend amount ($4) remains the same, the only way that the yield can rise to 5 percent is for the stock price to fall—in this case, to $80 ($4 ÷ $80 = 5 percent).

Figure 16-12 shows that a 1 percent reduction in the expected growth rate will trigger a 20 percent reduction in the stock price.

Example 4—The company cuts its dividend: If the company reduced its dividend from $4 to $3, the stock dividend yield would be only 3 percent if the price remained at $100. And this 3 percent yield plus the 11 percent expected growth rate would total only 14 percent instead of the required 15 percent total return.

Accordingly, the stock price would fall such that a $3 dividend would produce the 4 percent yield that is required to balance the equation. In this case, that price would be $75 per share since $3 ÷ $75 = 4 percent.

Example 4 shows that a 25 percent reduction in the dividend payment produces a 25 percent decline in the stock price. (See Figure 16-13.)

Example 5—Combined effect: In each of these four examples, we looked at the isolated effects of a change in one component of the relative return equation. But the world never

Figure 16-11. Risk Premium Increases by 1 Percent: Example 2

	Return on T-Bonds	+	Stock Risk Premium	=	Total Return on Stocks	=	Stock Dividend Yield	+	Expected Growth (%) of Stock Price
	RT	+	rp	=	RS	=	$\dfrac{d}{p}$	+	G
Base case	8%	+	7%	=	15%	=	$\dfrac{\$4}{\$100}$	+	11%
	or								
	8%	+	7%	=	15%	=	4%	+	11%
Example 2	8%	+	8%	=	16%	=	5%	+	11%
	or								
	8%	+	8%	=	16%	=	$\dfrac{\$4}{\$80}$	+	11%

New price = $80

Figure 16-12. Expected Growth Rate Falls by 1 Percent: Example 3

	Return on T-Bonds	+	Stock Risk Premium	=	Total Return on Stocks	=	Stock Dividend Yield	+	Expected Growth (%) of Stock Price
	RT	+	rp	=	RS	=	$\frac{d}{p}$	+	G
Base case	8%	+	7%	=	15%	=	$\frac{\$4}{\$100}$	+	11%
	or								
	8%	+	7%	=	15%	=	4%	+	11%
Example 3	8%	+	7%	=	15%	=	5%	+	10%
	or								
	8%	+	7%	=	15%	=	$\frac{\$4}{\$80}$	+	10%

New price = $80

Figure 16-13. The Company Cuts Its Dividend by $1: Example 4

	Return on T-Bonds RT	+	Stock Risk Premium rp	=	Total Return on Stocks RS	=	Stock Dividend Yield $\frac{d}{p}$	+	Expected Growth (%) of Stock Price G
Base case	8%	+	7%	=	15%	=	$\frac{\$4}{\$100}$	+	11%
	or								
	8%	+	7%	=	15%	=	4%	+	11%
Example 4	8%	+	7%	=	15%	=	$\frac{\$3}{\$75}$	+	11%
	or								
	8%	+	7%	=	15%	=	4%	+	11%

New price = $75

operates with "all other things being equal." In the dynamic financial markets, many things are always changing at once.

What would be the combined effect of all the negative changes that we just looked at? A pretty sad effect, indeed. The price of our hypothetical stock would plummet from $100 to $42.85 if (1) interest rates rose by 1 percent, (2) the risk premium increased by 1 percent (3) the growth rate estimates were cut from 11 percent to 10 percent, and (4) the dividend was cut by $1. While this appears to be an unrealistic disaster, it is not unlike the situation that many growth companies face when a runaway bull market in stocks comes to an end. The numbers for Example 5 are shown in Figure 16-14.

Of course, similar changes in interest rates, risk premiums, estimated growth rates, and dividend payouts in the positive direction would produce proportionate increases in a stock's price.

The Relative Attractiveness of the Whole Stock Market

In the last section, we looked at some individual types of stocks with different risk premiums and then traced the stock price reactions of a typical stock to changes in interest rates, risk premiums, growth rate estimates, and dividend payouts. However, the purpose of this book is not to concentrate on the analysis of individual stocks, but to focus on tracking, forecasting, and investing money in financial markets and the stock market as a whole at the right times in the business cycle. The relative return equation applies to the whole market, as measured by the Dow Jones industrials or the S&P 500 Stock Index, just as it does to individual companies. The long-term T-bond yield is still the risk-free baseline against which the potential return of the stock market can be measured. The risk premium for stocks is the premium that stocks, in general, must return to attract shareholders. And the only two sources of stock market return are still the dividend yield and the expected growth in stock prices.

Not only do the principles of the relative return equation apply to the whole market, but this equation can be used to

Figure 16-14. Combined Effects of Examples 1–4: Example 5

	Return on T-Bonds RT	+	Stock Risk Premium rp	=	Total Return on Stocks RS	=	Stock Dividend Yield $\frac{d}{p}$	+	Expected Growth (%) of Stock Price G
Base case	8% **or** 8%	+ +	7% 7%	= =	15% 15%	= =	$\frac{\$4}{\$100}$ 4%	+ +	11% 11%
Effects of Examples 1–4	9% **or** 9%	+ +	8% 8%	= =	17% 17%	= =	7% $\frac{\$3}{\$42.85}$	+ +	10% 10%

New price = $42.85

238

Figure 16-15. *Dividend Yields*

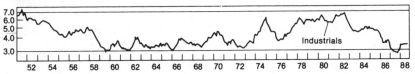

Source: Securities Research Company.

provide some useful insights into the identification of major stock market turning points. The following material shows that there is a practical way to answer definitively the question, "When is the stock market *really* overvalued and when is it *really* undervalued?"

We answer this question by looking at the historical relationships between the four components of the relative return equation: dividend yields, risk premiums, interest rates, and expected growth rates.

Dividend Yields. Our first insight into stock market behavior can be gained by looking at the history of dividend yields. Figure 16-15 shows the yield on the Dow Jones Industrial Average since 1951. The range of this yield is very clearly defined between 3 percent (at market tops) and 7 percent (at market bottoms).

With the Dow Jones Industrial Average rising from about 250 in 1951 to over 2,700 in 1987 and the dramatic changes that we have witnessed in every aspect of our lives and our economy over the last 35 years, it is remarkable that dividend yields have moved in such a narrow range. Why should such a well-defined set of boundaries exist in our complex financial world? The answer lies in the fact that stock market dividend yields are structurally linked to stock market risk premiums in the relative return equation.

The Stock Market Risk Premium. Two facts about stock risk premiums were noted in the last section. First, the average risk premium for an average stock is about 5 percent, so investors will be looking for a total rate of return equal to the T-bond rate plus about 5 percent. Second, the risk premium is higher when companies pay a low dividend yield, because a greater portion of the stock's total return has to come from price growth—which is much more speculative than dividends. Similarly, the risk premium is lower when the dividend yield is high because a greater portion of the total return is provided by relatively secure dividends.

These principles also apply to the market as a whole as it rises and falls in every business cycle. As the *stock market rises, the dividend yield falls* and the *risk premium rises* because, with a lower dividend yield, the total return from the stock market is more dependent on continued price growth. And when the *stock market falls,* the *dividend yield increases* and the *risk premium declines* because, with a higher dividend yield, the total return from the stock market is less dependent on price growth.

Here, we can reconstruct the yield-risk table in Figure 16-7, which linked dividend yields and risk premiums, to apply to the stock market as a whole (Figure 16-16).

The yield-risk table ties several specific historical findings together. We can see that the normal range of dividend yields is from 3 percent to 7 percent, with an average of 5 percent, and that the related risk premiums cover a range from 1 percent to 9

Figure 16-16. *The Yield-Risk Table for the Stock Market as a Whole*

	y	rp	
	If the Stock Dividend Yield Is	Then the Stock Risk Premium Is	
	0%	15%	
	1	13	
	2	11	
	3	9	
Historical	4	7	Normal
Market ——→	5	5	Historical
Average	6	3	Range
	7	1	
	8	−1	
	9	−3	
	10	−5	

Figure 16-17.

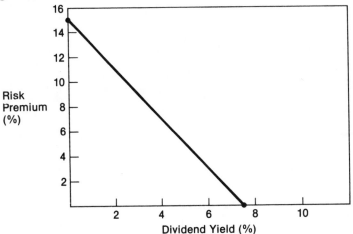

percent, with an average of 5 percent. But this relationship between dividend yields and risk premiums also serves as the essential key to understanding stock market valuation.

If we plot the two columns of the table on a graph, we see the inverse relationship between risk premiums and dividend yields.

Since the line in Figure 16-17 is straight, it can be turned into a simple equation linking the risk premium to the market dividend yield. That equation is shown in Figure 16-18.

The Valuation Map

The Valuation Equation. Now, by combining the yield-risk equation with the relative return equation, we can produce the last equation that we need to completely address the stock

---

Figure 16-18. *The Yield-Risk Equation*

Risk Premium $= 15\% - (2 \times \text{Yield})$
$\qquad\quad rp = 15\% - 2y$

Examples:
$\qquad\quad 9\% = 15\% - (2 \times 3\%)$
$\qquad\quad 1\% = 15\% - (2 \times 7\%)$

market valuation question. This brief algebraic exercise is as follows:

- *Step 1*—The relative return equation is:

$$RT + rp = y + g$$

- *Step 2*—The yield-risk equation is:

$$rp = 15\% - 2y$$

- *Step 3*—Substitute (15 percent − 2y) for rp in the relative return equation to get:

$$RT + (15\% - 2y) = y + g$$

- *Step 4*—Transpose terms and solve the equation to get the valuation equation, which is shown in Figure 16-19.

Figure 16-19. *The Valuation Equation*

T-Bond Rate	+	15%	=	3	×	Dividends / Stock Price	+	Expected Growth Rate
RT	+	15%	=			3y	+	g
RT	+	15%	=			$3\dfrac{d}{p}$	+	g

The valuation equation says that if an investor knows the current T-bond rate and the current stock market dividend yield, both of which are published on a regular (daily or weekly) basis, then the expected growth rate that is currently built into the price of the stock market can be calculated. And since the risk premium is already built into this equation, all of the elements of the relative return equation are captured in this single equation.

This is significant because we can now plot *all* of the relationships between risk and reward, stock yields (and stock prices), interest rates, and the market's expected growth rates on a single chart. This chart, which we call the valuation map, is somewhat unusual and requires a little explanation. However, once it is understood, the investor can tell at a glance whether the stock market is overpriced, underpriced, or correctly priced based on proven historical relationships. The valuation map is shown in Figure 16-20.

What the Valuation Map Says. Along the bottom of the valuation map is the Dow Jones industrials dividend yield; the

Figure 16-20. *The Stock Market Valuation Map*

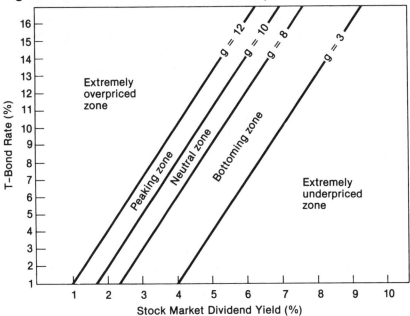

left-hand side measures the T-bond interest rate. The diagonal lines are the result of solving the valuation equation, using different values for dividend yields and T-bond rates and calculating the required growth rate. The leftmost diagonal line represents an expected 12 percent growth in stock prices, and the rightmost diagonal represents a 3 percent growth rate. The two middle diagonals represent a market growth rate expectation of 8 percent and 10 percent.

The entire history of the stock and bond markets can be placed on this valuation map, which is divided into five zones: the extremely overpriced zone, the peaking zone, the neutral zone, the bottoming zone, and the extremely underpriced zone.

We can see that the market gets more overpriced as we move up to the left on the map, where dividend yields are very low and interest rates are very high. The market becomes increasingly underpriced as we move down and to the right on the map, where dividend yields are high and interest rates are low. Let's look at what happens in each zone of the valuation map:

- *The peaking zone*—Most stock market peaks occur in the peaking zone. The combination of dividend yields and interest rates contained in this zone requires investors to believe that a growth rate of 10 percent to 12 percent in stock prices can be sustained. But since history shows that such growth rates cannot be sustained for very long, the stock market will tend to peak out here.

- *The bottoming zone*—Major stock market bottoms occur in this zone. The combination of dividend yields and interest rates in this zone requires investors to believe that only a 3 percent to 8 percent growth rate will prevail in the future. Since this is a modest expectation based on history, investors see that the risk in investing at that point is quite low, and the stock market tends to bottom out.

- *The neutral zone*—Neither stock market peaks nor bottoms occur in this zone. The combination of dividend yields and interest rates produces a required growth rate expectation between 8 percent and 10 percent—very near the long-term historical average of 8.59 percent. In moving from a bottom to a peak, the stock market will pass through this zone, but won't peak out until it enters the peaking zone. Similarly, after the market peaks out, it will pass through the neutral zone, but won't hit bottom until it reaches the bottoming zone. In other words, when the market is in this zone, it will continue its long-term trend until it moves into either the peaking or bottoming zone.

- *The extremely overpriced zone*—The market rarely enters this zone; when it does, this is a signal to investors that stock prices are dangerously high based on the fundamentals. To keep stock prices at this level, investors must believe that the market will grow by more than 12 percent per year for the next several years. And history shows that this is not a rational expectation. As indicated earlier, most bull markets end when the market enters the peaking zone. Even the speculative bull market of 1929 ended in September, when dividend yields and interest rates were in the peaking zone. The only time that the stock market entered this extremely overpriced zone was— you guessed it—in 1987, preceding the October crash.

- *The extremely underpriced zone*—Sometimes, the general level of depression and despair that surrounds difficult economic times becomes so great that investors do not have the confidence to buy back into the market in the bottoming zone—even though the pure investment opportunity is very handsome. Although an expected growth rate of only 3 percent to 8 percent is needed to justify an investment in stocks, investors won't take the risk because prevailing conditions are so poor. In these cases, the stock market declines and the dividend yields increase even though interest rates fall to a very low level. This decline continues until investors need to believe in only a 1 percent or 2 percent growth rate to start buying stocks again. The classic case of this situation occurred in 1932—after the crash of 1929 and in the midst of the depression. In such situations, a pragmatic investor can see and capitalize on a tremendous buying opportunity.

If one were to plot the T-bond rate and dividend yield over a typical business cycle, the plotted points would tend to move from one diagonal line (say, the 3 percent growth line at the stock market bottom) to another diagonal line (for example, the 12 percent growth line at the stock market peak) and then move back toward a lower diagonal growth rate line.

For example, a typical stock market bottom might occur with the dividend yield at a fairly high 6 percent rate and interest rates at the peak at 10 percent. Plotting on the valuation map puts this bottom in the market bottoming zone. Then, as interest rates fall and the stock market rises, the dividend yield begins to decline; a midway point in the cycle might be reached when interest rates equal 7 percent and the dividend yield equals 4.5 percent. This puts the market into the neutral zone. Finally, as we reach the stock market peak, interest rates are rising again, while the dividend yield is quite low since stock prices have risen. The peak might occur with interest rates back up to 8 percent and rising, while the dividend yield has fallen to 4 percent or so, which is in the stock market peaking zone. We tie the valuation map to the business cycle in more detail later in this chapter.

Mapping the Historical Stock Market Turning Points. We can now develop a new and unique perspective on the major stock market peaks and bottoms over the last 80 years by placing them on the valuation map. The points on the map were derived by using the dates of the historical market turning points, finding the Dow Jones industrials dividend yield and the T-bond rates on those dates, and plotting these points on the map. This historical view of market peaks and bottoms is shown in Figure 16-21.

We can see from Figure 16-21 that most of the major stock market peaks and bottoms have fallen into the peaking zone and the bottoming zone, respectively, of the valuation map. But there are two notable exceptions. In each case, this map would have made it extremely clear to investors that extraordinary buying and selling opportunities were waiting to be exploited:

• *Incredibly cheap stocks in 1932*—In 1929, the stock market reached a peak in September, with a dividend yield of 2.92

Figure 16-21. *Major Stock Market Turning Points on the Valuation Map*

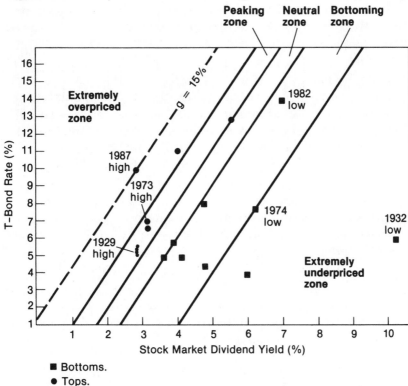

■ Bottoms.
● Tops.

percent and a T-bond rate of 4.5 percent. This clearly occurred in the peaking zone of the valuation map. But after the crash of 1929, the stock market declined to one-sixth of its 1929 value, even though the dividend rate increased to over 10 percent. By mid-1932, the dividend rate was 10.3 percent while the T-bond rate was only 5 percent. In the valuation map, it is very clear that stocks were incredibly cheap at this point. An unemotional investor with this map would have had the buying opportunity of a lifetime.

• *Outrageously high-priced stocks in 1987*—Earlier in the book, we said that the market was outrageously and visibly overvalued in August 1987, just prior to the October crash. We can now see why this degree of overvaluation was so easy to identify. In August 1987, the T-bond rate was rising and reached a rate of 8.9 percent. Meanwhile, the stock market was soaring and, accordingly, the dividend yield was plummeting. By August 1987, the dividend yield was at a ridiculously low 2.9 percent—just as it was in 1929. But look at where the combination of 8.9 percent interest rates and a 2.9 percent dividend yield puts the market on the valuation map: Remembering that as we move up and to the left as the market gets more and more overvalued, we can see that the August 1987 stock market peak occurred with the market far outside of the normal overpriced peaking zone and well into the extremely overpriced zone. To justify a Dow Jones industrial stock price of 2,700 in 1987 with a dividend yield of 2.9 percent and a T-bond rate of 8.9 percent, investors had to believe that the market could continue to grow at a rate of 15 percent—nearly double the historical growth rate. Therefore, at that time, just two months before the crash, the market was visibly and outrageously overpriced, as seen on this valuation map.

Using the Valuation Map to Evaluate the Stock Market. There are two easy ways to use this map to assess the condition of the stock market at any time:

- *The graphic method*—To determine the condition of the stock market, look up the current T-bond rate and the latest Dow Jones industrial dividend yield. Then plot that point on the valuation map to determine which zone it is in. A blank valuation map is provided in Appendix E of this book so that the reader can use this tracking method in the future.
- *The equation method*—To calculate the degree of overvaluation or undervaluation, look up the same two numbers: the T-bond rate and the stock market dividend yield. Then substitute those numbers into the valuation equation and solve for the expected growth rate.

Example: The valuation equation is:

$$RT + 15\% = 3y + g$$

If the T-bond rate is 10 percent and the stock market dividend yield is 4 percent:

$$10\% + 15\% = (3 \times 4\%) + g$$
$$25\% = 12\% + g$$
$$13\% = g$$

The investment decision associated with any answer that the investor may get by either method is summarized in Figure 16-22.

Answering the Yield Barrier Question. In addition to telling us whether the stock market is overpriced or underpriced at any point in time, the map can help us solve some other riddles. We

Figure 16-22.

Graphic Method	Equation Method	Investment Action
Market is in the extremely overpriced zone	g is greater than 12%	Sell
Market is in the peaking zone	g is between 10% and 12%	Prepare to sell; wait for business cycle events and technical indicators for final warnings
Market is in the neutral zone	g is between 8% and 10%	Do nothing
Market is in the bottoming zone	g is between 8% and 3%	Prepare to buy; wait for business cycle events and technical indicators for final warnings
Market is in the extremely underpriced zone	g is less than 3%	Buy

can begin with the question we asked earlier: Why are stock dividend yields so well defined in the 3 percent to 7 percent range?

Looking at the valuation map, we can see that given a 3 percent dividend yield, the T-bond rate would have to be 4 percent or less for the market to be in the neutral or bottoming zone. Since we haven't seen a 4 percent T-bond rate since the early 1960s, it is very likely that whenever the market dividend yield hits 3 percent, the market will be in the peaking zone and very near a major peak. Furthermore, using more normal (6 percent to 12 percent) T-bond rates with a 3 percent dividend yield always puts the market in the extremely overpriced zone.

On the other side of the map, when the market dividend yield hits 7 percent, T-bond rates would have to be 14 percent or higher to put the market into the neutral or peaking zone. But long-term T-bond rates have never exceeded 14 percent (not even in 1981). Thus, any time in which the market yield hits 7 percent, we are always in the bottoming or extremely underpriced zone for any T-bond rate between 0 percent and 14 percent.

The Yield Spread Myth. Before leaving the valuation map, we want to expose one additional myth that many investors use as a guide to stock market valuation: the yield spread myth. The yield spread, which is calculated and reported by many financial publishers, represents the difference between the prevailing bond interest rate and the stock market dividend yield. The idea is that if the yield spread is very high, bond yields are very attractive relative to stocks, which is bad for the stock market outlook. Conversely, if the yield spread is low, bond yields are not too attractive relative to stocks, which is good for the stock market outlook.

We can now look at the yield spread in terms of the relative return equation:

$$RT + rp = y + g$$

Transposing terms, we get:

$$RT - y = \underbrace{g - rp}$$

$$\text{Yield}$$
$$\text{Spread}$$

The T-bond rate (RT) minus the dividend yield (y) is the well-known yield spread.

But we can now see what's wrong with using the yield spread as an indicator of stock market overvaluation or under-valuation. Suppose that the prevailing yield spread is six percentage points, which is considered fairly high. By looking at the valuation map, we can see that a 6 percent yield spread can occur in almost any zone on the map, as shown in Figure 16-23.

Similarly, if the yield spread is only 3 percent, the market could also be in almost any zone on the valuation map. (See Figure 16-24.)

The conclusion of this exercise is that when a famous analyst says that the market is overvalued or undervalued and backs his argument with either a high or low yield spread, investors should not take that simplistic assessment too seriously. In and of itself, the yield spread tells the investor nothing with respect to market valuation.

Linking the Valuation Map to the Business Cycle. The valuation map provides investors with a useful, easy-to-use

Figure 16-23.

If the T-Bond Rate Is	And the Dividend Yield Is	Then the Yield Spread Is	And the Market Is in
13%	7%	6%	Bottoming zone
12	6	6	Neutral zone
11	5	6	Peaking zone
10	4	6	Extremely overpriced zone

Figure 16-24.

If the T-Bond Rate Is	And the Dividend Yield Is	Then the Yield Spread Is	And the Market Is in
9%	6%	3%	Bottoming zone
8	5	3	Neutral zone
7	4	3	Peaking zone
6	3	3	Extremely overpriced zone

device to assess the current valuation level of the stock market. But this map is only one tool for making investment decisions. To play the business cycle properly, you must link it to the events of the business cycle and then, at certain critical points in the cycle, supplement it with some specific technical analyses, which we describe later in this chapter.

As a first step in this process, we can resurrect the road map of stock prices and interest rates.

The road map showed that stock market bottoms and interest rate tops occurred at nearly the same time (Points B and C on Figure 16-25). However, as interest rates declined, bot-

Figure 16-25. *The Road Map of Stock Prices and Interest Rates*

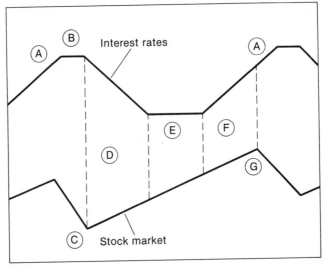

Figure 16-26. *The Business Cycle and the Relative Return Equation*

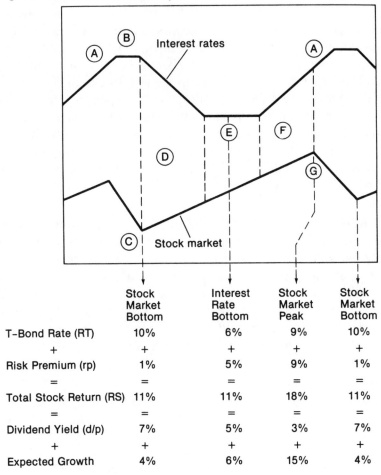

	Stock Market Bottom	Interest Rate Bottom	Stock Market Peak	Stock Market Bottom
T–Bond Rate (RT)	10%	6%	9%	10%
+	+	+	+	+
Risk Premium (rp)	1%	5%	9%	1%
=	=	=	=	=
Total Stock Return (RS)	11%	11%	18%	11%
=	=	=	=	=
Dividend Yield (d/p)	7%	5%	3%	7%
+	+	+	+	+
Expected Growth	4%	6%	15%	4%

tomed out (Point E), and rose again, the stock market climbed steadily (from Point C to Point G) and then peaked *before* the next interest rate peak.

Using this framework, we can now set up the relative return equation to see what happens to interest rates, risk premiums, dividend yields, and expected growth rates at stock market tops and bottoms. Figure 16-26 traces the components of the relative return equation through a typical business cycle.

The events in Figure 16-26 are as follows:

- *At stock market bottoms*—The first column of Figure 16-26 shows that at the stock market bottom, the T-bond rate is at its peak (10 percent) and the stock risk premium is at a minimum (1 percent) because the falling prices of stocks have boosted the dividend yield to a peak (in this example, 7 percent). To balance the equation, investors have to expect only a 4 percent annual growth rate to be motivated to buy stocks and achieve a total return of 11 percent. Since the stock market has grown at an average nominal rate of 8.6 percent for the last 40 years, this is a very reasonable expectation. The stock market bottoms out and then moves up.

- *At interest rate bottoms*—While the market is rising, interest rates are falling to their low points. But by the time that the interest rate bottom is reached (say, at 6 percent), the risk premium on stocks has risen (to 5 percent) because increasing stock prices have reduced the dividend yield (to 5 percent). At this point, the falling interest rates and the rising risk premium have offset each other and have kept the total stock return at 11 percent; with a 5 percent dividend yield, the investor now needs to expect a 6 percent growth rate to balance the equation.

- *At stock market tops*—As we move into the final phase of the bull market (Phase F in Figure 16-26), the balancing act becomes much more difficult. Both interest rates and the risk premium are rising, which sharply increases the required total stock return to 18 percent. In addition, the stock dividend yield is falling (to 3 percent), leaving most of the burden of providing the total stock return of 18 percent to the expected growth rate of 15 percent in the stock market. Every day in which interest rates rise and stock prices rise, the dividend yield falls further and the risk premium rises. To balance the equation, the investor must believe in a higher and higher stock market growth rate.

Eventually, hopes for higher growth rates reach an unsustainable level and the market breaks. In our example, the breaking point occurs when the growth rate expectation reaches

15 percent—almost four times what it was at the market bottom, nearly twice the average historical growth rate, and a clearly unsustainable growth rate for investors to expect.

When any signals of a weakening economy, such as a decline in the leading indicators or a cutback in the money supply (which drive interest rates up even further) first appear, the growth expectations for stock prices are seen to be too high and the stock market peaks out and declines in recognition of reality. In the last section, we saw that a mild reduction in expected growth from 11 percent to 10 percent produced a stock price decline of 20 percent. If the expected growth rates were extremely overrated at the market peak, the adjustment to reality will be even more severe.

Conclusions. We can reach several conclusions from this analysis:

- From the valuation map, we know that the stock market and the bond market are inseparably linked through the market mechanism of balancing the risk-adjusted returns from each market.

- In addition to the stock market falling into the bottoming zone of the valuation map, stock market bottoms are characterized by peaking interest rates and high dividend yields in the 6 percent to 7 percent range. They are also easy to recognize because these bottoms occur in the *midst of a recession.*

- In addition to the stock market moving into the peaking zone of the valuation map, stock market tops are characterized by rising interest rates—after they have bottomed out in the middle of a bull stock market—and low dividend yields. The 3 percent dividend yield level for any of the major market averages should always be taken as an automatic "sell" signal. Stock market tops are more difficult to recognize because they occur when the money supply, inflation, interest rates, the economy, and stock prices are all moving up—but at an unsustainable rate. However, by following—coldly and un-emotionally—the business cycle status, the valuation map, and some technical indicators, investors can avoid misguided euphoria and sell stocks at or very near the major market peaks.

SOME UNUSUAL STOCK MARKET PERSPECTIVES

Stock Market Growth Rates

How much can you expect to make in the stock market in one year? How much could you lose in one year if you remained in the market during a one-year decline? Long bull markets can often double or triple one's investment over the full length of the bull market. But history shows that *over a one-year period, the most that you can expect the stock market as a whole to appreciate is 50 percent. And the largest one-year decline that is likely to occur is about 40 percent.* These conclusions are drawn from the historical evidence presented in Figure 16-27.

Looking at the major peaks in the annual growth rates of the S&P 500 Stock Index since 1953, we can see that a 30 percent annual growth rate is the most frequent peak, which has been exceeded only three times in the last 35 years. The infamous crash of October 1987 occurred when the 12-month growth rate was at 33 percent.

Figure 16-27. *Twelve-Month Percentage Change in the S&P 500 Stock Index: 1953–1988*

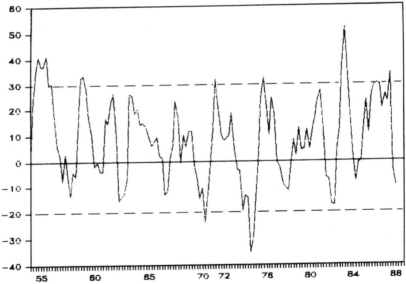

Source of raw data: *Business Conditions Digest.*

Most one-year stock market declines fall in the 10 percent to 20 percent range, with the major exception being the 35 percent decline of 1974. And since most stock market declines run their full course in one year or less, this is about the worst that an investor would have to face during any decline.

Having said that, we need to comment about the current business cycle and the stock market as they stand in the summer of 1988.

How Far Could the Market Fall During the Next Decline?

At the current time, the Dow Jones Industrial Average is at about 2,100. The current dividend yield is 3.5 percent, which means that the annual dividend rate of the Dow Jones industrials is $73.50. The 20-year T-bond is currently providing a 9.4 percent yield to maturity. With the dividend yield at 3.5 percent, the stock market risk premium is fairly high at 8 percent. Using our relative return equation, we can set up July 1988 as our base case, as shown in Figure 16-28.

The relative return equation shows that stock market investors must expect an annual growth rate in stock prices of 13.9 percent to balance the equation. As discussed later in the book, our current position (summer 1988) in the business cycle is nearing the top of the economic and stock market cycles. Plotting a 3.5 percent dividend yield and a 9.4 percent T-bond rate on the valuation map shows that *we are still in the extremely overpriced zone.* Since the economy has grown for almost six years, it is not unreasonable to assume that the next stock market decline will be accompanied by a recession. Therefore, we will set up a hypothetical scenario for a market downturn:

Scenario 1: *Interest rates rise to 10 percent, which is enough to trigger a recession. The stock market declines, and the Dow Jones industrial yield rises to 6 percent. The economic decline is only mild, and all dividends are maintained at July 1988 levels.*

Figure 16-28. *Base Case*

	Return on T-Bonds	+	Stock Risk Premium	=	Total Return on Stocks	=	Stock Dividend Yield	+	Expected Growth (%) of Stock Price
	RT	+	rp	=	RS	=	$\dfrac{d}{p}$	+	G
Base case	9.4%	+	8%	=	17.4%	=	$\dfrac{\$73.50}{\$2,100}$	+	13.9%
or	9.4%	+	8%	=	17.4%	=	3.5%	+	13.9%

Figure 16-29. Downturn: Scenario 1

	Return on T-Bonds	+	Stock Risk Premium	=	Total Return on Stocks	=	Stock Dividend Yield	+	Expected Growth (%) of Stock Price
	RT	+	rp	=	RS	=	$\dfrac{d}{p}$	+	G
Base case	9.4%	+	8%	=	17.4%	=	$\dfrac{\$73.50}{\$2{,}100}$	+	13.9%
	or								
	9.4%	+	8%	=	17.4%	=	3.5%	+	13.9%
Scenario 1	10%	+	3%	=	13%	=	6%	+	7%
	or								
	10%	+	3%	=	13%	=	$\dfrac{\$73.50}{\$1{,}225}$	+	7%

Dow Jones industrial average at bottom = $1,225

Where will the stock market be at the bottom? We'll use the relative return equation to get our answer. We know that stock market bottoms occur at interest rate tops; thus, when the T-bond rate peaks out at 10 percent, the stock market bottom will occur with a dividend yield of 6 percent. With a dividend yield of 6 percent, the risk premium will be low—at 3 percent—which leaves an expected stock price growth rate of 7 percent to balance the equation. For $73.50 in dividends to equal 6 percent of the stock market price (for a 6 percent yield), the market must fall to 1,225, representing a 42 percent decline under Scenario 1, as seen in Figure 16-29.

However, this is not the worst case. Let's look at another downturn scenario.

Scenario 2: *Suppose that the recession is deep enough to cause the Dow Jones industrial stocks to cut their dividends by 10 percent to $66.15, and suppose that the stock yield at the bottom is 7 percent, as it was in 1982.*

In Scenario 2, the market would have to fall to a level at which $66.15 was equal to 7 percent of the market price, and *this bottoming price would be reached when the Dow hit 945*—a whopping 55 percent decline. But in the last section, history showed us that such a decline would not be likely to occur in one year. Even during the years of the 1929 crash and the depression, one-year declines in the stock market did not exceed 42 percent. The total drop in the stock market from September 1929 to September 1932 was 74.5 percent, but the annual declines were 35 percent (from 1929 to 1930), 42 percent (from 1930 to 1931), and 30 percent (from 1931 to 1932).

This brings us to our next subject: the fear of being caught in a massive, sudden stock market decline.

The True Nature of Stock Market Crashes

The information presented below should provide some degree of comfort to investors who have nightmares about a one-day crash that could leave them in financial ruin.

The Crash of 1929. The famous, or infamous, crash of 1929 has been portrayed in movies and books for years and has subliminally left an impression on many investors. The image that the crash of 1929 conjures up is that of a nonstop, raging, soaring bull market that suddenly crashed, taking everyone by surprise and plummeting so fast that no one could react before it was too late.

As with many Wall Street myths, the facts show an entirely different picture. History shows that the October 1929 market crash was, in reality, characterized by:

- A market peak on September 7, 1929
- Several failed attempts to rise above that peak, followed by a full month of declining prices that produced a 10 percent decline from the September 7 peak
- A three-day rally that regained 7 percent, or about two-thirds, of the 10 percent decline
- A further decline to a three-month low
- Then, a week later, the crash of October 28 and 29, which produced a 21 percent loss in market value in two days

Figure 16-30 is a daily price chart for the S&P Composite Stock Index for the months before, during, and after the October crash.

The Crash of 1987. Coincidently, the most recent debacle occurred in October 1987. During this crash, millions of investors lost millions of dollars during the two trading days of Friday, October 16, and "Black Monday," October 19, 1987. This event has also been portrayed as a complete surprise to most Wall Street analysts. However, a review of the daily market activity reveals that the "crash of 1987" was characterized by:

- A market peak on August 25, 1987
- Several failed attempts to rise above that peak, followed by a month of declining prices that produced a 7.5 percent decline from the August 25 peak

Figure 16-30. *The Crash of 1929*

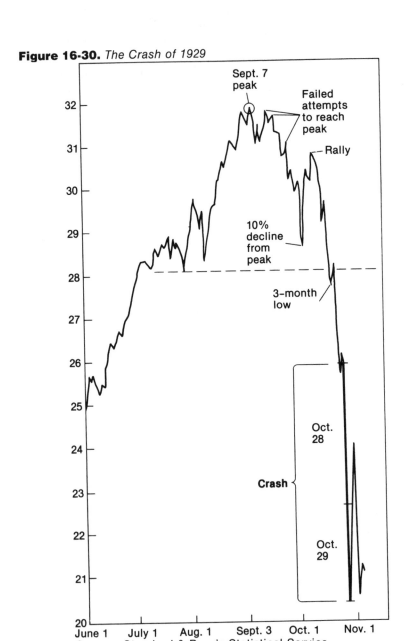

Source: Standard & Poor's Statistical Service.

- An eight-day rally, which regained 5 percent, or two-thirds, of the 7.5 percent decline
- A further decline to a three-month low
- Then, two days later, the crash of October 16 and 19, which produced a 26 percent loss in market value in two days

The S&P stock price chart for the crash of 1987 is shown in Figure 16-31.

Figure 16-31. *The Crash of 1987*

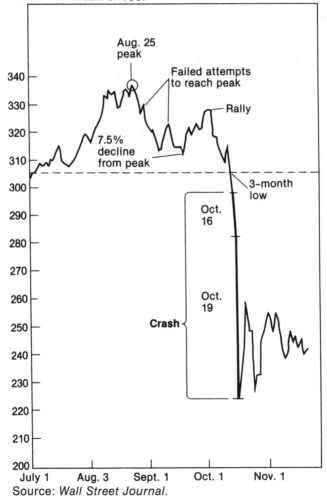

Source: *Wall Street Journal.*

Learning from the Crashes

Conclusions About Crashes. While we are working with a very limited sample size, the evidence at hand suggests some useful and comforting conclusions about crashes in the stock market:

- Crashes do not occur at market peaks, but well after market peaks.
- Crashes occur after several failed attempts to reach new highs and a period of substantial price erosion.
- Therefore, the notion that stock prices simply rise and rise and then crash suddenly and without warning is erroneous.
- The actual damage done in the brief periods (two days) of crashes is in the area of a 20 percent to 25 percent loss in value. Of course, this is a serious loss, but it is not in and of itself a devastating or suicide-inducing loss. The two crashes cited earlier would only be that disastrous for people who were engaged in options and futures options or who were highly leveraged in their stock positions without sufficient liquid funds elsewhere in their portfolio to cover their losses.
- Both of these historic crashes would have had *no serious impact on investors that*:
  —Simply held nonleveraged positions in stocks or mutual funds, and
  —Had pre-programmed a 10 percent stop-loss provision into their investment strategy.
- From a more fundamental point of view, both of these crashes occurred at precisely the right phase in the Primary Business Cycle, when a stock market peak was visibly in the cards.
- Both of these crashes occurred at a time of very serious overvaluation, according to our relative return equation.
- The crash of 1987 was also accompanied by several technically oriented supply and demand indicators (to be discussed next) that clearly foreshadowed a major downturn.

Rules for Escaping Market Crashes. Based on this information, it is fair to state that any investor can avoid being exposed to or financially injured by serious market crashes by:

- Following the current status of the Primary Business Cycle
- Following the degree of overvaluation of the market by using the relative return equation
- Following some short-term supply and demand indicators that are discussed in the next section
- Avoiding highly leveraged stock positions
- Avoiding options and futures
- Monitoring the market price level and placing stop-loss orders at a level 10 percent below the current price

THE PROPER PLACE OF TECHNICAL ANALYSIS

Technical analysis has been a source of fascination for stock market analysts for generations. And why shouldn't it be? You don't have to understand economics, high finance, corporate income statements and balance sheets, or business to do a perfectly competent job of technical analysis. In fact, the foundation of technical analysis is the premise that none of these things matter when predicting stock market behavior. To a pure technical analyst, the only thing that matters is the market action itself.

Technical analysis, which has its own jargon, speaks frequently of support and resistance lines, pricing formations, triple tops, high poles, momentum, breadth, oscillations, and breakouts. At the root of technical analysis is the concept that *future* market moves are predictable based on *past* and *present* market moves. When the majority of the technical analyst's indicators turn down, the analyst says that we're in a technical decline. And we'll stay in a technical decline until the analyst's technical indicators turn up. Then he says that we're in a technical rally, where we'll stay until the indicators turn down again. But from the perspective of an investor trying to identify the major tops and bottoms in the stock market, technical analysis has several inherent problems.

First, technical analysis tends to be very short term in nature. Many technical indicators can move from a bullish position to a bearish position in a matter of days or weeks. This means that during a single two- or three-year bull market, there could be dozens of technical upturns and downturns. And unless the investor is a very active trader of stocks, these frequent buy and sell signals are of little value.

Second, the multitude of technical indicators that are widely used often present a mixed picture. Anyone who has ever watched the weekly reading of the technical index on "Wall Street Week" has seen months and months go by with the index reading of four bullish, two neutral, and four bearish indicators. This information cannot be readily acted on.

Third, indicators are often late or wrong. Because they are essentially recording what has already happened, by the time that an indicator reaches a recognizable turning point and reverses direction, the short-term market move may be over.

Fourth, technical indicators cover a very wide spectrum. Some indicators have solid foundations in terms of supply and demand and cause and effect. Others are less reasonable, and some require a significant leap of faith to be accepted as plausible indicators of things to come. A technical analyst may be doing purely statistical research or may be studying time cycles, phases of the moon, hemline theories, contrarian principles, "waves," or psychological indicators. They are all referred to as technical analysis. So if a technical analyst makes a market forecast, it's relatively important to find out which approach he or she is using before buying into that forecast.

As an example of how far the field has extended, one of the favorite technical indicators of many analysts is a measure of how many other analysts are bullish or bearish at any point in time. If most technical analysts are *bullish*, this technical sentiment index is interpreted as *bearish*, based on the logic that most other technical analysts are usually wrong.

Finally, technical analysis has restricted itself to analyzing stock market *effects*—not causes or cause-and-effect relationships. A decline in stock prices that is caused by the rumor of a political scandal looks identical to a decline in stock prices that is caused by the onset of a major recession on the technical charts. Stated another way, every major top will begin with what looks like a technical decline, and every major bottom will begin with what looks like a technical rally. But between the major tops and major bottoms, there may be several technical tops and bottoms that are of no significance at all.

Therefore, it is impossible to use technical analysis in isolation to identify major peaks and bottoms in the stock market. However, used in conjunction with the business cycle and the relative return equation, some specific, well-founded technical indicators can be used as decisive, final signals of a major peak or bottom in the stock market.

To use technical analysis properly, the investor should:

- Track the Primary Business Cycle until we are in the right phase of the cycle for a stock market peak
- Track the stock market dividend yield and the long-term bond rates with the relative return equation until stock prices become overvalued
- Then—and only then—look for significant declines in some specific technical indicators to signal an imminent major stock market peak and subsequent downturn
- As the market declines, track the Primary Business Cycle until we are in the right phase of the cycle for a stock market bottom
- Track the dividend yield and long-term bond rates with the relative return equation until stock prices are undervalued
- Then—and only then—look for significant increases in some specific technical indicators to signal the imminent major stock market bottom and subsequent upturn

Three Short-Term Indicators

Three short-term indicators that have proven to be very useful in confirming long-term turning point signals generated by the business cycle are described in this section. These indicators are not tied to stock prices themselves, but, instead, are reflections of supply and demand and of the strength and breadth of the money moving through the stock market.

On-Balance Volume. On-balance volume (OBV) is a common technical indicator used by many analysts. This series is calculated by cumulatively adding each day's New York Stock Exchange (NYSE) volume on days in which the S&P 500 rises or subtracting each day's volume on days in which the S&P 500 falls. It is a good reflection of the amount of money flowing into

Figure 16-32.

	Daily Market Change	NYSE Volume (Shares)	OBV
Day 1	Up (+)	150,000	150,000
Day 2	Up (+)	180,000	330,000
Day 3	Up (+)	200,000	530,000
Day 4	Down (−)	−130,000	400,000
Day 5	Down (−)	−200,000	200,000
Day 6	Up (+)	150,000	350,000
Day 7	Down (−)	−140,000	210,000

and out of the market, as well as the cumulative buying or selling pressure that the market is experiencing. An example is shown in Figure 16-32.

A technical *downturn* is signaled if the OBV index declines and penetrates a previous low point or breaks a previous support level. (See Figure 16-33.)

If we are not in the right phase of the business cycle for a major stock market peak or if the market is not overvalued, a downturn in OBV will trigger a "technical decline" that will be brief and limited. If we are in the correct phase of the business cycle for a major peak and if stocks are overvalued as per the

Figure 16-33. *OBV Index*

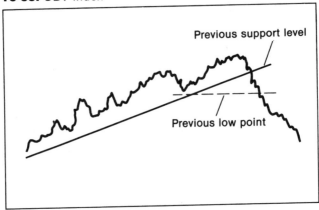

Figure 16-34. *OBV: 1987*

relative return equation, a downturn in OBV will signal a major decline in the stock market. The same rules hold in reverse for stock market bottoms.

In September and October 1987, OBV broke through both a previous low point and a previous support level well before the crash of 1987, as shown in Figure 16-34.

Cumulative Advances and Declines. This classic measure of market breadth accumulates the daily number of advancing stocks, less declining stocks on the NYSE. It is a legitimate reflection of how *widely* money is being spread among the stocks on the entire stock exchange.

The advance-decline line reflects the degree of interest that investors have in all sectors of the market and gives a true picture of how many stocks are actively rising or falling across the entire NYSE. Typically, as we approach market tops, more stocks appear to be overpriced and fewer stocks appear attractive to institutional investors. Thus, the advance-decline line weakens as bullish money is invested in fewer and fewer stocks.

Figure 16-35 shows an example of the construction of the advance-decline line.

There are other more complicated ways to compute the advance-decline line, but they are no more accurate than this

Figure 16-35.

	NYSE Advancing Issues	NYSE Declining Issues	Net Advances Less Declines	Advance-Decline Line Cumulative Net Advances Less Declines
Day 1	600	400	200	200
Day 2	700	400	300	500
Day 3	600	500	100	600
Day 4	400	700	−300	300
Day 5	500	600	−100	200
Day 6	600	900	−300	−100
Day 7	500	700	−200	−300
Day 8	800	700	100	−200

method. The absolute number of the advance-decline line has no meaning; only the direction of the line is relevant. Like the OBV indicator, turning point signals are given if the indicator breaks (1) a previous low (going down) or high (going up) or (2) a previously established support line (going down) or resistance line (going up).

In the fall of 1987, the advance-decline line broke a previous low, broke a previous support line, and declined sharply well before the October 19 crash, as shown in Figure 16-36.

Figure 16-36. *Advance-Decline Line: 1987*

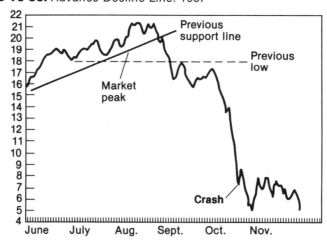

Cumulative New Highs and Lows. This index measures the number of stocks reaching new 52-week highs and lows on the NYSE. Like the advance-decline line, it is measured cumulatively. (Seé Figure 16-37.)

The cumulative high-low index is also a measure of the momentum of the money entering the market. If the market average is rising but fewer and fewer specific stocks are reaching new highs, the cumulative high-low index reflects the increasing selectivity of attractive stocks. As such, it is an indicator of a forthcoming peak.

In 1987, the cumulative high-low index also peaked and declined long before the October crash, as shown in Figure 16-38.

Figure 16-37.

	Stocks Reaching New 52-Week Highs (a)	Stocks Reaching New 52-Week Lows (b)	Net Highs and Lows (a – b)	Cumulative Net Highs and Lows
Day 1	30	10	20	20
Day 2	40	8	32	52
Day 3	44	12	32	84
Day 4	60	6	56	140
Day 5	52	10	42	182
Day 6	30	14	16	198
Day 7	20	22	-2	196
Day 8	8	28	-20	176

The Raw Data for These Indicators

The numbers used to develop all these indicators are presented everyday in the *Wall Street Journal*. Inside the back section of the *Wall Street Journal* is a column entitled "Stock Market Data Bank," which carries all the price, volume, and

Figure 16-38. *Cumulative Net New Highs and Lows: 1987*

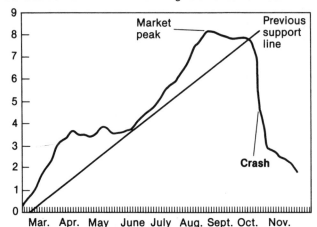

other statistical data for the market action of the previous day. These data include all of the advance, decline, new high, new low, and volume numbers needed to construct the indicators described in this chapter (see Figure 16-39). The same data can be obtained on a weekly basis from the "Market Laboratory" section of *Barron's* (see Figure 16-40).

Combining the Technical Indicators

The three technical indicators discussed in this chapter tend to be coincident market indicators that reach peaks and bottoms at just about the same time as the S&P 500 index or the Dow Jones industrial index. However, at major turning points, they can be significant *leading* indicators of the future market direction. For example, prior to the crash of 1987, these indicators, taken together, virtually *collapsed well before stock prices collapsed* on October 16 and October 19, 1987.

Figure 16-41 shows two lines: One is the S&P 500 index, and the other is a combined technical index. This combined index is a (proprietary) mathematical combination of the three indexes discussed earlier. What is remarkable about this index is how dramatically it led the stock market down during September and October 1987. Through September and then again after the crash, the combined technical index and the stock market track almost identically. But prior to the crash, a huge gap opened up between the combined technical index and the stock market.

Figure 16-39. *Daily Technical Data from the* Wall Street Journal

DIARIES			
NYSE	**FRI**	**THUR**	**9/30 WK**
Issues traded	1,944	1,955	2,140
Advances	853	1,065	1,134
Declines	613	412	680
Unchanged	478	478	326
New highs	32	24	68
New lows	10	12	44
zAdv vol (000)	73,579	123,555	341,310
zDecl vol (000)	77,505	19,163	233,893
zTotal vol (000)	175,750	115,790	634,690
Closing tick[1]	+273	+54	
Closing trin[2]	1.49	.40	
zBlock trades	3,445	3,379	14,012
NASDAQ NMS			
Issues traded	4,595	4,598	4,595
Advances	1,172	1,119	1,536
Declines	801	822	1,482
Unchanged	2,622	2,657	1,577
New highs	120	93	208
New lows	51	45	171
Adv vol (000)	58,158	54,978	215,464
Decl vol (000)	27,995	27,148	159,217
Total vol (000)	135,438	121,490	565,164
Block trades	2,039	1,968	8,888
AMEX			
Issues traded	872	829	1,035
Advances	376	350	467
Declines	221	208	336
Unchanged	275	271	232
New highs	23	17	42
New lows	10	10	32
zAdv vol (000)	4,576	4,619	17,386
zDecl vol (000)	2,909	1,791	13,697
zTotal vol (000)	9,100	8,620	39,530
Comp vol (000)	10,402	9,839	45,344
zBlock trades	144	145	658

Labels pointing to the NYSE section: Advances, Declines, New highs, New lows

BREAKDOWN OF TRADING IN NYSE STOCKS			
BY MARKET	**Fri**	**Thur**	**WK AGO**
New York	175,750,000	155,790,000	145,100,000
Midwest	13,475,100	10,493,800	9,049,100
Pacific	5,974,600	5,434,700	5,563,100
NASD	3,786,530	3,858,760	5,302,370
Phila	3,085,500	2,544,800	2,366,300
Boston	2,512,700	2,139,500	3,745,500
Cincinnati	586,900	985,200	713,600
Instinet	249,700	48,500	239,900
Composite	205,421,030	181,295,260	172,079,870

Label pointing to Composite row: Volume

Source: *Wall Street Journal* (October 3, 1988).

Figure 16-40. *Weekly Technical Data from* Barron's

BARRON'S
MARKET LABORATORY

Market Advance/Decline Totals

Weekly Comp.	NYSE	AMEX	NASDAQ
Total Issues	2,140	1,035	4,595
Advances	1,134	467	1,536
Declines	680	336	1,482
Unchanged	326	232	1,577
New Highs	68	42	208
New Lows	44	32	171

Weekly figures { → Advances → Declines → Unchanged → New Highs → New Lows

NYSE Composite

	Sept. 26	27	28	29	30
Issues Traded	1,928	1,929	1,938	1,955	1,944
Advances	550	620	750	1,065	853
Declines	845	764	642	412	613
Unchanged	533	545	546	478	478
New Highs	21	15	16	24	32
New Lows	12	16	15	12	10
Blocks	2,199	2,455	2,534	3,379	3,445
Total (000)	135,369	137,361	134,605	181,295	205,421

Daily figures { → Advances → Declines → Unchanged → New Highs → New Lows

Weekly Volume By Markets
In NYSE-Listed Stocks

Shares in thousands

	Last Week	Prev. Week	Year Ago
NYSE	674,692	701,240	927,004
Midwest	52,200	46,095	63,996
Pacific	25,451	25,424	33,744
NASDAQ	16,453	20,442	22,303
Phila.	11,563	14,129	16,847
Boston	9,133	12,383	13,894
Cincinnati	3,784	3,647	5,215
Instinet	776	1,037	368
Total	794,052	824,397	1,083,371

Weekly volume →

Source: *Barron's* (October 3, 1988).

This gap was signaling a major decline in stock prices. When the stock market plunged and finally caught up with the combined index, it was 600 Dow Jones industrial points later.

All of these technical indicators show us that the true supply and demand story of the market is not always reflected in stock market prices. All of these indicators are valid reflections of the level, direction, and momentum of investment dollars hitting the stock market, and they all peaked out (1) well before the crash, (2) at a point in the business cycle when a stock market peak was predictably imminent, and (3) when the low dividend yields and high interest rates clearly showed that the market was seriously overvalued.

Figure 16-41. *Combined Technical Index*

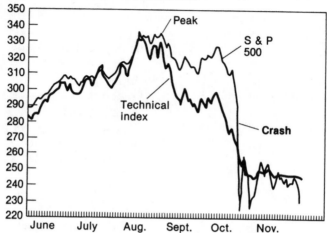

The conclusion to be drawn from this analysis is that tops or bottoms in the stock market can be readily identified through a combination of:

• Business cycle analysis
• Valuation analysis (the relative return equation)
• Analysis of some specific technical indicators

We can now look at all of these indicators as they typically present themselves at major stock market bottoms and tops.

RECOGNIZING THE MAJOR BOTTOMS

Identifying major stock market bottoms is a lot easier than identifying the stock market tops. Stock market bottoms occur while we are *in the midst of an officially declared recession.* The leading and coincident economic indicators are headed down. Meanwhile, inflation and interest rates are rising, the money supply is falling, and stock dividend yields are rising as the stock market declines.

Then the bottoming indicators develop in a relatively short period of time, as shown in Figure 16-42.

Figure 16-42. *Bottom Finders*

Business cycle indicators	Inflation indicators turn down. Interest rates turn down. The annual percentage change in the money supply turns up. The actual nominal M2 money supply turns up. The leading indicators turn up (but not the coincident indicators—we are still in a recession). The C/L ratio turns up.
Valuation map	High stock market dividend yields and low interest rates fall into the bottoming zone of the valuation map.
Technical indicators	OBV turns up. The advance-decline line turns up. The cumulative high-low line turns up.
Stock market	The stock market bottoms out and turns up.

With all of these key indicators moving decisively within a few months, it should be simple to invest in the stock market within one or two months of every major stock market bottom. And it is simple, but emotionally difficult, to invest money in the stock market when:

- Depressing news about the economy, which is now near bottom, is printed, broadcast, and discussed every day.
- The high inflation rate, which is near its peak, is frightening.
- High interest rates, which are also at their peaks, are dismal and depressing reading.
- Bearish technical analysts dominate the airwaves.

In other words, to buy into the stock market at the absolute bottom, you must invest in the face of a bombardment of bad fundamental and technical news. If investors wait until all of the bad news turns good, the bottom will be well behind them.

Therefore, the keys to success in investing in stocks at market bottoms are:

- To follow the business cycle indicators, the valuation indicators, and the technical indicators in a cold, pragmatic, and unemotional way.

- Tc invest based on the indicators themselves, while ignoring the forecasters, the newscasters, and the *current* economic situation. You are betting on the *future* economic situation; *all of the news in the coming months will show improvements because you are investing at rock bottom.*

Although this may sound like contrarian investing, it is not. It is simply recognition of a multitude of bottom signals that are clear to a trained eye with the emotional control to recognize that when "things just can't get any worse, they must get better"—that is the time to buy. In summary, the way to get rich is to buy snow shovels in July.

RECOGNIZING THE MAJOR TOPS

Finding stock market peaks is harder. Stocks hit their peaks *before* recessions begin, which means that the stock market peaks out while everything is still rosy. The problem is that bull markets can last from one year to seven or eight years—unlike bear markets, which are usually fairly brief. Where are the signs of a market top in this long period of expansion?

The first sign comes from the road map of stock prices and interest rates and the sequence of events in the Primary Business Cycle. The last recession will have ended as inflation and interest rates peaked and then declined. And after the recession is over, we hit a section of the business cycle in which the economy is expanding and inflation and interest rates are still falling.

But then the growing economy finally begins to pull inflation and interest rates up again. Remembering the road map, we are then in the phase of the business cycle in which everything is going up: the money supply, the economy, inflation, interest rates, and the stock market are all rising at the same time. This phase, which marks the homestretch of the business cycle, sets the stage for the next stock market peak. But this phase can also last a few months or a few years, so it is not enough to tell investors when to sell. It is enough only to let investors see that we are in the right "season" for a stock market peak.

Then things finally begin to happen. The M2 money supply peaks, as the Fed moves to curb inflation. The stock market dividend yield falls, and interest rates rise into the peaking zone of the valuation map. If the stock market dividend yield drops to 3 percent or below, investors can be sure that the peak is virtually imminent.

At this point, we can look to the technical indicators for final sell signals. OBV, advances and declines, and the high-low index will fall back and penetrate previously established support levels. And that is the time to be *completely* out of the market—no matter who says it's only a technical decline. The sequence is fully described in Figure 16-43.

THE CRASH OF 1987: A CASE STUDY IN TOP FINDING

The surprise crash of October 1987 is a classic case of a shock that should not have been a shock. The events of the business cycle of the 1980s unfolded precisely in accordance with the Primary Business Cycle sequence, and the crash occurred well after all of the necessary sell signals were seen. The *Business Cycle Monitor* explained this situation fully in the September 15, 1987, edition, which is included in Appendix F in this book. But to state the situation succinctly here:

• The previous recession ended in 1982, and the stock market exploded from a level in the 800s to over 1,100 on the Dow

Figure 16-43. *Top Finders*

Business cycle indicators	After the recession ends, the money supply, the stock market, and the economic indicators all rise as inflation and interest rates fall. The homestretch of the business cycle develops as inflation and interest rates rise, the percentage change in M2 declines, and the stock market continues to rise. Now all of the key business cycle indicators are rising together. The nominal M2 money supply declines as we near the economic peak.
Valuation map	Stock yields fall and interest rates rise into the peaking zone of the valuation map.
Technical indicators	OBV turns down. The advance-decline line turns down. The cumulative high-low line turns down.
Stock market	The stock market peaks out and turns down.
Economy	If this is a full primary business cycle, the leading indicators and the C/L index will turn down within one or two months followed by downturns in the coincident indicators and capacity utilization. If it is a partial cycle, the coincident indicators and capacity utilization will continue to rise. Then the stock market will hit bottom in just a few months and resume its upward movement until the next major peaking phase occurs.

Jones industrials in just a few months. The money supply expanded, and the economic indicators all turned up as inflation and interest rates fell. This condition lasted from 1983 to late 1986.

- On September 11 and 12, 1986, the Dow Jones industrials fell 140 points in two days, driven by market fears of rising interest rates. But this decline was clearly technical because the final expansion phase—the homestretch in which everything rises together until the next stock market peak—had not yet developed. Our newsletter of September 15, 1986, issued an all-out buy recommendation because we were clearly in the wrong phase of the business cycle for a major stock market top. In late 1986, inflation and interest rates reached their bottoms and set the stage for the homestretch of the cycle, in which the money supply, the economy, the stock market, inflation, and interest rates all rise together to the next peak.

- By January 1987, the money supply peaked out, but the leading indicators and the C/L index still continued to rise— and the stock market soared to over 2,700 by August 1987.

- However, in rising to over 2,700, the stock market dividend yield crashed through the 3 percent yield barrier to 2.9 percent, while interest rates rose to 9 percent—putting us into the extremely overpriced zone of the valuation map.

- At the same time, OBV, advance-decline, and high-low indicators all peaked out and crossed previous support levels. In addition, the combined technical index showed a huge disparity between the index and the stock market, signaling a *major correction* at the very least.

- By mid-September, it was clear that one of two things had to happen: Either (1) the stock market had to decline sharply, followed almost immediately by declines in the leading indicators and the C/L index, which would lead us directly into a full-scale recession to complete the Primary Business Cycle, or (2) the stock market had to decline sharply as we entered a partial cycle. However, our position in the business cycle, the outrageous overvaluation of the market (2.9 percent dividend yield and a required growth rate of over 15 percent to balance the relative return equation), and three out of three technical

Figure 16-44. *History of Primary Business Cycles: Through July 1988*

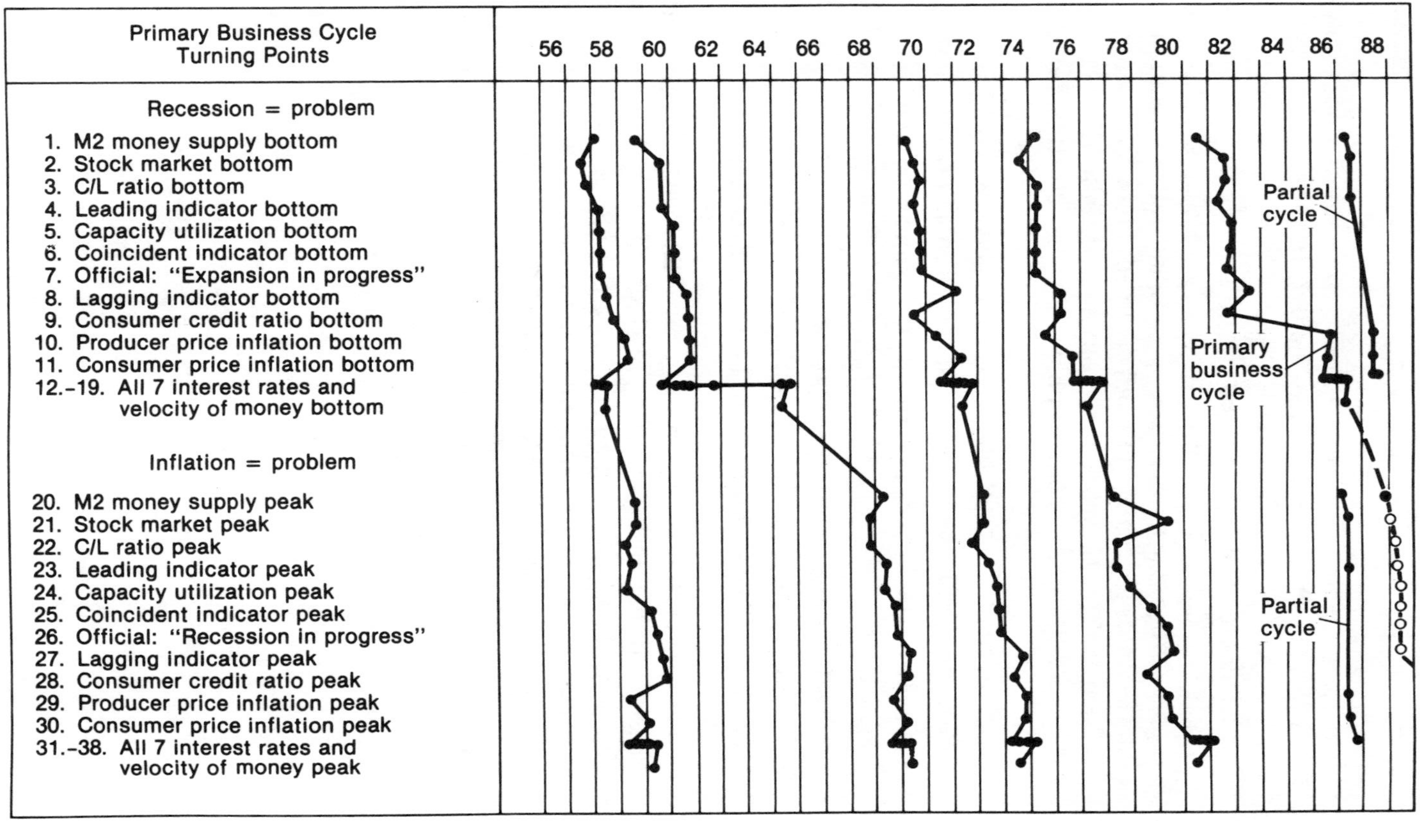

Primary Business Cycle
Turning Points
56
58
60
62
64
66
68
70
72
74
76
78
80
82
84
86
88
Recession = problem
1. M2 money supply bottom
2. Stock market bottom
3. C/L ratio bottom
4. Leading indicator bottom
5. Capacity utilization bottom
6. Coincident indicator bottom
7. Official: "Expansion in progress"
8. Lagging indicator bottom
9. Consumer credit ratio bottom
10. Producer price inflation bottom
11. Consumer price inflation bottom
12.–19. All 7 interest rates and velocity of money bottom
Inflation = problem
20. M2 money supply peak
21. Stock market peak
22. C/L ratio peak
23. Leading indicator peak
24. Capacity utilization peak
25. Coincident indicator peak
26. Official: "Recession in progress"
27. Lagging indicator peak
28. Consumer credit ratio peak
29. Producer price inflation peak
30. Consumer price inflation peak
31.–38. All 7 interest rates and velocity of money peak
Partial cycle
Primary business cycle
Partial cycle

indicators showing serious deterioration left no doubt that the stock market had to fall significantly. It did.

The crash of 1987 turned out to be only a partial cycle in which we did not go directly into a recession. The money supply, the stock market, the leading indicators, inflation, and interest rates all peaked out and declined; however, later in 1987 and early 1988, they bottomed out and began to rise again.

To sum up this catastrophic event, the crash of 1987:

- Occurred at the right phase of the business cycle
- Was caused by massive overspeculation and overvaluation
- Was foreshadowed by all of the valuation and technical indicators
- Was, therefore, quite predictable
- Turned out to be only a partial cycle
- Caused millions of dollars to be lost—needlessly

As this is being written (summer 1988), we have returned to Phase 19 of the business cycle, in which all of the business cycle components have bottomed out and are rising. At 2,000 to 2,100, the market is still in the extremely overpriced zone of the valuation map, and we are now awaiting the next peaks in the money supply, the stock market, and the economy, as shown in Figure 16-44. The current situation and the outlook for the future are described in detail in the last chapter of this book.

Chapter 17

Investing in Gold:
Glitter and Volatility

A BRIEF HISTORY

During the early part of this century, most of the nations of the world were officially on a gold standard, which meant that each paper dollar of currency was backed by and could be redeemed for a fixed amount of gold in the country's treasury. In 1933, the United States officially went off the gold standard, but the value of the dollar was still based on a defined number of ounces of gold. By the 1970s, the conversion ratio was $35 per ounce of gold; by 1973, the official price of gold in the United States was $42 per ounce.

Prices of gold rose dramatically to almost $200 an ounce during the inflationary years of 1973 and 1974. Gold then fell back to $100 per ounce in 1976. But in that year, the United States completely severed the link between the dollar and gold. With no foundation remaining to stabilize the dollar, federal policy makers were free to create or debase dollars at will. Since that time, both the dollar and the price of gold have roller-coastered their way through the world economies—with the dollar soaring to new highs in 1985 and then plummeting to new lows in 1987, and with gold soaring to over $800 per ounce in 1980, then declining to $300 per ounce in 1982, and finally rising to about $450 an ounce in 1988. With this kind of volatility, gold has significant profit potential if it can be bought and sold at appropriate times within the business cycle.

SOME GOLDEN RELATIONSHIPS

Gold and Inflation

Several known factors move the price of gold up and down. The factor that is most commonly known is inflation. The fundamental reason that gold rises during periods of inflation is that the amount of gold in circulation at any point in time is relatively fixed and stable, while the supply of money is increasing during a period of inflation. If we had only $1 million in money and one million ounces of gold in the world, the price of gold would be $1.00 per ounce. But if we had $2 million and the same one million ounces of gold, the price of gold would rise to $2.00 per ounce. This relationship is clearly established, as shown in Figure 17-1, which compares the price of gold with the consumer and producer inflation rates from 1970 to 1988.

Figure 17-1. *Gold Prices and Inflation*

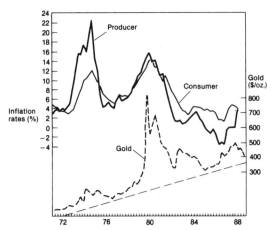

Source of inflation rates: *Business Conditions Digest.*
Source of gold prices: International Investors Inc. (London), gold price charts.

Figure 17-2. *Gold, Inflation, and M2 Annual Growth Rates*

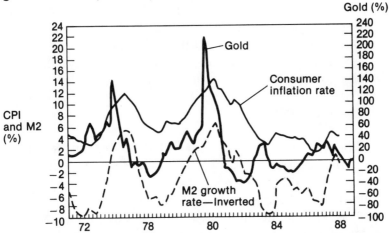

This relationship is even clearer if we compare apples with apples—that is, the annual *rate* of inflation with the annual *rate* of growth in gold prices. Figure 17-2 shows this comparison, as well as the annual growth rate M2—inverted as it was in Figure 10-11.

In Figure 17-2, the inflation rate moves between 0 percent and 15 percent, while the annual percentage change in the price of gold ranges from −50 percent to over 200 percent. Also, gold prices tend to *lead* the inflation rate and the inverted growth rate of M2.

Looking further, we can see that the big moves in gold occur only after the inflation rate moves up past 5 percent or 6 percent. Therefore, we can find very profitable turning point signals for gold by tracking the M2 and inflation indicators throughout the business cycle. The time to buy gold is when (1) inflation has clearly bottomed out and moved up past 5 percent and (2) the *inverted* M2 growth rate bottoms out (which means when the *actual* M2 growth rate peaks out). We know from the business cycle sequence that these events occur after the beginning of an economic expansion period, following the end of a recession. The time to sell gold is just after we enter a recession, when the producer and consumer price indexes peak out and the percentage change in M2 bottoms out.

One final observation about gold is noteworthy. Refer back

to Figure 17-1 and look at the dashed line underneath the gold price chart. The underlying growth rate of this base support level has been 15 percent per year since 1972. This suggests that having some part of one's portfolio invested in gold (or gold stocks) as a permanent inflation and panic hedge is not a bad idea, based on gold's historical track record.

Gold and Oil

For a while, several people tried to connect the price of gold with the price of oil. This became popular in 1979–1981, when gold soared to $800 per ounce while OPEC raised oil prices to over $34 per barrel during the Iranian crisis. However, this is a case of incidental—not direct—cause and effect. The fundamental supply and demand characteristics of oil and gold have little in common.

Gold is used in luxury products and is a surrogate for money during times of high inflation or national crises. Gold is supplied by many countries; its largest supplier is South Africa, which has not tried to manipulate the price of gold by controlling supply.

On the other hand, oil is a vital, necessary commodity whose demand is a function of the energy requirements of all the industrialized nations of the world. And the supply of oil is dictated by the control or lack of control of oil production by the member nations of OPEC. Structurally, it would be difficult to identify two products that are more fundamentally different than gold and oil.

The only commonality of gold and oil is that, in the long run, they are depleting resources, in that there is a finite amount of both buried in the earth that is economically practical to extract. Thus, over the very long term, the prices of both will tend to rise as we approach the limits of each.

So why the connection? The answer lies in two links to a third variable: inflation. As we have just seen, gold tends to rise and fall with inflation. And since oil is such a dominant commodity in every industrialized nation in the world, an increase in crude oil prices, which raises the production costs of just about everything, causes an increase in inflation.

Tension in the Persian Gulf always seems to cause upturns in the price of gold. But the underlying reason still goes back to supply, demand, and prices. If Iran and Iraq raise such a fury as to shut down the shipping channels in the Persian Gulf, the free-flowing supply of oil to the world would be curtailed. A smaller supply of oil would necessarily raise the price of oil, which would increase inflation; then gold would rise because of inflationary expectations. Thus, gold and oil would both go up together. However, other fighting in the Mideast that does not actually threaten to disrupt the oil supply has little or no effect on the price of gold or oil. Therefore, the effect of Mideast tension on gold prices is just another extension of the link between gold and inflation.

Gold and the Dollar

No discussion of gold would be complete without touching specifically on the basic relationship between gold and the dollar. That basic relationship is: *When the dollar weakens, gold goes up, and when the dollar strengthens, gold goes down.*

While the value of the dollar in terms of other countries' currencies tends to move up and down over time, these movements are not a distinct part of the Primary Business Cycle. Exchange rates are treated as an external influence of the business cycle, since they are, in effect, a reflection of discontinuities between the U.S. business cycle and the business cycles of other nations and are influenced by inflation, interest rates, economic growth rates, trade balances, and other factors.

In terms of currency valuations, gold is the great equalizer. In this respect, it must be discussed on two levels. The first level is the "real money" level. Every economy is driven by a currency that is normally considered "as good as gold"—it is expected to hold its value from day to day. But if confidence in that currency were to erode suddenly, there would be nowhere else to turn to but gold. Therefore, if a nation's currency becomes worthless as a basis for internal or international trade, a great amount of that currency would be required to buy an ounce of gold, which could then be given to someone else to complete a financial transaction. So, in the final analysis, gold is the money of last resort when a currency loses its acceptance. Under those conditions, the price of gold in terms of that currency will rise dramatically as the currency weakens and degenerates. We discuss gold with respect to panics and crises in the next section.

The second level is a less extreme level of transactions that reflects the relationship between currencies and gold during the more or less normal swings in national exchange rates and the worldwide supply and demand for gold. Consider first what would happen if only one worldwide currency was accepted by all people and all national banks around the world. In this situation, the price of gold would be dictated by nothing more than (1) the worldwide demand for gold and (2) the worldwide supply of gold. Whenever someone found a new gold deposit in the outbacks of Australia or in Alaska, the price of gold would go down. And if a military or political situation, such as a miner's strike in South Africa, should develop, the price would temporarily rise because of the reduced supply. If any new developments in electronic technology required the use of gold, this new demand would push the price of gold up. Also, if this hypothetical worldwide government were to inflate this hypothetical worldwide currency, there would be more money and the same supply of gold. This would increase the price of gold in direct proportion to the inflation rate.

To develop the exchange rate situation, let's now imagine that there are only two currencies in the world: the U.S. dollar and another currency used by all the other nations of the world. In this scenario, the price of gold in both currencies would go up if either worldwide demand went up or worldwide supply went down. And the price of gold would go down in both currencies if worldwide demand went down or worldwide supply went up.

But what would happen if the U.S. inflation rate went up twice as much as that of the other currency and nothing else happened to the supply and demand for gold? Since we "cheapened" our money by producing too much of it, it would be less valuable than the other currency; many more U.S. dollars would be needed to buy an ounce of gold.

To illustrate this situation, let's assume that the other worldwide currency is the German deutsche mark and that, during last year (which we'll call the base case), $1 could purchase 4 deutsche marks. At that time, the price of gold was $100 per ounce, or 400 deutsche marks per ounce. As shown in Figure 17-3, the world of money is now in balance. Four hundred deutsche marks can buy one ounce of gold. Four hundred deutsche marks can also be exchanged for $100, and then $100 can buy one ounce of gold.

But now, a year later in Example 1, we have inflated (or weakened) the U.S. dollar to the point at which it takes twice as many dollars to buy 1 deutsche mark. The exchange rate is now 2 deutsche marks per dollar (or $0.50 per deutsche mark). This new situation is summarized in Figure 17-4.

With a weakened U.S. dollar and a new exchange rate, what happens to the price of gold in U.S. dollars? The free market will raise the price in U.S. dollars to $200 per ounce to keep the currencies in equilibrium. At $200 per ounce, there is

Figure 17-3. *Base Case*

Dollars Needed to Buy DM 4	DM Needed to Buy $1	Exchange rate		Price of Gold	
		In $/DM	In DM/$	In $/Oz.	In DM/Oz.
$1	DM 4	0.25	4	$100	DM 400

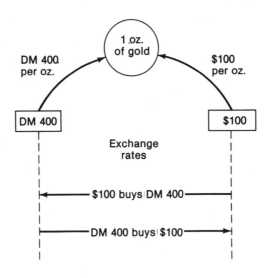

Figure 17-4. *A Weaker Dollar: Example 1*

Dollars Needed to Buy DM 4	DM Needed to Buy $1	Exchange rate		Price of Gold	
		In $/DM	In DM/$	In $/Oz.	In DM/Oz.
$2	DM 2	0.50	2	$200	DM 400

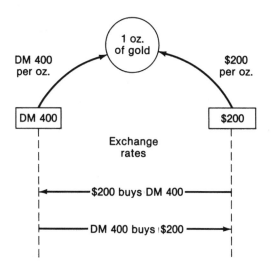

balance in the gold market of both currencies. A foreigner can take 400 deutsche marks and buy one ounce of gold. An American can take $200 and buy one ounce of gold. A foreigner can convert 400 deutsche marks to $200 (at $0.50 per deutsche mark) and buy one ounce of gold, and an American can convert $200 to 400 deutsche marks (at 2 deutsche marks per dollar) and buy one ounce of gold. With the new exchange rate, all is fair and in balance with the price of gold at $200 per ounce.

If the exchange rate had changed from 4 deutsche marks per dollar to 2 deutsche marks per dollar but the price of gold had remained at $100 per ounce, an unsustainable arbitrage situation would have been created. A foreigner could take 400 deutsche marks and convert it to $200 (at $0.50 per deutsche mark), purchase *two* ounces of gold (at $100 per ounce), sell the two ounces of gold in a foreign country at 400 deutsche marks apiece, and receive a total of 800 deutsche marks for his trouble.

Figure 17-5. *Unsustainable Imbalance*

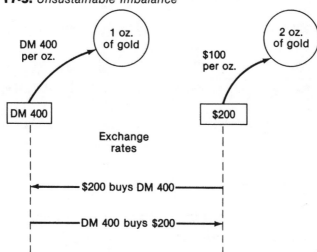

100% profit in arbitrage.
Market will not allow to be sustained.

This is a nifty way to double one's money in a day or so. But, of course, the free market will not allow anyone to make this easy money; the price of gold in terms of U.S. dollars will rise until this trading advantage is eliminated—in this case to $200 per ounce. (Figure 17-5)

The real-life parallel to our hypothetical second currency, which we called the deutsche mark in the example, is an index or a basket of international currencies referred to as the "trade-weighted dollar index." This index shows the value of the dollar against an average of all the other major currencies as if it were one currency used by all our trading partners.

The recent history of the relationship between the price of gold and the dollar index is shown in Figure 17-6. As the dollar index is plotted inversely, the plot of the index moves down as the dollar gets stronger and moves up as the dollar gets weaker. This chart shows that the major turning points of gold prices and the dollar index are closely linked and that gold prices tend to reach peaks just as the dollar hits a bottom, and vice versa. The most recent bottom in gold prices occurred in early 1985, when

Figure 17-6. *Gold Versus the Dollar: Gold Prices and the Federal Reserve Board Dollar Index*

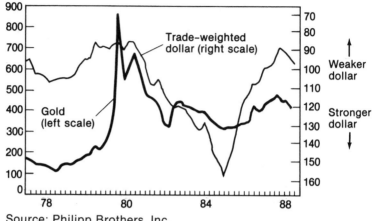

Source: Philipp Brothers, Inc.

the dollar peaked. Since then, the price of gold has steadily risen, as the dollar has declined.

Gold and Panic

Gold has always been mankind's refuge in times of national crisis. This has been true over the centuries because gold is the only true form of money. When you think about the real purpose of money and the characteristics that money must possess to be accepted and used as money, gold emerges as the only candidate.

Gold became a medium of exchange when the bartering system that was used centuries ago became unmanageable. People traded chickens and cows for wood and leather to meet their individual needs. But if you needed wood and had only chickens and the people who had wood didn't need chickens, you would have to find someone else to take your chickens in exchange for something that the wood owners wanted. When this became untenable, the world sought an item that would hold its value between exchange transactions and also meet six criteria:

• It had to be recognized and accepted by everyone.
• It had to be difficult to counterfeit.

- It had to be convenient to carry around.
- It had to be divisible into different units for both cheap and expensive transactions.
- There had to be a limited supply of it so that it wouldn't be devalued.
- It had to be durable.

The answer was gold. Few people would recognize titanium, anyone could make a wooden coin, rocks were too heavy, paper wouldn't last, living things would die, and sand was too common. Thus, gold emerged as true money for exchange transactions.

As we became more civilized, we invented paper currency backed by gold deposits in the national banks; finally, we've progressed to paper currency backed by the full faith and credit of the nation's government. Accordingly, whenever a country bursts into civil war or communist incursions or military overthrows threaten the existence of the nation's government, the full faith and credit of the government become suspect and the citizens of that country revert to gold. People trying to flee the country cash in all their possessions for gold coins to buy their way out because no one will accept the suspect currency. During such times, the price of gold in terms of *that nation's currency* soars because the currency's value is uncertain and the local demand for gold is so high.

The important words in the last sentence are "that nation's currency"—not everyone's currency. If a revolution in Turkey should shatter the nation's confidence in the Turkish lira, the price of gold in lira per ounce skyrockets. But if the U.S. dollar is stable and the worldwide supply of gold is stable, the price of gold in dollars per ounce does not change significantly because of the Turkish revolution. The added demand for gold by Turkish refugees would put a little upward pressure on the price, but not enough to create a significant investment opportunity.

Therefore, when investors hear about military disruptions in one country or another, they should not run out and buy gold based on the old cliché that world tension drives up the price of gold. On the other hand, if the United States ever fell into a similar situation or we found ourselves in a banking or debt crisis

that undermined the full faith and credit of the U.S. dollar, gold
in terms of dollars per ounce would rise dramatically.

But even in such a situation, we believe that investors have
been seriously misled about the practical value of gold and silver
coins as a permanent part of their portfolios.

The Myth of Gold and Silver Coins

Virtually every "financial disaster" book contains a chapter about the ultimate panic hedge of gold and silver coins.
Investors and concerned citizens are advised to acquire a
small portfolio of Krugerrands and U.S. silver dollars, half
dollars, and quarters minted before 1965 and to stash them
away for the day when banks close and confidence in the dollar
disappears.

While the purchase of gold and silver coins might be a good
short-term money-making investment for wealthy investors with
excess cash during a financial panic, both logic and evidence
suggest that the "security blanket" aspect of these coins is not
only overrated, but totally invalid from a pragmatic and practical
standpoint.

Consider the following scenario: The worst nightmares of
government officials around the world have come true. A
plunging stock market has stripped consumers of their paper
wealth. Consumer spending plunges, which throws the United
States into a massive recession. The federal deficit soars as tax
revenues fall and social costs climb. Foreign investors withdraw
billions from U.S. banks, triggering a massive run on banks
across the country that ultimately forces the government to
declare a bank holiday, leaving all access to banks' funds closed
for four weeks.

But, of course, you do not need to worry because you have
cleverly hidden away ten Krugerrands (at about $400 each,
that's $4,000 worth of gold in today's dollars), as well as $100 in
face value of 1963 U.S. silver coins (at about $5 per face value
dollar, that's another $500 in liquid silver spending money). So
you gingerly drive down to your local A&P or Krogers; select
about a week's worth of vital food supplies, soap, toilet paper,
and other necessities; stand in line; and eventually reach the

cashier. The cashier—19 years old, on summer vacation, and with 2½ months' experience at checking out groceries—rings up your total and says with a smile, "$43.95, please."

After having seen numerous people turned away because they tried unsuccessfully to buy things with personal checks or credit cards, you confidently and proudly slap down a shiny new Krugerrand.

"What's that?"

"That's a gold Krugerrand."

"So what?"

"So what? This is one pure ounce of gold, and it's worth ten times the $43.95 that I owe you."

"That's very nice, but this is 20 pounds of groceries here, and I'd like the $43.95 in cash."

"Cash? I have pure gold here!"

"Listen, I'm a cashier—not a coin dealer. That thing could have come out of a Cracker Jack box as far as I'm concerned. Do you have any real cash?"

"OK! If you don't like gold, I also have some 1963 silver dollars, and I'm sure you're familiar with those. They're worth a lot more than a dollar just on the value of their silver content."

"Well, I wasn't born until 1969, but I know that's a silver dollar. So, if you just have 43 more of them, you can have your groceries."

"43 more of them? Listen, I paid more than $5 each for those coins."

"Well, perhaps you should go back to your coin dealer and try to get $5 each for them now. You see, I have 100 more people in line here, and I'm not in a position to appraise everybody's coin collection. If you like, I'll put these groceries aside until you come back with some cash."

Crushed, you leave the store and return to your car with the intention of taking a trip to the coin dealer's shop. But, alas, you're out of gas. Now, if you think you had a liquidity problem at the A&P, wait until you see the gas station attendant's face when you cross his palm with a Krugerrand. Finally, when you've traded your highly recognizable Rolex watch for a tankful of gas, you make your way to the coin dealer's. There, you see a line of 50 or 60 people holding attache cases, large purses, and little bags filled with coins. After an hour and a half in line, you finally reach the dealer.

"OK, what have you got?"

"I have ten Krugerrands."

After he carefully inspects each coin, he says, "That's fine, I'll give you $2,000 for them."

"$2,000? I paid $4,000 for them and, according to the *Wall Street Journal,* the going price of gold is now $450. You're only offering $200 an ounce."

"Take it or leave it."

"That's highway robbery."

"You can always try another dealer."

"You're a crook!"

"Have you been to the A&P yet? You won't get much with those coins."

"This is an outrage! You should be arrested."

"You should try a bowl of Krugerrands for dinner sometime."

"I refuse to give you these coins for $200 an ounce."

"Next!"

Totally demoralized, fit to be tied, and ready to sue all of the panic scenario book writers, you return home—a beaten human being—with no food and no Rolex watch.

After explaining the situation to your family, your 12-year-old son, Midas, speaks: "Mom and Dad, I've been saving my Christmas money and allowance in a duck bank for the last year, and I have $52 in there now. Would that be any help?"

With tears of joy rolling down your cheeks, you embrace your son, knowing that you can survive the next week in relative comfort due to his frugal nature and long-term savings habit.

There are two key points to this story:

• In a real bank crisis or financial panic, cash will be king because it is the only recognizable medium of exchange that can be physically transferred from one person to another without an element of trust being brought into the transaction. When a true panic exists, trust will totally evaporate and cash on the barrel head will be the only way to buy daily necessities.

• The real winners in our story are the coin dealers who have access to international coin exchanges on one end and a helpless, starving public who will take whatever they can get to survive on the other end, which results in a huge profit spread in between. If you're looking for a hobby, try gold and silver coin appraisal. It could have a huge payoff during a financial panic.

A recent example of this phenomenon occurred in March 1988, when the United States impounded Panamanian funds in U.S. banks and withheld payments for the use of the Panama Canal to shut off the supply of money to banks in Panama. Checks, credit cards, and funny-looking coins did not allow ordinary people seeking food, gas, and other basic necessities to buy what they needed. Only those with cash had access to goods and services for sale. On the other hand, those who had cash, which was very scarce and very much in demand, could buy whatever they wanted at deeply discounted prices from desperate people who were willing to sell any asset for a few dollars to buy food.

The logical flaw in the argument that supports the gold and silver coin theory is that it assumes that total financial chaos has swept the nation, but that business goes on as usual. Stores are still open, people are still driving to work, producers are still producing and distributing goods to retail stores, and everyone does their job. But no one trusts money anymore, so they all use and accept gold coins.

This is simply an unrealistic and inconsistent scenario on which to build an investment strategy. In Vietnam, people sold all of their goods for gold to escape the country, but the nation was torn apart by war. During the German hyperinflation, business went on as usual but with paper money that rapidly depreciated. During our own Great Depression, business came to a standstill but a few dollars could keep a family alive. However, nowhere in history have we seen a situation in which (1) there is total financial chaos while (2) life goes on as usual, but (3) people do business with gold and silver coins instead of currency. Even if a government creates a new currency, it will be valued in terms of the old currency—not gold.

In our view, only two panic hedges make sense in case of any realistic panic scenario that might develop in the United States. The first is cash in small bills. How much? Take any recent typical month and add up all your costs for groceries, drugstore items, and gasoline. The total is the minimum amount of cash that you should keep where you can gain access to it without depending on anyone else.

Under different panic scenarios, prices of goods could escalate rapidly if the Fed decided to print money as a way out, or prices could plunge to very depressed levels if the Fed took some other route. Therefore, the *absolute* amount of cash that one might need is difficult to pinpoint. But in a world suddenly thrown into panic, the *absolute* amount of money is not as important as the *relative* amount of cash that you have available. If you have more cash than most other people in your immediate neighborhood, you will do quite well. Even if you live in a relatively affluent area, you would find very few people who have as much as $1,000 in cold cash lying around.

Therefore, a minimum total of $1,000 to $2,000 in ones, fives, tens, and twenties that are kept in a safe but accessible place would serve investors very well in a temporary bank panic or a dollar crisis. Investors would be giving up a 5 percent to 6 percent interest rate by taking this money out of the bank, but the ability to survive comfortably a scenario such as that presented earlier is certainly worth $50 or $100 a year in forgone profits.

The second panic hedge is gold stocks. If a superinflationary scenario should unfold due to a governmental lapse of responsibility that led to massive printings of paper money, the price of gold would rise in terms of dollars per ounce, as indicated earlier. If that were the case, would you rather own a few gold coins or a piece of a gold mine? Since one can authenticate a stock certificate in a well-known gold mining company with proven gold reserves much more easily than a bar of bullion or a Canadian Maple Leaf coin and since you can buy or sell gold stock shares at any time at a known market price by making a phone call, gold stocks are a much more practical way to hedge a portfolio against a hyperinflation scenario.

Therefore, we believe that the combination of real cash in a secure place plus gold stocks represents a far more practical and simple approach to panic hedging than the widely touted gold and silver coin approach.

Gold and Gold Stocks

Having suggested that gold stocks are a more practical investment than gold coins or bullion—as both an investment in the inflation cycle and a panic hedge—we now have to ask a few more questions. What about performance? Do gold stocks do as well as gold itself during an upswing? If gold stocks are easier to buy and sell and avoid such problems as storage and recognition, what does an investor give up by choosing gold stocks instead of gold?

To answer these questions, we begin by comparing the price history of gold with that of an index of listed gold stocks from 1970 to 1988. The comparison of actual prices is shown in Figure 17-7, and the annual growth rates or annual percentage changes in the prices are shown in Figure 17-8.

Figure 17-7. *London Gold Spot Price Versus U.S. Gold Stock Index*

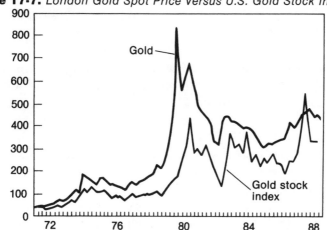

Source of stock index data: Securities Research Company, gold stock index price charts.

Figure 17-8. *Annual Percentage Changes in Gold and Gold Stocks*

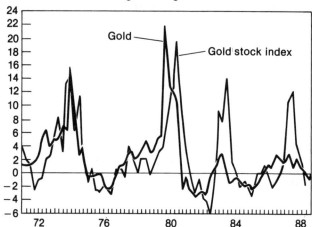

These charts show three things quite clearly:

- As one would expect, the turning points for gold and gold stocks are almost identical.
- During 1980–1981, gold rose more than gold stocks. However, during the other three upturns since 1970, gold stocks climbed as much as or more than gold itself on an annual percentage increase basis.
- During all four surges since 1970, gold stocks rose *more than* 100 percent during the upturn, which illustrates the profit potential of gold stocks with proper timing. On the other hand, gold rose less than 50 percent in the last two upswings in 1983 and 1987.

In addition, gold stocks pay dividends—small dividends, but dividends. On the other hand, gold usually has a storage cost.

From this comparison, we can conclude that investors might lose a little upside potential by investing in gold stocks rather than gold during a major inflation crisis, but would gain liquidity, flexibility, and dividends as opposed to storage costs and resale difficulties for gold coins and bullion.

INVESTING IN GOLD STOCKS

There are two primary ways to invest in gold stocks:

- Individual gold mining company stocks
- Mutual funds that focus exclusively on gold and precious metals

Individual Gold Stocks

Gold is mined in many places throughout the world, but the lion's share of the world's gold supply comes from South Africa, which produces approximately two-thirds of the world's gold each year. Next come the U.S.S.R., Canada, the United States, Ghana, Australia, and the Philippines.

Reducing the Political Risks. South Africa frequently makes headlines. While South Africa boasts the largest proven gold reserves in the world, it also is the home of apartheid. This national policy of racial segregation has prompted sit-ins, demonstrations, and political rhetoric promoting actions that range from economic sanctions and trade restrictions to boycotts of the South African Krugerrand.

Apartheid has also led to a systematic shifting of pension funds and mutual funds out of South African gold stocks and into American, Canadian, and other politically stable gold stocks. This shift is totally independent of all the other factors that influence the gold market. Fund managers that do not want to change the total amount of money that they have invested in gold stocks are shifting funds away from South African mines to companies that are more politically safe. However, moving billions of dollars from one set of investments to another without causing the price to fall requires this transaction to be a long, slow, systematic process. Thus, there will be long-term upward price pressure on the "safe" gold stocks of the United States, Canada, and Australia—independent of other events that might influence the prices of these stocks.

Scanning the list of major gold producers, we can see some additional problem areas. Following South Africa is the U.S.S.R.—not the best game in town for U.S. investments. Then we have Canada, the United States, Ghana, Australia, and the Philippines. Ghana lies in a relatively unstable African region, and the Philippines are far from politically stable.

For investors who want to invest in an individual gold mining operation that could at least be counted on in terms of political and military stability, our first rule would be to restrict those investments to companies located in the United States, Canada, and Australia.

Reducing the Financial Risks. It must be remembered that the history of gold prices is a volatile one, with dramatic moves in both directions. For a gold mining company, price is only one of the key factors in its profit equation. Of course, the other is cost. Like manufacturing, mining involves labor, equipment, and energy costs, which all rise during a period of inflation and fall a little during times of disinflation or deflation.

A gold mining company can be viewed as an operation with relatively fixed costs and highly volatile prices. Therefore, during a period of rapidly rising gold prices, profits soar for quite a while before costs begin to escalate. Also, a prolonged decline in gold prices can drive revenues well below costs and produce substantial losses. With this in mind, our second rule of investment in gold mining companies is, "Bigger is better." Small, poorly capitalized companies may not survive downturns or may not be able to invest in equipment or technology to reap full profits during upturns.

Accordingly, our recommended list of individual gold mining stocks is limited to those that are listed on the NYSE and whose mining operations are located in the United States or Canada. The gold mining stocks that meet these criteria are listed in Figure 17-9.

Gold Mutual Funds

Among the hundreds of stock funds, bond funds, and money market funds, only a few solid mutual fund families have created mutual funds that are pure gold plays.

Figure 17-9. *Most Secure Gold and Silver Mining Stocks*

Company	Primary Product	Headquarters of Primary Mining Operations
Callahan	Gold	Arizona
Hecla	Silver	Idaho
Homestake	Gold	California
Newmont	Gold, oil, and gas	New York
PlacerDome*	Gold and silver	Canada
Sunshine	Silver	Texas

* A new company comprising Placer, Dome Mining, and Campbell Redlake Mines.
Source: Value Line.

The advantages of using a gold fund are numerous. First, the individual portfolio risk is greatly reduced by investing in a fund that owns shares in 50 to 100 different gold companies. The investor doesn't have to research all of the gold mining and processing companies in the world; instead, professionals do it on a daily basis. The fund has access to international gold mining companies that individual investors would have difficulty in finding or researching. Notable among these foreign gold stocks are those of Australia, which are profitable and free from political tension. Finally, many of these funds allow investors to switch into gold and then switch back into cash on one day's notice—offering flexibility and liquidity at a nominal cost.

Figure 7-10 is a list of 24 gold and precious metal funds that are now available and whose net asset values are listed daily in the *Wall Street Journal* for tracking purposes.

Since gold and gold stocks are highly correlated and gold stock funds offer the performance characteristics of gold—plus flexibility, liquidity, and dividends—without the disadvantages and inconvenience of gold coins or bullion, we suggest that gold mutual funds are the most practical and profitable way to invest in gold during the inflation cycle and as a panic hedge.

Summary

Gold is driven by inflation, localized political instability, Mideast tension that actually threatens to curtail the oil supply,

Figure 17-10. *Gold and Hard Asset Funds*

Fund	Telephone	State
Bull-Bear Golconda	800-847-4200	N.Y.
Colonial Advanced Strategies Gold	800-225-2365	Mass.
Fidelity Select American Gold	800-544-6666	Mass.
Fidelity Select Precious Metals	800-225-6190	Mass.
Financial Programs—Gold	800-525-8085	Colo.
First Investors Natural Resources	800-423-4036	N.Y.
Franklin Gold	800-632-2180	Calif.
Freedom Gold and Government	800-225-6190	Mass.
Hutton Precious Metals	800-334-2626	N.Y.
IDS Precious Metals	800-328-8300	Minn.
Keystone Precious Metals	800-343-2898	Mass.
Lexington Goldfund	800-526-0056	N.J.
Midas Gold Shares and Bullion	800-328-1010	Minn.
Oppenheimer Gold	800-525-7048	N.Y.
Permanent Portfolio	800-531-5142	Tex.
Strategic Investments	800-527-5027	Tex.
Strategic Silver	800-527-5027	Tex.
United Services Gold Shares	800-824-4653	Tex.
United Services New Prospector	800-824-4653	Tex.
United Gold and Government	816-283-4400	Mo.
USAA Gold	800-531-8000	Tex.
Van Eck Gold Resources	800-221-2220	N.Y.
Van Eck International Investors	800-221-2220	N.Y.
Vanguard VSP Gold	800-662-7447	Pa.

Source: *The Mutual Fund Advisor.*

currency devaluations, and national financial panics. Gold rises and falls over a complete business cycle, and these large cyclical moves can be played with gold stocks or gold stock funds, using the Primary Business Cycle as a timing guide. Our recommended approach to investing in the inflation cycle is to use gold mutual funds. Our suggested hedge against financial crises and panics is a combination of hard, real cash and gold stock fund investments.

In the next chapter, we discuss the different ways in which individual investors can integrate gold mutual funds into an easy-to-manage, total portfolio management system.

Putting It All Together: The Business Cycle Money Management System

OVERVIEW

The ultimate purpose of this book is to provide investors with a *timely, practical,* and *workable* system of investing money profitably over the long term. We have constructed the various components of the system with some economic theory and long-term historical evidence to show that the system is based on a solid foundation. But even the best theories are valueless without *action*—in this case, a systematic, pragmatic, and disciplined set of actions to place specific amounts of money into specific kinds of investments at specifically defined times in every business cycle.

In this section of the book, we combine all the pieces discussed so far in a complete, step-by-step investment process that can be *acted on* by investors with relative ease.

The Business Cycle Money Management System

The complete business cycle money management system consists of six steps, which are summarized as follows:

• *Step 1: Portfolio creation*—The first step in developing a money management system is to identify the funds that are to be used in a long-term investment system. An investment portfolio is only a part of a total portfolio of assets, and the portion to be used for investment needs to be defined and isolated for investment purposes.

- *Step 2: Data collection*—Once a pool of investment funds has been defined, the investor is ready to begin the systematic process of collecting and tracking some specific, selected pieces of economic and financial information every month to monitor our position in the business cycle.

- *Step 3: Analysis*—When the appropriate data have been collected, the investor needs to analyze those data on three different levels:

  —To determine where we are in the business cycle by using the turning point sequence of the Primary Business Cycle

  —To determine if the stock market is overvalued or undervalued, based on the relative return equation and the valuation map

  —To examine the stock market technical indicators for the final turning point signals—but only if we are in the stock market peaking or bottoming phase of the business cycle and the valuation map

- *Step 4: Decision*—After having performed the appropriate analysis, the investor can now decide which phase of the business cycle we are in and whether we are approaching a major peak or bottom in either stocks, bonds, or gold.

- *Step 5: Portfolio allocation*—As major peaks and bottoms are reached in stocks, bonds, and gold, the investor's portfolio must be reapportioned or reallocated to exit markets that are heading down and to move into markets that have bottomed out and are moving up. At different points in the business cycle, there are specific ideal apportionments of funds—or "ideal portfolios"—for different kinds of investors. These specific ideal portfolios are defined later in this chapter.

- *Step 6: Execution*—Given an analysis of our position in the business cycle and an ideal portfolio for that phase of the cycle, the investor needs a quick, easy, inexpensive, and efficient way to switch money between stocks, bonds, gold,

Figure 18-1. *The Business Cycle Money Management System*

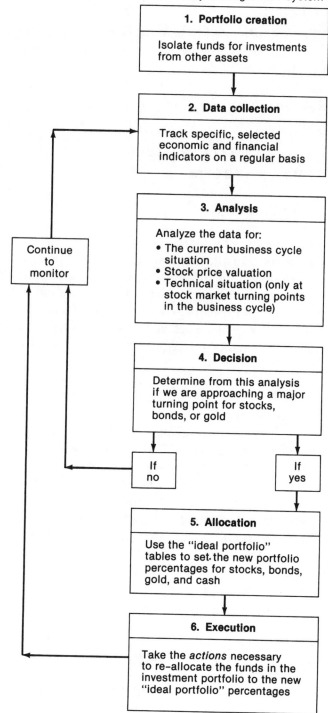

and cash in conformity with the ideal portfolio at that time. We describe several ways to execute the portfolio switches in this section of the book.

This six-step process is shown in Figure 18-1.

THE BUSINESS CYCLE MONEY MANAGEMENT SYSTEM

Portfolio Creation

A tourist who visits the casinos in Las Vegas or Atlantic City is well advised to allocate a specific amount of money, or a budget, for playing the casino games. Ideally, that budget should be money that is not needed for home mortgage or life insurance payments, retirement income, or children's educational funds. People who do not make such an allocation often find themselves in serious financial trouble unless they are extremely lucky.

Setting up a portfolio of assets to manage for profit is much the same and is a very personal thing that can only be done judiciously by the investors themselves. As everyone has a unique set of financial responsibilities, financial resources, and financial priorities, it's impossible to recommend any specific set of investment priorities that are right for everyone.

However, we can offer a way to segment the assets or financial needs of investors into some specific categories to provide investors with a guide to structuring their total portfolio of assets. Fundamentally, everyone can define their total assets in terms of four categories, as shown in Figure 18-2.

The investor's total assets represent the sum of everything he or she owns; this total can be broken down into assets for living and liquid assets.

Assets for Living. This category would include all of the *things* that a person wants and uses in life: homes, cars, furniture, art (for the beauty of it), vacation houses, real estate, business assets, boats, and so on. In other words, these assets

Figure 18-2. *Asset Categories for Individual Investors*

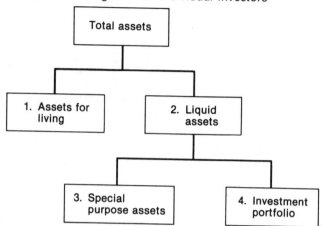

are purchased from the income that a person earns from a job and from an investment portfolio. They are not part of an investment portfolio, but are the spoils of a good portfolio.

This category should also include *nonliquid* investments that an individual wishes to own as either a part of his or her life-style or estate. Vacation homes, property, coin collections, art objects, and antiques properly belong in this category, even though they are viewed as investments that should appreciate over time. They cannot be put into the investment portfolio that is tied to the business cycle because they are not liquid and do not offer the flexibility that should be a key characteristic of an investment portfolio. Anyone in Texas that owned property or oil wells in 1986 can quickly attest to the illiquidity and inflexibility of these investment-oriented assets. Therefore, an asset that cannot be sold quickly without an erosion of value should be viewed as an asset for living that is separate from liquid assets that must be managed in a timely and efficient way.

Total Liquid Assets. This category includes all financial assets that one possesses. These assets are cash, near cash, or readily convertible to cash. This pool of money can either be spent, saved for something special, or invested in a portfolio. The most prudent approach to structuring a complete liquid asset portfolio is to list all of the liquid funds you have in different places on a sheet of paper, showing each account, where it is, and how much money it contains.

Special Purpose Accounts. The money in special purpose accounts, a part of total liquid assets, can be defined by separating all those accounts that have specific objectives in the investor's life. This category would include:

- A checking account for basic daily living
- Some small savings accounts for reserve cash needs
- Savings bonds
- Retirement accounts
- Specific accounts for children's college educations, a new boat, a special vacation, and so on

In other words, special purpose accounts are not designed to generate high returns, but to isolate, accumulate, and preserve money for specific purposes. These accounts carry a very low investment risk and, accordingly, generate a low return, but they serve their designated purpose by preserving the investor's capital in liquid form until it is needed.

Investment Portfolio. After special purpose funds have been identified, *all other financial assets* can be placed into the investment portfolio. This pool of money needs to be managed for maximum return. The business cycle money management system is primarily intended for the management of these financial assets.

The system can also be used to manage long-term retirement accounts (in special purpose accounts) if those accounts are established with mutual funds or brokerage firms that allow investors to switch money between different kinds of investments during a typical business cycle. While these retirement accounts must be established as separate, isolated accounts for legal reasons, there is no reason why an IRA or Keogh account could not be managed in the same way that the investment portfolio is managed as we progress through each business cycle.

Figure 18-3. *How the Business Cycle Money Management System Fits into the Investor's Portfolio of Total Assets*

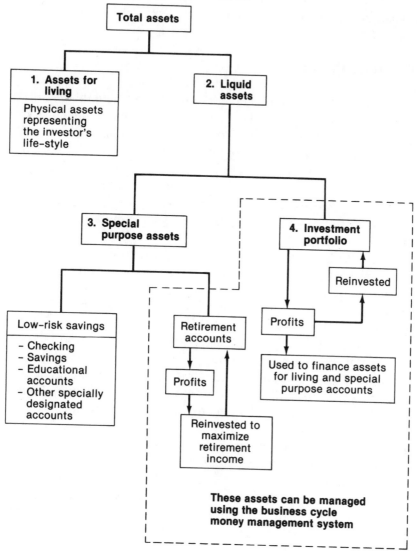

Figure 18-3 is a restatement of the investor's total assets; it shows the purpose of each category of assets and the segments for which the business cycle money management system can be used.

Having defined our investment portfolio, we can focus on

managing it. The rest of this chapter is devoted to the remaining five steps (data collection, analysis, decision, allocation, and execution) involved in using the business cycle money management system.

Data Collection

The first step in managing the portfolio, the data *collection* step, could aptly be called the data *selection* step. One of the key findings of our business cycle research is that many news events, media commentaries, and regularly published statistics are either unnecessary or misleading in assessing our true position in the business cycle. The trick, then, is to simultaneously reject the useless information and systematically collect and track the vital statistics that paint the true picture of our economic and financial situation.

We've looked at three types of information throughout the book: first, Commerce Department statistics pertaining to the business cycle; second, interest rate and stock yield information pertaining to the overvaluation or undervaluation of stock prices; and third, some specific technical data that are useful only when we are approaching major peaks or bottoms in the stock market. With only three publications at a very modest price, investors can collect *all* of the data that are necessary to see our position and to make appropriate investments. Figure 18-4 lists every item of data needed for a complete analysis and the specific sources of those data. Figure 18-5 then lists the addresses and phone numbers of the publishers of these data, along with annual subscription fees of these publications.

As shown in Figures 18-4 and 18-5, all the information necessary to completely assess the business cycle and the key financial markets can be found in just three publications at a total annual cost of only $255. An additional source available to investors is a monthly newsletter, *Business Cycle Monitor*. This advisory letter tracks the movements of the economic, financial, and technical indicators; monitors our position in the Primary Business Cycle; and provides portfolio recommendations accordingly. It is available for an annual subscription rate of $120 (see Appendix F for details).

Analysis

Now that we have access to all the data that we'll need, we have to analyze those data in a systematic and disciplined way to answer three questions:

- Where are we in the business cycle?
- Are we approaching any major turning points in stocks, bonds, or gold?
- If so, what investment actions should be taken?

As we see in this chapter, once the first question has been answered, the answers to the other two questions fall into place quickly and easily.

Where Are We in the Business Cycle? To see our position in the business cycle at any point in time requires a little effort. However, considering the complexity of the question and the financial benefits of knowing the answer, an hour or so of work each month doesn't seem like too much to ask.

The first step consists of finding and plotting our position on the business cycle Gantt chart. We've made some small changes to the format of the Gantt chart shown earlier in the text to make it easier to track the progress of each future cycle. The new Gantt chart includes the bottoms and peaks of the annual percentage change in the M2 money supply, since Chapter 10 showed us that this indicator can confirm peaks and bottoms in inflation and interest rates. We've also split the interest rate turning points into three separate events to make it easier to monitor: short-term interest rate turning points, long-term interest rate turning points, and velocity of money turning points. The short-term interest rates are the prime rate, the T-bill rate, and the federal funds rate. The long-term interest rates are the T-bond, corporate bond, municipal bond, and FHA mortgage rates.

The new business cycle Gantt chart shows the 40 events— 20 peaks and 20 bottoms—that make up the complete business cycle. Figure 18-6 shows the new version of the Primary

Figure 18-4. *Specific Sources of Data*

Data Needed	Source	Frequency of Data Reported
For business cycle analysis:		
M2 money supply	*Business Conditions Digest*	Monthly
S&P 500 stock prices (monthly average)	"	"
Leading economic indicators	"	"
C/L ratio	"	"
Capacity utilization rate	"	"
Coincident economic indicators	"	"
Commerce Department economic status:	"	"
Expansion or recession	"	"
Lagging economic indicators	"	"
Consumer credit ratio	"	"
Producer price index	"	"
Consumer price index	"	"
Federal funds rate	"	"
T-bill rate	"	"

	Source	Frequency
Prime rate	"	"
T-bond rate	"	"
Corporate bond rate	"	"
Municipal bond rate	"	"
FHA mortgage rate	"	"
Velocity of money	"	"
For valuation analysis:		
T-bond rate	Business Conditions Digest	Monthly
S&P stock dividend yield	Barron's or Wall Street Journal	Weekly Every Monday
Risk premium	Calculations	
Estimated stock growth rate	Calculations	
For technical analysis:		
NYSE volume	Barron's or Wall Street Journal	Weekly Daily
NYSE advances	"	"
NYSE declines	"	"
NYSE new highs	"	"
NYSE new lows	"	"
For current market conditions:		
Stock prices	Wall Street Journal	Daily
Gold prices	"	"
Bond prices	"	"

Figure 18-5. *Summary of Sources Required for Complete Business Cycle Analysis*

Source	Address and/or Phone	Annual Subscription	Frequency
Business Conditions Digest, published by the U.S. Commerce Department	Superintendent of Documents U.S. Government Printing Office Washington, D.C. 20402 For questions on data series, call 202-523-0541 at the U.S. Commerce Department	$ 44	Monthly
Barron's	*Barron's* 200 Burnett Road Chicopee, MA 01020	92	Weekly
Wall Street Journal	*Wall Street Journal* 200 Liberty Street New York, NY 10281	119	Daily
Total annual cost		$255	

Business Cycle. Each turning point is denoted by a black circle when the event occurs. The sequence of events for each business cycle begins with Event 1, the bottoming of the M2 money supply, moves down the list until we reach the peak in interest rates and velocity, and then recycles back to the first event at the top of the chart. The shaded areas represent periods of recession.

Each month, on receiving the *Business Conditions Digest* from the Commerce Department, investors should study the components of the business cycle that are listed in Figure 18-4 to see if any have reached a turning point that needs to be plotted on the Gantt chart. Investors could do this by simply examining the graphs and the data given in the *Business Conditions Digest* and noting any bottoms or peaks that have developed. Investors could also do this by plotting the latest data on separate charts that they maintain. Since there are only 20 data points to update and the process takes place only once a month, this is really a relatively easy task. It takes only a few minutes on a personal computer, and not much longer on 20 separate pieces of graph paper.

Once the charts are updated, they can be quickly analyzed to see if any indicators are reversing direction. When a clear reversal is seen in one indicator, such as the money supply, a dot is placed on the Gantt chart in the appropriate month.

For example, Figure 18-7 shows the business cycle Gantt chart as it would appear if we were at Event 21 in the cycle, when the money supply had just peaked and we were waiting for the next stock market peak.

Figure 18-6. *The Primary Business Cycle for Tracking Purposes*

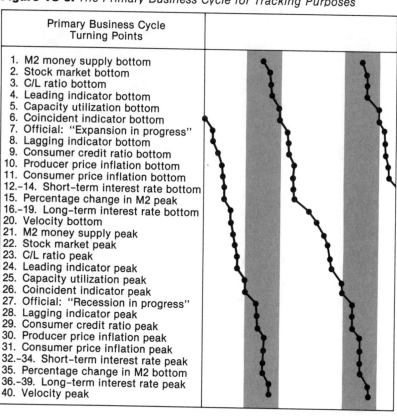

Primary Business Cycle Turning Points	
1. M2 money supply bottom	
2. Stock market bottom	
3. C/L ratio bottom	
4. Leading indicator bottom	
5. Capacity utilization bottom	
6. Coincident indicator bottom	
7. Official: "Expansion in progress"	
8. Lagging indicator bottom	
9. Consumer credit ratio bottom	
10. Producer price inflation bottom	
11. Consumer price inflation bottom	
12.–14. Short–term interest rate bottom	
15. Percentage change in M2 peak	
16.–19. Long–term interest rate bottom	
20. Velocity bottom	
21. M2 money supply peak	
22. Stock market peak	
23. C/L ratio peak	
24. Leading indicator peak	
25. Capacity utilization peak	
26. Coincident indicator peak	
27. Official: "Recession in progress"	
28. Lagging indicator peak	
29. Consumer credit ratio peak	
30. Producer price inflation peak	
31. Consumer price inflation peak	
32.–34. Short–term interest rate peak	
35. Percentage change in M2 bottom	
36.–39. Long–term interest rate peak	
40. Velocity peak	

Figure 18-7. *Business Cycle Gantt Chart at Event 21 of the Cycle*

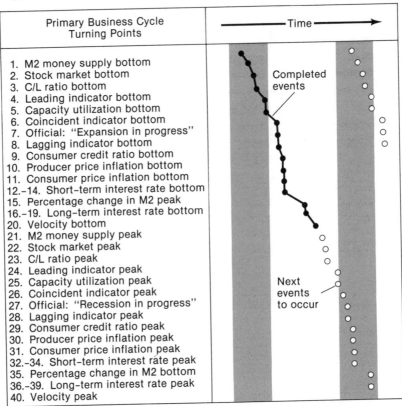

Primary Business Cycle Turning Points	Time ⟶
1. M2 money supply bottom 2. Stock market bottom 3. C/L ratio bottom 4. Leading indicator bottom 5. Capacity utilization bottom 6. Coincident indicator bottom 7. Official: "Expansion in progress" 8. Lagging indicator bottom 9. Consumer credit ratio bottom 10. Producer price inflation bottom 11. Consumer price inflation bottom 12.–14. Short–term interest rate bottom 15. Percentage change in M2 peak 16.–19. Long–term interest rate bottom 20. Velocity bottom 21. M2 money supply peak 22. Stock market peak 23. C/L ratio peak 24. Leading indicator peak 25. Capacity utilization peak 26. Coincident indicator peak 27. Official: "Recession in progress" 28. Lagging indicator peak 29. Consumer credit ratio peak 30. Producer price inflation peak 31. Consumer price inflation peak 32.–34. Short–term interest rate peak 35. Percentage change in M2 bottom 36.–39. Long–term interest rate peak 40. Velocity peak	Completed events Next events to occur

Later, as we progressed through the cycle and entered a recession, we would reach the peaks in the stock market, the C/L ratio, the leading indicators, capacity utilization, and the coincident indicators. Then, midway through the recession, inflation would peak out and we would be at Event 31 of the cycle, waiting for the peak in interest rates; the Gantt chart would appear as shown in Figure 18-8.

But, are the bottoms and tops of the business cycle indicators easy to see? What is clear reversal? Don't these indicators wiggle up and down, making decisive turning points difficult to see? Yes, they often wiggle up and down, but turning points are still quite easy to see for two reasons.

First, they are easy to see because you know *what to look for and when to look for it.* Have you ever had to drive somewhere that you've never been to before with a handwritten set of directions that someone gave you?

"Go south on the expressway to the first exit after the shopping mall. Go west on that street until you cross Route 10. Then go another two or three miles west until you see a white church on the right and an Exxon station on the left. Take the next right, go a half mile, and you'll be there."

These directions are not explicit, but they are clear enough to get you where you want to go because you know what to look

Figure 18-8. *The Business Cycle Gantt Chart at Event 27 of the Cycle*

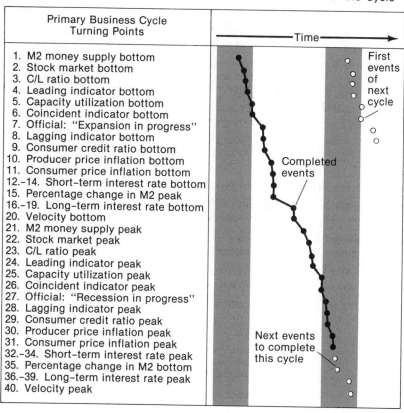

for and *approximately* when to look for it. You won't exit the expressway until you've passed the mall. You won't look for Route 10 until you have exited the expressway. You won't look for the church and the Exxon station until after you've crossed Route 10. The estimate of two or three miles from Route 10 to the church and the gas station might be a bad guess, and the true distance might be only one mile or as much as five miles, but you'll be prepared to see them once you've crossed Route 10. And if you happen to see a church and an Exxon station while you are still on the expressway, you'll know it is meaningless because they are in the wrong part of your direction sheet.

This analogy is very similar to the business cycle mileposts shown on the Gantt chart. Once we have established our position in the cycle, we watch specifically for the next mileposts so that they will be easy to identify.

The second reason is that the major turning points in the business cycle can be confirmed by multiple signals. Inflation is not just a single indicator. It is measured by the consumer price index and the producer price index. In addition, it is confirmed by gold prices, raw material costs, and the percentage change in the M2 indicator. When all these indicators reverse direction simultaneously, a turning point in inflation is clear.

Interest rate turning points are even more visible because we are tracking seven of them—not just one. By simply watching all seven rates and knowing when to look for peaks and when to look for bottoms, investors can easily see these major turning points. To illustrate this point, monthly charts for the seven interest rates from January 1986 to July 1988 are shown in Figure 18-9.

The last bottoming phase began with the short-term rates in September 1986 and ended when all the long-term rates started to rise in March 1987. Between September 1986 and January 1987, there was an apparent conflict in the interest rate trends because the short-term rates were headed up while the long-term rates were still going down. But since we know historically that the short-term rates tend to lead the long-term rates, we can resolve this conflict in favor of the short-term rates. Since inflation was also bottoming out in late 1986, once all three

Figure 18-9. *Short-Term Interest Rates*

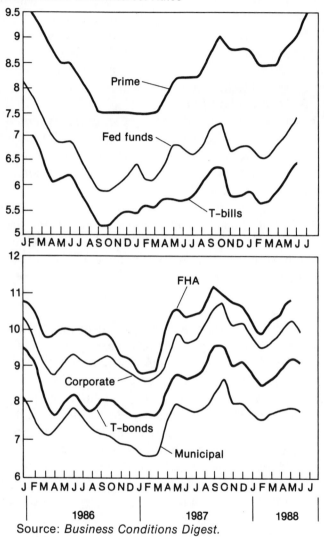

Source: *Business Conditions Digest.*

short-term rates began to move up, it was clear that we were in the interest rate bottoming phase of the cycle and that long-term rates would soon follow the upward trend. In addition, the velocity of money also bottomed out (predictably) in early 1987—a final confirmation.

The economic indicators also follow a very well-defined pattern. The C/L ratio and leading indicators turn first and are later followed by the coincident indicators. The official declaration of a period of recession or expansion does not occur until several months after the coincident economic indicators have reversed direction; the lagging indicators reach turning points shortly after the declaration.

The money supply tends to move in long, sweeping cycles and either leads or coincides with stock market turning points. Stock market bottoms coincide with interest rate peaks, and stock market peaks can be confirmed by the valuation map and some technical indicators.

By plotting the data for the components of the business cycle, identifying the key turning points, and plotting the recent history of those turning points on the business cycle Gantt chart, we can establish our initial position in the cycle. From there, the subsequent turning points can be plotted with relative ease as they develop.

Are We Approaching Any Major Turning Points? Doing this analysis and discovering where we are in the cycle is much like spotting our position on a map during a long car trip across the country, during which we have to face several forks in the road and make decisions as we come to them. Sometimes, there are long stretches of highway with no forks in the road, and no decisions are necessary. But then, suddenly, a fork appears in front of us, and we have to choose which way to go.

Our business cycle consists of 40 events, or stretches of road, over which we have to travel during every cycle. But as these 40 events occur, we have to make investment decisions at only six of them. As we progress through each cycle, we have to do something only at the points in the cycle in which we should (1) buy stocks, bonds, and gold and (2) sell stocks, bonds, and gold.

To get a better fix on these critical investment decision points, let's look more closely at the new business cycle Gantt chart shown in Figure 18-10.

In this chart, we've lined up the timing of the 40 events

Figure 18-10. *Investment Stages in the Business Cycle*

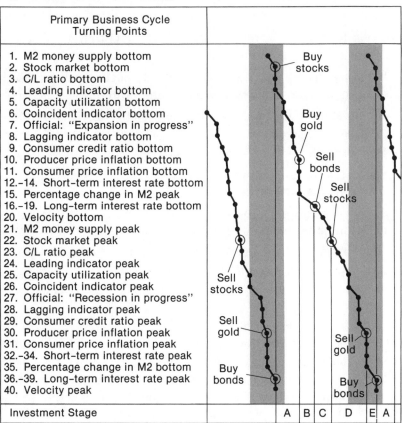

Primary Business Cycle Turning Points	
1. M2 money supply bottom 2. Stock market bottom 3. C/L ratio bottom 4. Leading indicator bottom 5. Capacity utilization bottom 6. Coincident indicator bottom 7. Official: "Expansion in progress" 8. Lagging indicator bottom 9. Consumer credit ratio bottom 10. Producer price inflation bottom 11. Consumer price inflation bottom 12.-14. Short–term interest rate bottom 15. Percentage change in M2 peak 16.-19. Long–term interest rate bottom 20. Velocity bottom 21. M2 money supply peak 22. Stock market peak 23. C/L ratio peak 24. Leading indicator peak 25. Capacity utilization peak 26. Coincident indicator peak 27. Official: "Recession in progress" 28. Lagging indicator peak 29. Consumer credit ratio peak 30. Producer price inflation peak 31. Consumer price inflation peak 32.-34. Short–term interest rate peak 35. Percentage change in M2 bottom 36.-39. Long–term interest rate peak 40. Velocity peak	
Investment Stage	A B C D E A

based on all the evidence and relationships presented earlier in the book. Twelve proven timing relationships have been used to plot the points in Figure 18-10:

• Inflation and short-term interest rate bottoms occur at almost the same time.

• Inflation and short-term interest rate peaks occur at the same time.

• Inflation and short-term interest rate bottoms occur at the same time as the peak in the annual percentage change in M2.

- Inflation and short-term interest rate peaks occur at the same time as the bottom in the annual percentage change in M2.
- Long-term interest rate peaks and bottoms follow short-term interest rate peaks and bottoms.
- Velocity of money peaks and bottoms occur near or shortly after long-term interest rate peaks and bottoms.
- Stock market bottoms occur at the same time as long-term interest rate peaks.
- Stock market peaks occur *after* interest rate bottoms.
- Economic peaks (or the beginning of recessions) occur before inflation and interest rate peaks.
- Economic bottoms (or the end of recessions) occur before inflation and interest rate bottoms.
- Stock market turning points occur very near the turning points in the C/L ratio and the leading indicators.
- Money supply turning points coincide with or precede stock market turning points.

We've also identified the buy and sell points for stocks, bonds, and gold as they relate to the Primary Business Cycle. Obviously, the buy and sell points for stocks occur at the stock market bottom (Event 2) and peak (Event 22), respectively. The buy point for bonds occurs at the long-term interest rate peak (Events 36–39), and their sell point occurs at the interest rate bottom (Events 16–19). Finally, the buy point for gold occurs at the inflation bottom (Event 11), and its sell point occurs at the inflation peak (Event 31).

The first thing to notice about Figure 18-10 is that the "buy stocks" turning point (near the top of the chart) coincides with the "buy bonds" turning point (near the bottom of the chart). This is the result of our earlier finding that stock market bottoms occur at interest rate peaks (which are bond market bottoms). Since these two buy decisions coincide, only five investment decisions must be made over a complete business cycle.

Accordingly, we have broken the business cycle into five distinct investment stages, which are shown along the bottom of

Figure 18-11. *Investment Stages of the Business Cycle*

	Beginning Point		Ending Point	
Investment Stage	Business Cycle Event	Investment Decision	Business Cycle Event	Investment Decision
A	Event 2	Buy stocks and bonds	Event 10	Buy gold
B	Event 10	Buy gold	Events 16–19	Sell bonds
C	Events 16–19	Sell bonds	Event 22	Sell stocks
D	Event 22	Sell stocks	Event 30	Sell gold
E	Event 30	Sell gold	Event 2 of next cycle	Buy stocks and bonds

Figure 18-10. These five investment stages, which represent the time between the five major investment decisions in each business cycle, are defined in Figure 18-11.

Given these five investment stages and the five major buy and sell points, we can begin to link the events of the business cycle to specific investment decisions and the ideal portfolio at each stage of the business cycle.

If you look at the beginning of Stage A in Figure 18-10, you can see that, at this point in the business cycle, *three* clearly defined events are happening simultaneously:

• A recession is in progress.
• The C/L ratio, the leading indicators, and the *stock market are bottoming out.*
• Long-term interest rates and velocity are peaking (which means that *bonds are bottoming out*).

Therefore, at the beginning of *Stage A* of the cycle, when we are in the depths of a recession, the correct investment and portfolio management strategy is to *buy stocks* and *long-term bonds.* While it usually takes a good deal of courage to make investments in stocks and bonds during a recession, historical evidence and the laws of supply and demand, which drive the business cycle, provide strong support for these investments during this part of the cycle.

Let's look next at *Stage B.* As we enter this stage of the business cycle, we have emerged from the recession, the economy is growing at a healthy rate, and stocks are rising. At the same time:

- Inflation is bottoming out (so *gold is hitting bottom*).
- Short-term interest rates are bottoming out. But long-term interest rates are still going down—approaching their cyclical bottoms—so long-term bonds are obviously still rising and approaching their cyclical peaks.
- The annual percentage change in M2 is peaking out, confirming an interest rate bottom.

Therefore, when we enter *Stage B* of the cycle, investors seeing these turning points develop would want to (1) *buy gold,* (2) *hold stocks,* and (3) *hold bonds a little longer.*

As we enter *Stage C* of the cycle, long-term interest rates finally bottom out, confirmed by the bottoming velocity of money. This is a *clear sell signal for bonds, but stocks and gold should still be held.* Later in Stage C, the M2 money supply peaks out, sending the first warning signals of an approaching stock market peak.

At the beginning of *Stage D,* stocks peak out and decline. This decline, which is closely tied to declines in the C/L ratio and the leading indicators, calls for *the immediate sale of all stocks,* as we prepare to enter a recession.

After we enter the recession, inflation peaks out at the beginning of *Stage E,* calling for the *sale of gold.* The inflation peaks are confirmed by peaks in the short-term interest rates and a bottom in the annual percentage change in M2. *In Stage E, there are no attractive investments* in sight. Inflation (and gold) is declining, long-term interest rates are still rising (so bonds are still falling), and the stock market is still falling. During this stage of the cycle, cash is the only viable investment.

Finally, at the depths of the recession, we return to Stage A when long-term interest rates peak out. Here we would buy both stocks and bonds.

The relationships defined in Figure 18-10 provide many clear confirming signals for:

- *Gold peaks* and *bottoms* (linked to inflation)
- *Bond peaks* and *bottoms* (linked inversely to interest rates)
- *Stock market bottoms* (linked to interest rate peaks)

The only investment decision point that is not clearly linked to other turning points in the cycle is the stock market peak. We know that stock market peaks are *preceded* by (1) a bottom in inflation, (2) a bottom in interest rates, and (3) a peak in the percentage change in M2. From earlier chapters, we also know that stock market peaks are either preceded by or coincide with (1) a peak in the actual M2 money supply figures, (2) a peak in the C/L ratio, and (3) a peak in the leading economic indicators. And we know that stock market peaks occur *before* the actual onset of a recession. This means that the correct time to sell stocks is during a period of great hope, prosperity, and economic growth with low unemployment, high corporate earnings, high capacity utilization, and growing inflation and interest rates.

However, periods of economic growth and prosperity can last for quite a long time. We need some additional information to help us close in on the timing of stock market peaks. Fortunately, we have some other tools to help us identify both peaks and bottoms in the stock market. First, we can determine the degree of undervaluation or overvaluation of the stock market by plotting the Dow Jones industrial dividend yield against the T-bond interest rate on the valuation map. Thus, after plotting the 20 data points for the business cycle, we have to obtain one more monthly fact: the stock market dividend yield. The Dow Jones dividend yield is provided in *Barron's* every week and is also shown in the back section of the *Wall*

Street Journal every Monday. The dividend yields presented in the "Market Laboratory" section of *Barron's* as of October 3, 1988, are shown in Figure 18-12.

The proper use of the valuation map is to *confirm* our business cycle position. Major stock market peaks occur when (1) we are in the right phase of the business cycle (Event 22) *and* (2) stocks are in the peaking zone or the extremely overpriced zone of the valuation map. Major bottoms occur when (1) we are in the right phase of the business cycle (Event 2) *and* (2) stocks are in the bottoming or extremely underpriced zone of the valuation map.

While the valuation map uses the Dow Jones industrial dividend yield to spot our position and determine the current

Figure 18-12.

Indexes' P/Es & Yields			
	Last Week	Prev. Week	Year Ago Week
DJ Ind.-P/E	12.5	12.4	20.9
Earns, $	168.54	168.54	126.23
Yield, %	3.66	3.70	2.61
Divs, $	77.33	77.31	69.00
DJ Tran.-P/E	12.6	12.4	19.0
Earns, $	72.15	72.15	56.03
Yield, %	5.73	5.82	1.37
Divs, $	52.01	51.96	14.59
DJ Util.-P/E	9.6	9.5	10.8
Earns, $	18.96	18.96	18.13
Yield, %	8.47	8.56	7.94
Divs, $	15.38	15.38	15.94
S&P 500-P/E	12.42	12.45	22.32
Earns, $	21.70	21.70	14.85
Yield, %	3.69	3.66	2.76
Divs, $	9.93	9.88	8.78
S&P Ind.-P/E	12.98	13.03	23.20
Earns, $	23.80	23.80	15.56
Yield, %	3.21	3.19	2.31
Divs, $	9.90	9.88	8.55

DJ trailing 12-month earnings ended June 30 and latest 52-week dividends based on Friday close. S&P trailing 12-month earnings ended June 30 and latest indicated dividends based on Wednesday close.

Source: *Barron's* (October 3, 1988).

degree of undervaluation or overvaluation, the results shown by our position on the map apply to the entire stock market. Therefore, *all* stocks should be sold when the valuation map and the business cycle indicate a peak, and all quality stocks can be bought when the valuation map and the business cycle point to a market bottom. The combined conditions for major stock market turning points are shown in Figure 18-13.

When these two conditions do not exist at the same time, the market is not at a major turning point. Instead, it is in one of the between-turning-point phases that are characterized by minor ups and downs. For example, if the business cycle events reach the point at which a stock market peak is approaching but the stock market is not yet overpriced (in Zone 4 or Zone 5 of the valuation map), any stock market decline will be *minor* and the fundamental bull market will continue. However, once stocks become overpriced, based on the valuation map, the next time that the business cycle events lead to an imminent stock market peak, that peak will be a *major* stock market peak when all stocks should be sold.

Similarly, if we are approaching the stock market bottom, according to the events of the business cycle, but stocks are not yet underpriced (Zone 1 or Zone 2 on the valuation map), any rally will be short lived; the bear market will continue until stocks become underpriced. The next time that the business cycle events lead to a stock market bottom, it will be a *major* bottom and a real buying opportunity.

Thus, if the events in the business cycle are leading to the stock market bottom (Event 2) *and* the valuation map confirms the stock market bottom (by being in the bottoming zone or the extremely underpriced zone), we know that a major buying opportunity is near. And if we are approaching the stock market peak (Event 22) in the business cycle *and* the valuation map confirms this position (by being in the peaking zone or the extremely overpriced zone), we know that an all-out sell signal is rapidly approaching.

To refine our timing of major stock market turning points even further, we have still one more tool—technical analysis— to tell us when these turning points are developing in the market itself. As discussed earlier, we should update the three technical

Figure 18-13. *Combined Signals from the Business Cycle and the Valuation Map*

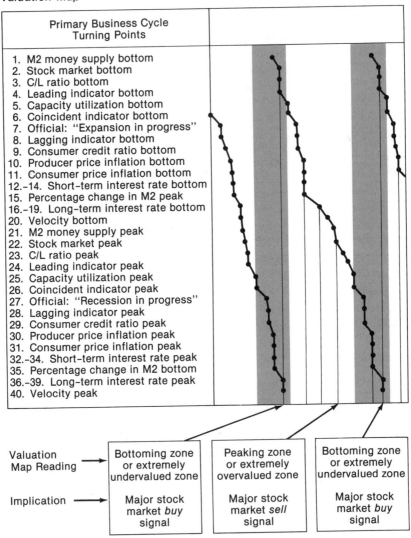

Primary Business Cycle Turning Points
1. M2 money supply bottom
2. Stock market bottom
3. C/L ratio bottom
4. Leading indicator bottom
5. Capacity utilization bottom
6. Coincident indicator bottom
7. Official: "Expansion in progress"
8. Lagging indicator bottom
9. Consumer credit ratio bottom
10. Producer price inflation bottom
11. Consumer price inflation bottom
12.-14. Short-term interest rate bottom
15. Percentage change in M2 peak
16.-19. Long-term interest rate bottom
20. Velocity bottom
21. M2 money supply peak
22. Stock market peak
23. C/L ratio peak
24. Leading indicator peak
25. Capacity utilization peak
26. Coincident indicator peak
27. Official: "Recession in progress"
28. Lagging indicator peak
29. Consumer credit ratio peak
30. Producer price inflation peak
31. Consumer price inflation peak
32.-34. Short-term interest rate peak
35. Percentage change in M2 bottom
36.-39. Long-term interest rate peak
40. Velocity peak

Valuation Map Reading	Bottoming zone or extremely undervalued zone	Peaking zone or extremely overvalued zone	Bottoming zone or extremely undervalued zone
Implication	Major stock market *buy* signal	Major stock market *sell* signal	Major stock market *buy* signal

charts throughout the cycle. *But it is critical to remember that they are only significant when the business cycle and the valuation map readings both indicate an imminent turning point.* Any upturns, downturns, or breakouts that happen at any other time in the cycle will result in the technical rallies or declines that happen so frequently and keep investors off balance. So we have to track continually (1) OBV, (2) the net advances and declines, and (3) the net new highs and lows, but we pay attention to them only when the business cycle and the valuation map tell us to do so.

The technical data can be tracked and plotted on a daily basis from the *Wall Street Journal* or on a weekly basis from *Barron's,* at the investor's discretion.

The three technical indicators should be viewed as the final signals triggering buy and sell actions for stocks. Referring back to our seasonal and weather analogy, the business cycle tells us that we're in the rainy season; the valuation map lets us see the big, black clouds coming over the horizon; and the technical indicators are the first claps of thunder preceding the rainstorm.

Decision: What Investment Actions Should Be Taken?

Translating our position in the business cycle into investment actions is a fairly simple task. Looking at the bottom of Figure 18-14, we can see that each investment stage has its own ideal mix of stocks, bonds, and gold. In Stage A, investors should be holding stocks and bonds. In Stage B, investors should own stocks, bonds, and gold. In Stage C, the bonds are sold and investors should be holding stocks and gold. In Stage D, only gold should be owned. And in Stage E, in which stocks, bonds, and gold are all declining, investors should be out of all three markets and invested safely in cash.

We now see when we should be in or out of the stock, bond, and gold markets over the five stages of a complete business cycle, and we have enough data and turning point signals to determine which stage of the cycle we are in at any point in time. The last two questions that must now be answered are: How much of our portfolio should we invest in these markets at different stages in the cycle and how can we set up a system that will allow us to switch our investments between stocks, bonds, and gold throughout the cycle?

Before we address those final questions, we want to ensure that the investor's understanding of the business cycle's se-

Figure 18-14. *Contents of the Ideal Portfolio Through a Complete Business Cycle*

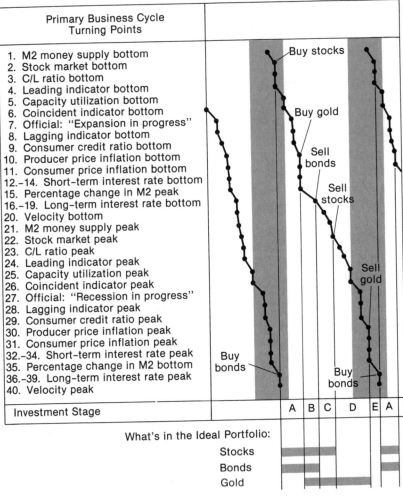

Primary Business Cycle Turning Points	
1. M2 money supply bottom	Buy stocks
2. Stock market bottom	
3. C/L ratio bottom	
4. Leading indicator bottom	
5. Capacity utilization bottom	
6. Coincident indicator bottom	Buy gold
7. Official: "Expansion in progress"	
8. Lagging indicator bottom	
9. Consumer credit ratio bottom	Sell bonds
10. Producer price inflation bottom	
11. Consumer price inflation bottom	
12.–14. Short-term interest rate bottom	Sell stocks
15. Percentage change in M2 peak	
16.–19. Long-term interest rate bottom	
20. Velocity bottom	
21. M2 money supply peak	
22. Stock market peak	
23. C/L ratio peak	
24. Leading indicator peak	
25. Capacity utilization peak	Sell gold
26. Coincident indicator peak	
27. Official: "Recession in progress"	
28. Lagging indicator peak	
29. Consumer credit ratio peak	
30. Producer price inflation peak	
31. Consumer price inflation peak	
32.–34. Short-term interest rate peak	Buy bonds
35. Percentage change in M2 bottom	
36.–39. Long-term interest rate peak	Buy bonds
40. Velocity peak	
Investment Stage	A B C D E A

What's in the Ideal Portfolio:
Stocks
Bonds
Gold

quence of events and of the cyclical investment decision points is absolutely clear. Throughout this book, we've used the business cycle Gantt chart (such as Figure 18-14) to convey the structure of the business cycle and the sequence of events within it. However, some people may visualize a cycle more clearly by looking at the actual upswings and downswings of the components of a business cycle as they would appear on a time chart. Figure 18-15 shows a typical business cycle and the ideal

Figure 18-15. *Time Chart of the Typical Business Cycle*

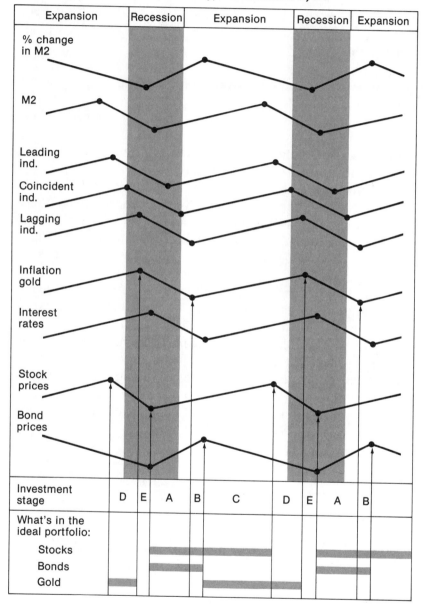

investments in each stage of the cycle, just as Figure 18-14 does.
But Figure 18-15 shows how all the key turning points would line
up over the course of a business cycle if an investor were
plotting them all on a graph, month by month. This figure
captures all the timing interrelationships that have been developed in this book.

Allocation: Building the Ideal Portfolio

We have just seen that, throughout the entire business
cycle, there are only five investment stages during which long-
term investors should have a completely different mix of investments in their portfolios. (See Figure 18-16.)

Within this framework, the next question is that of allocating specific percentages of the investment portfolio to stocks,
bonds, gold, and cash as we pass through these five stages. In
developing an ideal allocation of funds for each stage, we follow
our usual approach—seeking the answers by looking at some
underlying, guiding investment principles.

The first principle of portfolio allocation has been beauti-
fully captured in an advertisement by the Chicago Mercantile
Exchange, as shown in Figure 18-17.

The value of this ancient principle was amply demonstrated
during the crash of 1987, as well as the oil price crash of 1986. At
one level, we obeyed this principle by setting aside an investment portfolio that is not needed for other specific purposes. At
another level, within the investment portfolio itself, there is still

Figure 18-16.

Investment Stage	Business Cycle Events	Contents of Ideal Portfolio
A	2–9	Stocks and bonds
B	10–15	Stocks, bonds, and gold
C	16–21	Stocks and gold
D	22–29	Gold
E	30–1	Nothing but cash

Figure 18-17.

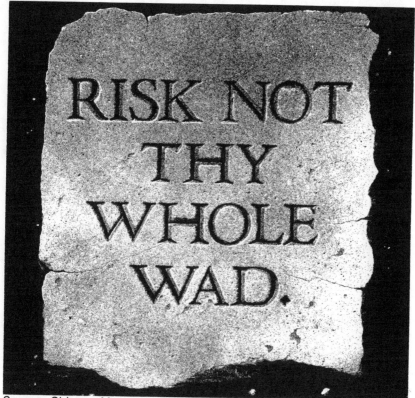

Source: Chicago Mercantile Exchange.

no need to take unnecessary portfolio risks by betting the entire ranch on stocks or bonds or gold. Following this principle a little further, history has shown us that although stocks and bonds possess considerable volatility, they are not nearly as volatile as gold. Since gold responds to panics and crises, as well as inflation, supply, and demand, it is subject to rapid and significant movements in either direction. And even though the business cycle indicators can provide some firm timing signals for gold, there is no need to expose a large percentage of an investor's portfolio to the unnecessary volatility risks that are inherent in gold to make substantial profits during the shiny metal's upswings.

Accordingly, we can use two rules to set up portfolio allocation limits:

- Never put more than 70 percent of the portfolio in a single investment category (stocks, bonds, or gold). The only exception to this rule is the safe haven of cash. During Stage E of the business cycle, when no other investment is attractive, 100 percent allocation of funds to cash is the only practical investment strategy.
- Never put more than 30 percent of the portfolio in the gold category.

To apply these rules, we begin by putting the words "yes" and "no" into Figure 18-18 to show which asset categories should be in the ideal portfolio at each investment stage of the business cycle.

As a first step in creating the ideal portfolio for each stage, we can apply our two portfolio rules and:

- Substitute a 70 percent portfolio allocation for the word "yes" in the table when it applies to either stocks or bonds.
- Substitute a 30 percent portfolio allocation for the word "yes" when it applies to gold.
- Add the fourth element of the ideal portfolio—namely, cash— and put any funds that are not assigned to stocks, bonds, or gold into the cash category during any stage of the cycle.

The result is shown in Figure 18-19.

Moving from right to left in Figure 18-19, this first draft of an ideal portfolio shows that we have all the portfolio in cash in

Figure 18-18. *Contents of the Ideal Portfolio*

	Stage A	*Stage B*	*Stage C*	*Stage D*	*Stage E*
Stocks	Yes	Yes	Yes	No	No
Bonds	Yes	Yes	No	No	No
Gold	No	Yes	Yes	Yes	No

Figure 18-19. *The Ideal Portfolio: First Draft*

	Stage A	Stage B	Stage C	Stage D	Stage E
Stocks	70%	70%	70%	0%	0%
Cash	0	0	0	70	100
Bonds	70	70	0	0	0
Gold	0	30	30	30	0
Total	140%	170%	100%	100%	100%

Stage E, when everything is going down. We have 30 percent in gold and the rest in cash during Stage D, when the stock market is falling, inflation is rising, interest rates are rising, and bonds are falling. In Stage C, we have 70 percent in stocks (our maximum) and 30 percent in gold (also our maximum) as stocks, the economy, and inflation are all rising.

However, in Stage B, we have 70 percent in both stocks and bonds and another 30 percent in gold for a total of 170 percent. In Stage A, we have 70 percent in both stocks and bonds for a total of 140 percent. Since we obviously cannot have more than 100 percent of the portfolio invested, we now have to make some choices in Stages A and B. Our research has shown that, in Stage A (coming off the bottom of a recession), stocks perform much better than bonds. For example, in the 1982 recovery, the Dow Jones industrials rose from 800 to 1,100 in five months. This rise was caused in part by falling interest rates, which also helped bonds. However, the interest rate decline and subsequent bond price increase were more prolonged processes. The big "bang for the buck" is in stocks during Stage A. Therefore, we recommend keeping our maximum 70 percent investment in stocks and allocating the remaining 30 percent to bonds.

In Stage B, after the recession has ended, stocks and bonds both outperform gold, and stocks still tend to outperform bonds. Stage B, which is the time between the inflation bottom and the interest rate bottom, is often a very brief period. Since inflation is low here, gold does not appreciate rapidly even though inflation may be picking up a bit. As a result, we can maximize our returns by keeping 70 percent invested in stocks and 30 percent in bonds, while forgoing the smaller increases in gold that would occur in this part of the cycle.

By following these rules, we can produce a finalized ideal portfolio for each of the five stages. Figure 18-20 shows the ideal portfolio as we move through two complete business cycles.

Figure 18-20 shows us that, for purposes of investing money, only four different portfolios are needed because the portfolios for Stages A and B are the same. Thus, over an entire business cycle, funds in the portfolio have to be reallocated or switched only four times. And a closer look at Figure 18-20 shows that these switches are extremely easy to execute.

- *Starting point*—The investor is in Stage A with 70 percent stocks and 30 percent bonds.
- *Switch 1*—As we move from Stage A through Stage B and into Stage C, the 70 percent investment in stocks remains unchanged and the 30 percent investment in bonds is switched into gold.
- *Switch 2*—As we move from Stage C to Stage D, the 30 percent investment in gold remains unchanged and the 70 percent investment in stocks is switched into cash.
- *Switch 3*—When we move into Stage E, the 70 percent investment in cash remains unchanged and the 30 percent investment in gold is switched into cash.
- *Switch 4*—Finally, as we move back into Stage A of the cycle, 70 percent of the money in cash is switched into stocks. The other 30 percent is switched into gold.

This approach makes the calculations involved in making switches extremely simple. In fact, no calculations are necessary for Switches 1, 2, and 3. The entire pool of money in one investment is simply moved to another investment. In Switch 4, when the entire portfolio is in cash, calculation of the 70 percent/30 percent split to move into stocks and bonds is all that is required. Figure 18-21 shows the business cycle Gantt chart and the ideal portfolio percentages that are associated with each event in the business cycle.

Figure 18-20. The Ideal Portfolio: Final

	First Business Cycle					Second Business Cycle				
Stage	A	B	C	D	E	A	B	C	D	E
Stocks	70%	70%	70%	0%	0%	70%	70%	70%	0%	0%
Cash	0	0	0	70	100	0	0	0	70	100
Bonds	30	30	0	0	0	30	30	0	0	0
Gold	0	0	30	30	0	0	0	30	30	0
Total	100%	100%	100%	100%	100%	100%	100%	100%	100%	100%

Switch 1 Switch 2 Switch 3 Switch 4

Switch 1 Switch 2 Switch 3

Figure 18-21. *The Ideal Portfolio at Each Event in the Business Cycle*

Primary Business Cycle Turning Points	*Stage*	*Ideal Portfolio*			
		Stocks	*Cash*	*Bonds*	*Gold*
1. M2 money supply bottom	E	0%	100%	0%	0%
2. Stock market bottom	A	70	0	30	0
3. C/L ratio bottom	A	70	0	30	0
4. Leading indicator bottom	A	70	0	30	0
5. Capacity utilization bottom	A	70	0	30	0
6. Coincident indicator bottom	A	70	0	30	0
7. Official: "Expansion in progress"	A	70	0	30	0
8. Lagging indicator bottom	A	70	0	30	0
9. Consumer credit ratio bottom	A	70	0	30	0
10. Producer price inflation bottom	B	70	0	30	0
11. Consumer price inflation bottom	B	70	0	30	0
12.–14. Short-term interest rate bottom	B	70	0	30	0
15. Percentage change in M2 peak	B	70	0	30	0
16.–19. Long-term interest rate bottom	C	70	0	0	30

20. Velocity bottom	C	70	0	0	30
21. M2 money supply peak	C	70	0	0	30
22. Stock market peak	D	0	70	0	30
23. C/L ratio peak	D	0	70	0	30
24. Leading indicator peak	D	0	70	0	30
25. Capacity utilization peak	D	0	70	0	30
26. Coincident indicator peak	D	0	70	0	30
27. Official: "Recession in progress"	D	0	70	0	30
28. Lagging indicator peak	D	0	70	0	30
29. Consumer credit ratio peak	D	0	70	0	30
30. Producer price inflation peak	E	0	100	0	0
31. Consumer price inflation peak	E	0	100	0	0
32.–34. Short-term interest rate peak	E	0	100	0	0
35. Percentage change in M2 bottom	E	0	100	0	0
36.–39. Long-term interest rate peak	E	0	100	0	0
40. Velocity peak	E	0	100	0	0

In describing this ideal portfolio, we've made switching money back and forth sound easy. But is it really that simple to switch money into and out of stocks, bonds, gold, and cash—just like that? You bet it is. And that brings us to the next key investment principle: flexibility. It is not just convenient for investors to have liquid assets that can be moved from one investment category to another on short notice. In fact, flexibility is a necessary feature of any portfolio in the volatile market environments that we now face.

Our advisory letter pulled the plug on the stock market on September 15, 1987—a full month before the crash. But suppose that an investor had only become concerned about the market when the Dow dropped 100 points on Friday, October 16, 1987—the last trading day before the 508-point debacle of Monday, October 19. That investor would still have been very well served by a portfolio management system that allowed him or her to be completely out of the market by the closing of Friday, October 16—before the 508-point massacre.

The volatile markets of recent years provide all the evidence necessary to convince investors that being able to get out of an investment rapidly, efficiently, inexpensively, and without affecting the price of the securities being sold is an absolute necessity in terms of profitability and peace of mind. In this light, the way in which an investor physically sets up his portfolio for flexibility and rapid *execution* can make all the difference in the world.

Execution: The Payoff

There are several ways to physically establish an investment portfolio or IRA and arrange to move funds between stocks, bonds, gold, and cash as we move through the business cycle. But some ways are clearly more advantageous than others when playing our system.

Since we are dealing with the stock market as a whole, interest rates and bonds as a whole, and gold as a fundamental commodity, it is not necessary to take the additional time and effort to try to evaluate specific stocks, bonds, or gold stocks. In fact, by doing this, an investor is taking on the additional risk of having money invested in individual situations that may or may not follow general market trends. In addition, the transaction costs of buying and selling individual securities can be significant; clearly, such switching costs should be minimized.

A Very Exclusive List of Mutual Funds. Based on our research, we believe that the easiest and most efficient way to invest and manage a pool of money in today's volatile markets is through the use of mutual funds. Entry costs are low, and you can move into and out of different markets (stocks, bonds, or gold) with much greater ease and *much lower costs* than you could by researching, buying, and selling individual securities.

Recently, we evaluated all the mutual fund companies that were rated by the Lipper Analytical Services and reported daily in the financial press. Our objective was to find all the fund companies that passed the following specific tests:

- The company had to have a growth stock fund, a bond fund, a gold fund, and a cash or money market fund.
- Telephone switching between all of the funds had to be allowed, with no practical limitations on the number of switches per year.
- If the company had a front-end sales load or a redemption fee, it had to be less than 5 percent.
- Investors had to be able to open an account with the company with less than $3,000.

Only five mutual fund companies passed all these tests. Figure 18-22 lists these five mutual fund companies and shows the best-performing fund for each company in each of the four investment categories of stocks, bonds, gold, and cash.

Figure 18-23 provides the specific cost, switching, and contact data for each mutual fund company, including their phone numbers for setting up an account.

Figure 18-22. *Recommended Mutual Funds for Telephone Switching Based on the Business Cycle*

| Mutual Fund Company | Specific Fund in Each Investment Category | | | |
	Growth Stocks	Bonds	Gold	Cash
Fidelity	Magellan	Ginnie Mae	Select American Gold	Cash Reserves
Franklin	Equity	U.S. Government Securities	Gold	Money Fund
Lexington	Growth Fund	GNMA Income Fund	Goldfund	Money Market Trust
United Services	U.S. Good and Bad Times	U.S. GNMA	U.S. New Prospector	U.S. Treasury Security
USAA	Growth	Income	Gold	Money Market Fund

To manage an investment portfolio or IRA account with this system, an investor needs only to:

- Select one of the five mutual fund companies listed in Figure 18-22 as a "home" for the investment portfolio and set up an account with them
- Put the recommended percentages of the portfolio into that company's stock, bond, gold, and cash funds, based on our position in the business cycle
- Switch the percentages in each of the four funds according to the ideal portfolio as we move through each business cycle

In this approach to investing, investors can be comfortable with the knowledge that they can move any part or all of their portfolios into or out of the stock, bond, or gold market in *one day* at a total cost of *$5 to $10*. As a point of comparison, it would cost $150 to $200 to buy and sell 100 shares of IBM.

Figure 18-23. Specific Information on Each Fund Family

	Fidelity	Franklin	Lexington	United Services	USAA
Sales load	0–3%	4%	None	None	None
Redemption fee	None	None	None	None except for gold (2%)	None
Minimum to open	$1,000–$2,500	Money fund is $500—All others are $100	$1,000	$100	$1,000
Telephone switching ability	Unlimited except for gold (4 switches per year)	Unlimited	Unlimited, but must stay for 7 days	After 12 switches per year, cost goes to $50/switch	Essentially unlimited—2 switches per month allowed
Cost per switch	Free except for gold ($25 per switch)	$5	$0	$5 up to 12 switches/year	$5
Phone number	800-544-6666	800-342-5236	800-526-0056	800-873-8637	800-531-8000

Alternative Ways to Manage Portfolios

Playing Without Gold. While the five mutual fund companies mentioned in Figure 18-22 are ideally suited to the business
cycle money management system, many investors now have
their portfolio(s) in one or more accounts with brokerage firms
or other mutual fund companies. If that is the case, the investor
will find that the limiting factor in most other accounts is an
inability to move money into or out of a gold fund to play the
inflation cycle. But since almost every family of funds has a
stock fund, a bond fund, and a money market or cash fund,
investors playing the business cycle must simply exclude the
gold investment from the portfolio.

Eliminating gold from the overall portfolio management
system, we can construct a different "modified ideal portfolio."
Presented in Figures 18-24 and 18-25 are (1) the original ideal
portfolio for each stage, as a point of reference, and (2) the
modified portfolio, in which the funds that were previously
invested in gold during Stages C and D have been diverted to
cash.

Using cash as a substitute for gold in the modified portfolio
is the only possible choice, given our investment rule of having
no more than 70 percent of the total portfolio in any single

Figure 18-24. *Original Ideal Portfolio*

	Stage A	*Stage B*	*Stage C*	*Stage D*	*Stage E*	*Stage A*
Stocks	70%	70%	70%	0%	0%	70%
Cash	0	0	0	70	100	0
Bonds	30	30	0	0	0	30
Gold	0	0	30	30	0	0
Total	100%	100%	100%	100%	100%	100%

Switch 1 Switch 2 Switch 3 Switch 4

Figure 18-25. *Modified Ideal Portfolio*

	Stage A	Stage B	Stage C	Stage D	Stage E	Stage A
Stocks	70%	70%	70%	0%	0%	70%
Cash	0	0	30	100	100	0
Bonds	30	30	0	0	0	30
Gold						
Total	100%	100%	100%	100%	100%	100%

Switch 1   Switch 2   Switch 3

investment category. In Stages A, B, and E, gold is not in the original ideal portfolio. Thus, no change is necessary. However, in Stage C, stocks are the only attractive investment other than gold, but we already have 70 percent of the portfolio in stocks. Therefore, unless we want to break the 70 percent rule, we have to put the other 30 percent in cash. In Stage D, neither stocks nor bonds are attractive, so the 30 percent that was in gold in the original ideal portfolio must definitely go into cash in the modified portfolio.

There is another noticeable difference between the modified portfolio and the original ideal portfolio. Between Stages D and E of the modified portfolio, there is no need to switch money between funds since the entire portfolio is invested in cash throughout both stages. Therefore, over an entire business cycle, only three switches are necessary for the modified portfolio.

Figure 18-26 shows the modified ideal portfolio at each stage of the business cycle.

Playing Only the Stock Market. For investors who are only interested in playing the stock market or whose investment portfolio only allows switches between stocks and cash, we can further modify the ideal portfolio. Since bonds are in the ideal portfolio only during Stages A and B, we can simply divert the

Figure 18-26. The Modified Ideal Portfolio at Each Event in the Business Cycle

Primary Business Cycle Turning Points	Stage	Ideal Portfolio			
		Stocks	Cash	Bonds	Gold
1. M2 money supply bottom	E	0%	100%	0%	
2. Stock market bottom	A	70	0	30	
3. C/L ratio bottom	A	70	0	30	
4. Leading indicator bottom	A	70	0	30	
5. Capacity utilization bottom	A	70	0	30	
6. Coincident indicator bottom	A	70	0	30	
7. Official: "Expansion in progress"	A	70	0	30	
8. Lagging indicator bottom	A	70	0	30	
9. Consumer credit ratio bottom	A	70	0	30	
10. Producer price inflation bottom	B	70	0	30	
11. Consumer price inflation bottom	B	70	0	30	
12.–14. Short-term interest rate bottom	B	70	0	30	
15. Percentage change in M2 peak	B	70	0	30	
16.–19. Long-term interest rate bottom	C	70	30	0	

20. Velocity bottom	C	0	30	70
21. M2 money supply peak	C	0	30	70
22. Stock market peak	D	0	100	0
23. C/L ratio peak	D	0	100	0
24. Leading indicator peak	D	0	100	0
25. Capacity utilization peak	D	0	100	0
26. Coincident indicator peak	D	0	100	0
27. Official: "Recession in progress"	D	0	100	0
28. Lagging indicator peak	D	0	100	0
29. Consumer credit ratio peak	D	0	100	0
30. Producer price inflation peak	E	0	100	0
31. Consumer price inflation peak	E	0	100	0
32.–34. Short-term interest rate peak	E	0	100	0
35. Percentage change in M2 bottom	E	0	100	0
36.–39. Long-term interest rate peak	E	0	100	0
40. Velocity peak	E	0	100	0

30 percent investment in bonds to cash during those stages of the cycle. This would retain our conservative investment rule of having only 70 percent of the total portfolio invested in one category (stocks) at any time. In this "ideal stock-only portfolio," 30 percent of the portfolio would always be invested in cash. While this may seem an unproductive investment, this 30 percent cash reserve can serve two useful purposes in a money management system. First, it generates risk-free profit. A 7 percent return on 30 percent of the portfolio generates a 2.1 percent return on the whole portfolio. If the other 70 percent were invested in the stock market and the market was absolutely flat for a year, the dividend yield from a stock fund would still be 4 percent or 5 percent. That dividend yield plus the 2.1 percent from the cash investment would provide a total return of 6–7 percent in a year in which the market was flat—and that's higher than the long-term inflation rate.

The second useful purpose for the 30 percent cash investment could be called the "opportunity cushion." If we read the business cycle indicators properly, we will be investing our 70 percent in stocks at the major market bottoms. But the path from the major bottoms to the major peaks is not always a smooth one. As discussed earlier, technical declines or unexpected events can trigger a temporary decline in the stock market while the fundamental trend is still up and while our 70 percent is invested in stocks. If such a decline were to occur during the wrong phase of the business cycle for a major peak, that decline would represent an outstanding, recognizable buying opportunity. Such an event happened in the two-day, 140-point (8 percent) drop in the Dow in September 1986. We were at Event 10 in the business cycle, well before the next expected stock market peak. At that time, an investor with a cash reserve could have used all or part of the 30 percent cash investment to buy stocks at a bargain price during a temporary decline. But it must be noted that this tactic should only be used by aggressive investors willing to break temporarily the 70 percent maximum investment rule.

The ideal stock-only portfolio is shown in Figure 18-27, using the 70 percent maximum investment rule. Investors who are less risk averse and who might wish to play a consistent all-or-nothing investment strategy can simply replace the 70 percent stock investments with 100 percent investments and change the 30 percent cash investments to 0 percent in Stages A, B, and C of the business cycle, as shown in Figure 18-27.

Of course, the 70 percent/30 percent splits in all the ideal portfolios are merely our recommendations, and investors may want to set up their own weightings for their portfolios. Use of any of our five selected mutual fund families offers the maximum benefits to investors who wish to profit from the upswings in stocks, bonds, and gold that develop during every business cycle. By using any of the modified ideal portfolios, investors can still outperform the stock and/or bond markets over the long run and manage their investments with virtually any well-run financial company. However, switching costs vary significantly, depending on whether the investor is using a full-service brokerage firm, a discount broker, or a fund family.

Investors who may have more than one portfolio established in different places (e.g., an investment portfolio with a mutual fund and an IRA account with a broker) can use the business cycle money management system to manage each portfolio separately. Once a business cycle switch signal is given, the investor would only have to make two phone calls—instead of one—to switch both portfolios to the correct mix of investments.

SUMMARY AND CONCLUSIONS

The business cycle money management system is designed to alert investors to when they should have money invested in stocks, bonds, gold, and cash. To effectively operate the system requires an annual investment of $200 to $300 in economic and financial publications that provide all of the data that are needed. The system also requires a monthly analysis of those data to:

• Assess our position in the business cycle
• Determine whether the stock market is undervalued or overvalued

Figure 18-27. *The Ideal Stock-Only Portfolio at Each Event in the Business Cycle*

Primary Business Cycle Turning Points	Stage	Ideal Portfolio			
		Stocks	Cash	Bonds	Gold
1. M2 money supply bottom	E	0%	100%		
2. Stock market bottom	A	70	30		
3. C/L ratio bottom	A	70	30		
4. Leading indicator bottom	A	70	30		
5. Capacity utilization bottom	A	70	30		
6. Coincident indicator bottom	A	70	30		
7. Official: "Expansion in progress"	A	70	30		
8. Lagging indicator bottom	A	70	30		
9. Consumer credit ratio bottom	A	70	30		
10. Producer price inflation bottom	B	70	30		
11. Consumer price inflation bottom	B	70	30		
12.–14. Short-term interest rate bottom	B	70	30		
15. Percentage change in M2 peak	B	70	30		
16.–19. Long-term interest rate bottom	C	70	30		

20.	Velocity bottom	C	70	30
21.	M2 money supply peak	C	70	30
22.	Stock market peak	D	0	100
23.	C/L ratio peak	D	0	100
24.	Leading indicator peak	D	0	100
25.	Capacity utilization peak	D	0	100
26.	Coincident indicator peak	D	0	100
27.	Official: "Recession in progress"	D	0	100
28.	Lagging indicator peak	D	0	100
29.	Consumer credit ratio peak	D	0	100
30.	Producer price inflation peak	E	0	100
31.	Consumer price inflation peak	E	0	100
32.–34.	Short-term interest rate peak	E	0	100
35.	Percentage change in M2 bottom	E	0	100
36.–39.	Long-term interest rate peak	E	0	100
40.	Velocity peak	E	0	100

- Track the three technical indicators that will generate the final buy and sell signals at major stock market bottoms and peaks

Once an investment portfolio has been set aside for profit-making purposes, the best of all investment worlds can be attained by:

- Using the business cycle, the valuation map, and the technical indicators to find the major bottoms in stocks, bonds, and gold
- Moving the investor's money into stocks, bonds, and gold at those major bottoms, in accordance with the ideal portfolio percentages
- Using the professional investment managers of the mutual fund companies to manage the individual stock, bond, and gold funds for maximum profit during their cyclical upswings
- Using the business cycle, the valuation map, and the technical indicators to find the major peaks in stocks, bonds, and gold
- Moving the investor's money out of those investments at their peaks and investing safely in cash during their cyclical downturns

Several years ago, it was discovered that a card-counting method could actually change the odds in favor of a gambler at a blackjack table in a casino. When the card count was right, the gambler increased his bets, knowing that the probability that he would win was high. When the card count was wrong, he would lower his bet to the minimum, knowing that the odds were now against him. This combination of big bets during winning streaks and little bets during losing streaks produced a very successful and very profitable long-term strategy for the blackjack player.

In the same vein, correct analysis of business cycle turning points can significantly change the performance of an investment portfolio. By investing in stocks, bonds, and gold at the right stages of the business cycle and by exiting those markets during their predictable cyclical downturns, the investor can achieve returns that are dramatically higher than the average market returns—without ever having invested in anything riskier than the market itself. As opposed to listening to hot tips and technical gurus or performing long, laborious, and detailed analyses of specific securities to try to improve investment profits, the strategic market-timing concept rests on proven economic laws, 80 years of historical evidence, and the wisdom provided in Kenny Rogers' famous song, "The Gambler," as applied to long-term investments: "You gotta know when to hold 'em, and know when to fold 'em."

Part V

EPILOG: DECEMBER 1989—
THE BUSINESS CYCLE—
WHERE WE ARE NOW AND
WHERE WE ARE GOING

"For everything there is a season . . . a time to keep, and a time to cast away . . ."

–Ecclesiastes 3:6

WHERE WE ARE NOW

We are presently on the leading edge of an economic decline. The current budget deficit remains at the $150 billion level and, as we discussed in Chapter 11, Congress was forced to raise the statutory debt ceiling again in November to avoid the technical shutdown of government operations and the delay of Social Security payments.

The stock market is in the peaking zone on our valuation map, with a current dividend yield of 3.87 percent and a T-bond yield of 7.9 percent (see page 247).

At the same time, we have seen several unprecedented events unfold in the Soviet Union and Eastern Europe in 1989. These events, largely political at this time, will have significant and lasting economic consequences throughout the world economies. Currently, the stock market is experiencing a "peace rally" that has pushed it to a level near its all-time high.

WHERE WE ARE GOING

We see the future unfolding in three distinct stages, each of which calls for a different investment strategy.

- Stage 1: Economic slowdown
- Stage 2: Financial restructuring
- Stage 3: International expansion

To illustrate this scenario, consider a conglomerate that has recently made several debt-financed acquisitions. The conglomerate is large in terms of assets, has foreign sales organizations in place, and produces several products that can be successfully marketed in the new international markets that will open in the future.

Although rich in terms of assets and opportunities, the conglomerate is laden with debt, and an economic slowdown will cut its revenues by 15 percent, which is enough to drive net income and operating cash flow into the red and make both principle and interest payments impossible to meet.

The tasks facing this hypothetical company are clear. The first step is to survive the economic decline and try to avoid going into bankruptcy by initiating layoffs and other large cost reductions which will ripple through the economy. Then, whether it goes into bankruptcy or not, it must restructure itself by shedding some assets, repaying some debt, and creating some additional debt capacity, putting it into a position to borrow money later for the financing of its international expansion program. Growth requires a great deal of cash, and the shorter-term financial problems of declining earnings and excessive debt must be dealt with before the international expansion can become a financially workable reality.

This illustration describes the fundamental situation which the federal government, a large segment of our economy, and many individuals now face—being burdened with debt, facing an economic slowdown with the knowledge that existing debt cannot be serviced if a full recession develops, but looking forward to a new era of international peace and economic expansion.

Stage 1: Economic Slowdown

The Current Economic Climate. The signs of economic weakness are now widespread: corporate earnings growth has been declining since May of this year; the leading economic indicators peaked out in January; and auto sales, aluminum production, durable goods orders, and retail sales are all declining at this time. Although the coincident economic indicators have not yet peaked out, some analysts believe that we are already in a recession. But this economic decline is marked with some very unusual characteristics.

- The current economic slowdown has *not* been caused by excessively high inflation or interest rates.
- The earlier expansion has *not* led to an excessive buildup of inventories which must be liquidated rapidly—a normal symptom of economic peaks.
- The real cause of the slowdown has been a combination of a consumer spending burnout and the limitations of federal, corporate, and personal debt. The excessive levels of consumer borrowing and the low levels of personal savings that have driven the expansion of the late 1980s are not sustainable, and are now reaching their limits.

We must remember that consumer spending, the key driver of economic growth, has three components. People spend (1) what they make, plus (2) what they can borrow, minus (3) what they save. So:

$$\text{Spending} = \text{Income} + \text{Borrowing} - \text{Saving}$$

If we were to try to create the maximum spending level possible from this equation, we would maximize income, maximize borrowing, and minimize saving—which is exactly what has happened since 1983. Incomes have been rising throughout this growth period, and borrowing as a percent of income, has hit a level that is unprecedented in U.S. history.

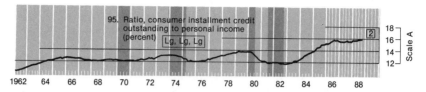

Source: *Business Conditions Digest.*

In addition, the savings level has been reduced to new historical lows.

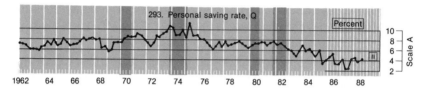

Source: *Business Conditions Digest.*

If borrowing and savings were both at normal levels, a recession would lower personal income, so one of the three components of spending would be adversely affected. But from where we are today, if a full recession develops, (1) incomes will drop, (2) people will stop borrowing as they sense financial trouble ahead, and (3) the public will start to save more as consumer fears rise. Suddenly, the consumer spending level will be hit with three out of three components moving in a negative direction as (1) incomes fall, (2) borrowing declines, and (3) savings increase. These three combined forces could produce a steep cutback in spending, which would lengthen and deepen the otherwise moderate economic downturn.

• Instead of waiting for an unacceptably high inflation rate or a deep recession to develop before taking action, the Fed, under Alan Greenspan, has now adopted a new policy stance which can best be described as *preventative*, rather than *reactive*. In the past two years, at the first signs of accelerating inflation the Fed has moderately tightened the money supply; when signals pointing to economic weakness became evident, the Fed has moderately expanded the money supply quickly to counteract the decline. Currently, the Fed is expanding money and credit as if we were at the bottom of a recession.

The Critical Question for 1990. It is clear that the Fed is not only aware of the dire consequences of entering a recession while the federal deficit is still in the $150 billion range, but it is highly motivated to prevent such a recession from developing. This leads to the critical question for 1990: Can the momentum of the current economic slowdown be stopped by the Fed's actions to ease credit and lower interest rates, when excessively high interest rates were not the cause of the economic slowdown?

Our Assessment. The stock market rally of 1989 is saying that the answer is yes. Current market valuations are based on the assumptions that (1) a recession can be forestalled by lowering interest rates, (2) a "soft landing" can be achieved, and (3) we can slide through this temporary decline directly into Stage 3—an extended period of international expansion. This is clearly the most optimistic scenario imaginable.

At the other extreme, we have the pessimistic scenario described earlier—a full recession that (1) begins with today's huge federal deficit, (2) generates an even higher deficit as tax revenues fall, and (3) puts us into an untenable position in which any fiscal policy actions to end the recession (lower taxes or higher government spending) will increase the deficit, and any actions to lower the deficit (higher taxes or lower spending) will deepen the recession. While the Fed will do everything in its power to prevent the latter from happening, we do not believe that the optimistic scenario is achievable without some period of economic decline and financial restructuring occurring first.

Given the Fed's recent track record, the nightmarish prospects of a near-term recession, and the glorious potential future of long-term international expansion, we believe that the Fed's future actions are now predictable. The Fed will continue to "massage" the economy and inflation with minor adjustments for as long as possible with a bias toward avoiding or postponing a major recession until the budget deficit can be reduced and the international expansion phase is underway. We believe that the result of this conflict between economic forces and money supply management will be a period of slow economic decline, or at best, stagnation. This implies a continuing series of partial cycles of fluctuating monetary policy and interest rate shifts in 1990. For traders, this points toward opportunities to play short-term swings in both the stock and bond markets. For long-term investors, it means a choppy, but essentially flat, stock market within a 200–400-point trading range on the Dow until either (1) the full recession develops and stocks plunge or (2) the budget deficit is reduced, we proceed to the international expansion stage, and stocks rise to new highs.

Stage 2: Financial Restructuring

Before a major expansion can take place, we must be in a "position to expand," and in order to be in that position, several structural changes must take place in the near future. These changes will begin to unfold during the period of economic slowdown.

At the federal level, the budget deficit is the key contraint to a major expansion. This deficit, unless reduced, will keep upward pressure on interest rates, which will constrain the financing of the international expansion in Stage 3. But the new era of peace and expanded trade now opens the door to substantive reductions in defense spending that could dramatically reduce the deficit over the long term—as long as there isn't a deep recession in the meantime.

Chapter 13 illustrated that the initial economic impact of "world peace breaking out" would be that "defense stocks would plummet." This is already happening and Secretary of Defense Dick Cheney is contemplating the reduction of nearly $200 billion from the defense budget in the next few years. If this program were carried out, some of the $200 billion reduction would be simply cut from the federal budget, reducing the deficit significantly, while the rest could be allocated to some of this country's more pressing domestic needs, such as environmental cleanups, rebuilding the infrastructure, education, and R&D for new technological improvements to keep the United States in a competitive position in the new, highly competitive world markets.

Naturally, we don't know if any of this will actually happen, but the stage is now set and the potential clearly exists for significant budget reductions that could pave the way to the Stage 3 expansion.

At the corporate level, the problem is not as easily solved. Any significant decline in economic activity has the potential to put many corporations in a severe financial bind. The aftermath of the recent S&L bailouts will constrain the government from engineering any significant number of additional bailouts. The restructuring that will take place here will be similar to other individual industry restructurings of the past. Companies with weaker balance sheets will be absorbed by those with financial resources, assets will change hands, jobs will be lost, and obsolete production facilities will be rationalized out of existence. While this is a painful process for many individuals and companies, it is a necessary prerequisite for future expansion.

At the individual level, a larger but easier adjustment is required.

The cure to the problem of excessive borrowing and the lack of savings is an economic slowdown during which people curtail their spending and borrowing, and increase their savings.

In summary, the economic slowdown in Stage 1 will lower interest rates and force the restructuring of corporate and individual balance sheets, while the prospect of peace and expansion in Stage 3 will allow the government the opportunity to reduce the deficit and reallocate government spending to support the future expansion.

Stage 3: International Expansion

The 1970s and 1980s were dominated by significant events originating in the Middle East. But, while we are now importing more oil than we have since 1984 and the possibility of another oil crisis still exists, the current Mideast situation pales in comparison to the events of 1989 in the Soviet Union and Europe.

The Gorbachev Effect. It is difficult to comprehend the scope of the implications resulting from these events. Since Mikhail Gorbachev initiated his new policies of *glasnost* (openness) and *perestroika* (restructuring), we have witnessed: dramatic reductions in nuclear weapons, Soviet troops removed from Afghanistan, vocalized opposition to party policies within the Soviet Union, baptisms permitted in the western Ukraine and a visit to the Vatican by Gorbachev, and a McDonald's in Moscow.

In the Soviet Union, citizens are exhilarated by the new political reality, but are still mired in the economic realities of a centrally planned economy. Severe shortages in basic items such as food, clothing, and soap still prevail and the people are now anxious to experience some economic benefits from these new policies.

The Freedom Wave. This, alone, would represent a historic departure from the former constraints imposed by the Cold War and the monolithic thinking of past Communist leaders. But, the spread of freedom has gone far beyond the borders of the Soviet Union. The abandonment of strict Communist rule has now developed in Hungary, Bulgaria, Poland, Czechoslavakia, and East Germany. While the situation in some of these nations is still chaotic, the direction of these movements is now unstoppable. From an economic standpoint, the population of these 5 countries totals over 90 million people—all of whom would like a credit card and the ability to consume a wider array of products and services. If the Soviet Union were to engage in the system of free world trade and create a currency that was acceptable in the world's markets, industrialized nations would have an open door to a new customer with a land area of 8.6 million square miles and a population of over 260 million people.

EEC—1992. The consolidation of the Western European nations which comprise the European Economic Community into a single economic enterprise represents still another historic change in the world's economic system. While the full ramifications of this endeavor are not well defined at this time, the directional impact is clearly *expansionary*. Whenever a group of diverse interests come together with a set of common objectives, the combined resources of the group will produce an economic power base that is far greater than the sum of the parts. The influence of OPEC in the past two decades is a clear example of this principle.

Economic Implications. In Chapter 13, we discussed a process of evaluating the impact of outside events. It consisted of (1) reacting first as a human being to changes such as those described above, and then (2) assessing the true economic impact on the supply, demand, and prices of goods or money.

Following this approach, the human reaction to *glasnost, perestroika,* and the new freedoms in Eastern Europe can only be those of relief, joy, and pride in the fact that the principles of human freedom, democracy, and market-based economies have prevailed over the strict principles of pure Communism.

The economic implications with respect to the United States economy, however, are both positive and negative.

On the plus side, a huge new set of potential markets for U.S. products and services has been created for any U.S. company with the ability to export and/or engage in joint ventures in these new untapped markets. Referring back to our economic model, the demand for goods will increase because the size of the free world market will expand significantly in the future.

On the minus side, these new customers can't buy our products unless they have money and are employed in their own countries. This means that the development of new foreign markets is linked with the development of new foreign economies. Consequently, new foreign factories must produce goods for both internal consumption and export to the United States and other free world countries. In economic terms, again, this means that eventually the supply of competitive goods will go up because the number of free world competitors will also increase significantly.

The combined economic resources of the EEC will also create both new markets and joint venture opportunities as well as new, stronger competitors. The advanced economy of West Germany, coupled with a weaker, poorer East Germany has the potential to create an extremely tough combined competitor with financial resources, technology and business savvy, linked with a low-paid work force producing a wide array of products (sounds a little like Japan, doesn't it?).

The bottom line is that we now look forward to a new era of international expansion, new trade channels, new markets, and new competitors, within a world political setting of lessened fears of nuclear disaster and a reduced need for military equipment and personnel. The challenge we face is that of positioning ourselves to best capitalize on these sweeping changes.

ADVICE TO INVESTORS

The three-stage scenario described earlier dictates a corresponding three-stage portfolio allocation.

During the *economic slowdown*, stock portfolios should be trimmed back significantly and concentrated on those companies with the highest, most stable dividend yields, and the lowest debt-to-capital ratios. Long-term bonds (government bonds or AAA-rated corporates) should be bought and a small amount of gold should be held as a hedge against any financial disruption that might occur during this period. Personal debt should be reduced and personal liquidity should be maximized.

During the period of *financial restructuring*, stocks of the companies doing the acquiring of the weaker stocks should be bought. Companies will become candidates for takeover during this phase because they are weak or insolvent, while the acquiring companies will be buying increased long-term market share positions for the future. The most desirable stocks in this stage will be those with (1) low debt, (2) an existing international presence, and (3) product lines that can be the most easily accepted in the new foreign markets (e.g., simple consumer goods). Raw material, natural resource, and gold stocks should also be bought at this point as we prepare for expanded demand for supply-constrained resources.

As we move into the *international expansion* stage, the stocks of companies producing the capital goods and technologies that will be integral to the development of the foreign economies will become the focus of attention and should be added to the portfolio. During this phase, inflation and interest rates will rise, so bonds should be sold and hard assets should be acquired.

STRATEGIC MARKET TIMING AND POSITIVE THINKING

It is essential to recognize that the downturn in the economy and the required financial restructuring will be temporary phases in the current long-term business cycle. At the bottom of the economic downturn, whenever it occurs, people and companies with investable cash will be in a position to capitalize on one of the greatest buying opportunities in stocks and hard assets in recent history.

While the immediate economic outlook is shaky and has the potential to become extremely harsh, it will not be the end of the world, even in the worst case. It will simply be the strategic time to "fold 'em." Later, when everything looks bleak and chaotic, the economic and financial turning point signals will be clearly evident to those who know how to read the business cycle. Those investors who see the bottoming signals will know that that's the time to "buy 'em" and "hold 'em" for the next, extended upturn of the Primary Business Cycle.

Appendix A

Business Cycle–Timed Portfolio Performance

Long-Term Performance of the Business Cycle-Timed Portfolio

Market Direction	Time Period	S&P 500 Value Bottom	S&P 500 Value Top	S&P 500 Value Bottom	BCT Portfolio "Perfect"	S&P 500 Value Bottom Plus 5%	S&P 500 Value Top Less 5%	S&P 500 Value Bottom Plus 5%	BCT Portfolio Imperfect by 5%	S&P 500 Value Bottom Plus 10%	S&P 500 Value Top Less 10%	S&P 500 Value Bottom Plus 10%	BCT Portfolio Imperfect by 10%	S&P Unmanaged Portfolio
					1,000[1]				1,000[1]				1,000[1]	1,000
Up	4/42–7/56	7.84	48.78		6,222	8.2320	46.341		5,629	8.624	43.902		5,091	6,222
Down	7/56–12/57		48.78	40.33	6,427[2]		46.341	42.3465	5,815[2]		43.902	44.363	5,259[2]	5,144
Up	12/57–7/59	40.33	59.74		9,521	42.3465	56.753		7,794	44.363	53.766		6,373	7,620
Down	7/59–10/60		59.74	55.73	9,906[3]		56.753	58.5165	8,109[3]		53.766	61.303	6,631[3]	7,108
Up	10/60–1/66	55.73	93.32		16,588	58.5165	88.654		12,286	61.303	83.988		9,085	11,903
Down	1/66–10/66		93.32	77.13	17,160[4]		88.654	80.9865	12,709[4]		83.988	84.843	9,399[4]	9,838
Up	10/66–12/68	77.13	106.50		23,695	80.9865	101.175		15,878	84.843	95.850		10,618	13,584
Down	12/68–6/70		106.50	75.59	25,799[5]		101.175	79.3695	17,288[5]		95.850	83.149	11,561[5]	9,642
Up	6/70–1/73	75.59	118.40		40,410	79.3695	112.480		24,500	83.149	106.560		14,816	15,102
Down	1/73–12/74		118.40	67.07	44,522[6]		112.480	70.4235	26,993[6]		106.560	73.777	16,324[6]	8,555
Up	12/74–11/80	67.07	135.70		90,081	70.4235	128.915		49,413	73.777	122.130		27,203	17,309
Down	11/80–7/82		135.70	109.40	110,934[7]		128.915	114.8700	60,851[7]		122.130	120.340	33,279[7]	13,954
Up	7/82–8/87	109.40	329.30		333,918	114.8700	312.835		165,722	120.340	296.370		81,957	42,003
Down	8/87–3/88		329.30	265.70[9]	345,605[8]		312.835	278.9850	171,522[8]		296.370	292.270	84,820[3]	33,850

(1) Initial $1,000 investment in April 1942.
(2) Using period beginning T-bill rate of 2.33% for 17 months.
(3) Using period beginning T-bill rate of 3.24% for 15 months.
(4) Using period beginning T-bill rate of 4.60% for 9 months.
(5) Using period beginning T-bill rate of 5.92% for 18 months.
(6) Using period beginning T-bill rate of 5.31% for 23 months.
(7) Using period beginning T-bill rate of 13.89% for 20 months.
(8) Using period beginning T-bill rate of 6.00% for 7 months.
(9) Average value in March 1988—not necessarily a bottom.

Economic Indexes and Their Components

Leading Economic Indicators

Series Number*	Series Name
1	Average weekly hours of production or nonsupervisory workers, manufacturing
5	Average weekly initial claims for unemployment insurance, state programs (inverted)
8	Manufacturers' new orders in 1982 dollars, consumer goods and materials industries
12	Index of net business formation
19	Stock prices, S&P 500 stocks
20	Contracts and orders for plant and equipment in 1982 dollars
29	New private housing units authorized by local building permits
32	Vendor performance, percentage of companies receiving slower deliveries
36	Change in manufacturing and trade inventories on hand and on order in 1982 dollars, smoothed
99	Change in sensitive material prices, smoothed
106	Money supply, M2, in 1982 dollars
111	Change in business and consumer credit outstanding

* As used by the Commerce Department in their monthly publication, *Business Conditions Digest.*

Coincident Economic Indicators

Series Number*	Series Name
41	Employees on nonagricultural payrolls
47	Industrial production index
51	Personal income, less transfer payments, in 1982 dollars
57	Manufacturing and trade sales in 1982 dollars

* As used by the Commerce Department in their monthly publication, *Business Conditions Digest.*

Lagging Economic Indicators

Series Number*	Series Name
62	Labor cost per unit of output, manufacturing— actual data as a percentage of trend
77	Ratio of manufacturing and trade inventories to sales in 1982 dollars
91	Average duration of unemployment (inverted)
95	Ratio of consumer installment credit to personal income
101	Commercial and industrial loans outstanding
109	Average prime rate charged by banks

* As used by the Commerce Department in their monthly publication, *Business Conditions Digest.*

*Graphic History of Leading, Coincident, and Lagging Indicator Indexes:
1952–1988*

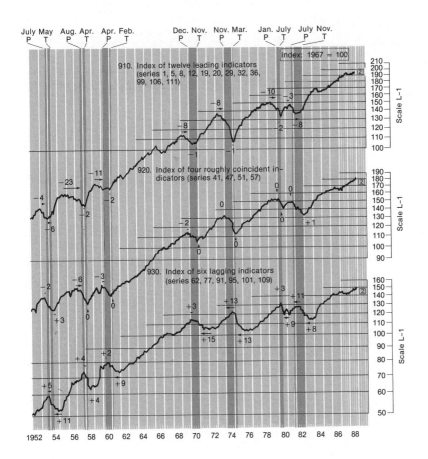

Source: *Business Conditions Digest.*

Historical Data for Economic Indexes

910. COMPOSITE INDEX OF 12 LEADING INDICATORS (1967=100)

Year	Jan.	Feb.	Mar.	Apr.	May	June	July	Aug.	Sept.	Oct.	Nov.	Dec.	I Q	II Q	III Q	IV Q	Annual
													AVERAGE FOR PERIOD				
1953	59.7	59.8	60.1	59.7	59.1	58.1	58.2	57.3	55.9	55.8	55.3	55.4	59.9	59.0	57.1	55.5	57.9
1954	55.5	56.1	56.0	56.7	57.3	57.9	58.1	58.3	59.7	60.9	62.3	63.2	55.9	57.3	58.4	62.1	58.4
1955	64.1	65.2	66.0	66.1	66.5	66.7	67.4	67.0	67.2	67.4	67.5	67.2	65.1	66.4	67.2	67.4	66.5
1956	67.0	66.3	67.1	67.4	65.0	66.7	66.4	65.1	64.2	65.3	66.7	62.1	66.4	66.4	65.4	65.2	66.1
1957	65.4	65.3	65.3	64.8	65.0	65.3	65.2	65.1	64.2	63.4	62.7	62.1	65.3	65.0	64.5	62.8	64.6
1958	62.1	61.6	62.0	62.2	63.4	65.5	66.2	67.1	68.7	69.4	70.4	73.2	61.9	63.7	67.5	70.8	65.7
1959	71.4	72.1	73.7	74.0	74.2	73.7	73.4	73.1	73.3	72.7	71.9	73.2	72.5	73.9	73.3	72.6	73.1
1960	72.9	72.1	70.8	70.9	71.0	71.1	71.4	71.4	71.5	71.2	70.8	70.4	71.9	71.0	71.4	70.8	71.3
1961	70.9	71.4	72.7	73.9	74.8	75.7	75.7	76.7	76.4	77.5	78.5	78.8	71.7	74.8	76.5	78.3	75.3
1962	78.8	79.6	80.0	79.6	78.7	77.9	78.7	79.5	79.9	79.9	80.8	81.0	79.6	78.7	79.3	80.5	79.6
1963	81.6	82.4	83.2	83.9	84.7	84.5	84.1	84.7	85.7	86.3	86.5	86.7	82.4	84.3	84.8	86.5	84.5
1964	87.2	88.5	88.2	89.3	90.2	90.4	90.8	91.8	92.7	92.8	93.0	91.7	87.6	89.9	91.7	92.5	90.6
1965	94.5	94.8	95.2	95.0	95.6	95.3	95.1	95.8	97.3	97.0	98.0	98.1	94.8	95.2	95.2	98.0	96.0
1966	99.3	100.8	101.5	101.5	100.2	99.2	100.1	101.3	101.2	96.7	98.0	96.4	100.9	101.2	101.2	98.9	99.0
1967	97.4	97.0	96.7	97.1	97.9	99.2	106.1	101.5	105.1	102.5	103.2	104.4	99.1	98.1	107.3	103.4	100.0
1968	104.4	105.3	105.7	104.7	105.4	106.0	106.5	105.3	108.1	105.5	108.2	107.3	105.2	105.1	107.2	107.0	107.2
1969	112.2	112.1	111.7	112.7	112.2	111.2	110.2	110.0	110.8	108.7	109.5	107.5	112.0	112.0	110.4	108.6	111.5
1970	107.3	106.3	105.3	104.5	105.1	105.5	104.5	104.7	104.5	104.5	106.5	107.3	106.2	105.1	104.5	106.2	105.3
1971	108.4	110.0	111.9	112.9	113.7	113.5	113.1	113.7	114.5	124.4	114.5	116.4	110.7	113.3	114.0	115.3	115.5
1972	119.2	120.7	123.0	123.0	122.9	123.1	124.1	126.0	127.5	124.6	130.7	131.6	120.7	123.0	125.9	130.1	125.0
1973	132.4	134.1	134.2	133.4	133.5	133.1	132.2	131.6	130.5	135.0	130.1	131.4	133.6	133.3	131.4	130.7	132.2
1974	128.7	128.0	127.8	126.1	125.5	123.8	123.3	120.3	116.5	113.5	111.2	109.2	128.1	125.1	120.0	111.3	121.0
1975	107.7	107.2	107.8	111.0	113.4	115.8	118.2	119.0	120.6	122.0	122.4	122.8	107.7	113.4	119.7	130.3	117.9
1976	126.1	128.0	128.6	129.3	130.5	131.6	132.1	131.9	132.4	132.0	133.5	132.8	127.6	130.2	132.2	133.4	130.3
1977	134.5	136.5	138.0	138.5	138.9	139.8	138.5	140.5	144.1	142.9	141.6	142.4	132.5	139.2	140.2	142.3	141.5
1978	147.7	147.3	149.3	146.4	147.6	146.5	145.2	144.6	144.5	147.9	147.6	147.2	148.5	146.1	144.7	147.6	145.5
1979	141.0	140.3	137.1	133.4	144.5	144.0	135.1	138.1	141.2	141.4	140.1	143.0	142.5	145.0	135.2	140.7	140.8
1980	142.1	140.7	141.7	133.9	134.5	132.0	142.0	142.4	139.7	136.6	143.0	140.2	135.7	144.3	135.4	139.7	138.1
1981	142.1	135.7	134.7	144.6	144.5	143.2	136.2	136.9	160.0	136.9	139.4	136.2	147.6	144.3	135.0	143.7	140.5
1982	135.2	147.1	150.2	152.5	154.4	157.3	158.2	163.4	164.1	163.4	162.5	163.8	142.6	154.7	165.0	153.6	151.2
1983	164.6	166.5	167.2	165.9	166.9	167.3	168.5	169.5	170.2	171.2	171.1	174.0	166.4	166.7	165.3	172.1	168.3

920. COMPOSITE INDEX OF 4 ROUGHLY COINCIDENT INDICATORS (1967=100)

Year	Jan.	Feb.	Mar.	Apr.	May	June	July	Aug.	Sept.	Oct.	Nov.	Dec.	I Q	II Q	III Q	IV Q	Annual
															AVERAGE FOR PERIOD		
1952	57.9	58.8	58.7	58.5	58.8	58.4	57.3	59.9	61.6	62.5	62.8	63.4	58.5	58.6	59.6	62.9	59.9
1953	63.0	64.3	64.4	64.9	65.0	64.7	64.1	64.1	63.4	63.1	61.9	60.8	64.3	64.9	64.1	61.9	63.8
1954	61.0	60.0	59.4	59.1	58.9	58.9	58.7	58.7	59.0	59.4	60.4	61.2	59.8	59.0	58.8	60.3	59.5
1955	61.3	62.2	63.2	64.3	65.2	65.6	65.9	66.2	66.7	67.4	67.8	68.2	62.6	65.0	66.4	67.8	65.5
1956	68.3	68.2	68.2	68.8	68.4	68.4	65.9	68.2	68.9	69.6	69.4	69.3	68.2	68.5	67.7	69.4	68.5
1957	68.6	70.0	69.9	69.3	68.9	69.1	69.1	69.1	68.4	67.7	66.2	65.4	69.1	69.1	68.9	66.6	68.4
1958	64.3	63.0	62.1	61.0	61.2	62.1	63.1	63.6	64.2	64.6	66.2	65.9	63.1	61.4	63.6	65.6	63.0
1959	67.0	67.7	68.8	69.8	70.6	70.8	70.2	68.1	67.9	67.6	68.3	70.9	67.8	70.4	68.7	68.9	70.0
1960	71.9	71.6	71.0	71.3	70.9	70.4	70.0	69.7	69.3	69.1	68.1	67.2	71.5	70.9	69.7	68.1	70.3
1961	67.0	66.8	67.2	67.5	68.3	69.3	69.4	70.1	70.2	71.0	72.0	72.4	67.0	68.4	69.9	71.8	69.5
1962	72.0	72.7	73.2	73.7	73.7	73.6	74.0	74.2	74.2	74.4	74.7	74.4	72.6	73.7	74.1	74.5	73.7
1963	74.5	75.1	75.4	76.0	76.3	76.6	76.8	76.9	77.4	78.0	77.7	78.3	75.0	76.3	77.0	78.0	76.5
1964	78.4	79.4	79.5	80.4	81.0	81.2	81.9	82.5	83.1	82.1	83.7	85.1	79.2	80.9	82.5	83.6	81.5
1965	85.4	86.3	86.8	87.3	87.9	88.5	89.4	89.6	90.2	91.2	92.2	93.0	86.1	87.9	89.7	92.1	76.5
1966	93.6	94.3	95.8	95.5	96.0	97.1	97.3	97.6	97.7	98.3	98.3	98.6	94.4	96.2	97.5	98.4	100.0
1967	102.8	103.5	104.0	104.4	105.2	106.0	106.6	106.8	107.1	107.7	102.0	103.3	103.8	105.2	106.8	101.4	100.0
1968	109.3	109.2	110.5	110.8	110.8	111.4	112.1	112.6	112.6	112.9	108.5	108.9	109.8	111.0	112.4	102.3	111.4
1969	110.8	110.8	110.8	110.1	110.1	109.7	109.8	109.3	109.0	106.7	111.9	112.0	110.8	110.1	109.4	106.7	110.7
1970	114.0	108.5	108.8	109.1	109.8	116.9	109.6	109.3	110.1	110.2	105.8	107.6	110.6	116.3	109.4	106.7	105.7
1971	114.0	114.4	115.6	116.6	117.2	116.9	117.8	119.3	119.9	121.8	111.0	112.2	114.7	116.9	119.0	111.1	118.4
1972	125.5	127.0	127.4	127.2	127.5	127.8	128.2	127.8	128.5	129.7	123.2	124.5	126.6	127.5	128.4	120.1	128.4
1973	128.7	128.0	127.8	127.6	128.2	128.3	128.2	127.3	126.5	125.2	130.7	129.8	127.5	128.0	127.3	130.1	116.2
1974	116.2	114.6	113.3	113.3	114.1	114.9	117.3	117.3	118.1	118.5	122.2	118.4	114.1	114.1	117.0	111.9	133.6
1975	121.4	122.0	123.0	124.3	125.2	128.3	125.3	125.5	125.6	125.3	118.2	119.5	122.6	124.6	125.5	119.0	114.6
1976	137.1	138.3	139.0	131.6	132.5	133.6	134.3	134.6	135.8	136.6	126.8	127.8	132.5	132.6	134.9	135.6	133.6
1977	137.1	138.3	140.0	143.0	143.1	144.2	145.0	145.6	146.1	147.4	137.2	138.1	138.5	143.4	145.7	145.3	144.6
1978	150.7	145.6	151.2	149.1	150.6	144.1	151.0	150.6	150.4	150.3	148.4	149.7	150.0	150.1	150.7	148.5	150.2
1979	150.7	145.6	148.1	143.0	142.4	141.1	140.8	141.2	142.7	144.2	149.9	150.0	149.5	142.9	141.6	150.1	144.8
1980	150.8	147.2	147.2	145.1	146.9	147.5	147.6	146.5	146.7	144.5	145.3	146.1	147.1	147.2	147.1	145.2	146.8
1981	136.5	135.3	139.6	138.0	138.8	137.3	136.4	135.2	134.5	132.9	132.7	140.9	139.2	138.0	135.4	132.7	146.1
1982	132.1	133.5	139.2	135.8	137.9	139.8	140.7	140.8	143.3	145.0	145.9	147.5	137.8	137.8	141.6	146.7	135.3
1983	145.3	150.6	151.1	152.6	153.9	155.4	155.7	156.0	156.5	156.5	157.7	158.8	150.4	154.0	156.1	146.7	134.5
1984	158.4	159.0	157.3	160.5	160.2	159.5	159.7	160.9	160.0	156.8	161.6	163.0	158.9	160.1	160.5	157.8	160.3

930. COMPOSITE INDEX OF 6 LAGGING INDICATORS (1967=100)

Year	Jan.	Feb.	Mar.	Apr.	May	June	July	Aug.	Sept.	Oct.	Nov.	Dec.	I Q	II Q	III Q	IV Q	Annual
													AVERAGE FOR PERIOD				
1953	53.3	53.8	54.1	55.2	56.5	56.8	56.9	57.3	57.9	58.1	58.3	58.5	53.7	56.2	57.4	58.3	56.4
1954	57.9	57.3	56.1	55.3	54.9	53.9	54.2	53.5	53.2	53.2	53.0	52.9	57.2	54.8	53.6	53.0	54.6
1955	52.6	52.7	53.0	52.6	53.2	53.9	54.2	55.5	56.9	58.2	59.4	59.4	52.8	53.2	55.9	59.0	55.2
1956	60.0	60.2	61.2	62.5	63.9	64.1	66.1	64.9	65.9	66.0	66.6	66.4	60.5	63.6	65.6	66.3	64.0
1957	67.0	66.6	67.0	67.8	68.1	68.1	68.4	71.0	72.3	71.8	72.6	73.2	66.9	68.0	70.6	72.5	69.5
1958	71.8	69.5	69.2	67.8	66.1	63.3	62.4	61.9	63.5	64.0	63.8	64.7	70.1	65.2	62.7	64.2	65.5
1959	64.1	64.0	64.3	64.3	66.1	65.2	73.2	71.4	75.1	75.8	76.4	77.2	64.1	65.2	72.0	76.0	69.6
1960	74.9	76.2	77.0	77.3	78.5	79.4	78.4	78.4	78.4	77.1	76.4	77.2	76.0	78.4	77.8	76.5	77.2
1961	76.7	76.4	75.8	75.0	74.5	73.7	73.2	73.4	73.6	73.1	72.6	73.0	76.3	74.4	73.3	72.9	74.2
1962	73.8	73.5	73.9	74.5	74.8	75.0	75.5	76.2	76.4	77.1	77.5	78.0	73.7	75.0	76.2	77.5	75.6
1963	77.9	78.1	78.3	78.3	78.5	79.0	79.5	80.0	80.3	80.7	82.1	82.4	78.1	78.6	79.9	81.7	79.6
1964	81.9	82.9	83.4	83.8	83.8	84.4	83.7	85.0	85.9	86.6	85.7	86.1	82.7	83.9	84.9	86.1	84.4
1965	87.0	87.7	88.2	88.6	89.8	90.4	89.7	90.7	90.5	91.2	91.9	92.3	87.6	89.5	90.3	91.8	89.8
1966	92.4	93.3	93.6	94.6	95.2	96.4	97.0	97.5	98.5	97.7	99.0	99.3	93.1	95.4	97.3	98.7	96.2
1967	99.3	99.4	100.3	100.2	100.2	100.4	100.5	99.8	100.5	100.5	99.6	99.3	99.7	100.3	100.2	99.8	100.0
1968	99.8	100.4	100.3	101.1	101.0	101.4	101.5	102.2	102.3	102.6	103.2	104.3	100.2	101.5	102.1	103.4	101.8
1969	104.8	104.6	105.9	107.0	108.0	109.2	109.5	109.2	110.5	111.5	111.3	111.0	105.1	108.1	109.9	111.1	108.7
1970	114.8	115.8	115.1	113.7	113.6	113.2	113.5	114.1	113.6	113.5	112.8	111.0	114.9	113.8	113.7	112.4	113.7
1971	109.1	108.8	108.3	107.2	107.3	107.7	106.9	107.0	106.9	106.4	108.0	105.9	108.7	106.9	106.6	106.1	107.0
1972	104.4	104.2	104.3	104.1	105.6	105.7	105.4	105.0	104.9	105.1	105.1	104.8	104.3	105.2	105.1	105.0	104.9
1973	106.2	107.3	107.6	108.1	109.4	110.7	112.0	112.0	113.2	113.3	113.6	114.5	107.0	109.9	112.4	113.8	110.8
1974	114.6	114.2	113.6	114.7	116.7	117.6	117.1	117.2	117.6	118.7	119.7	121.1	114.2	116.5	117.6	119.8	117.0
1975	121.0	119.0	118.6	116.5	112.8	107.1	108.1	106.3	105.9	106.0	105.1	104.8	119.5	112.2	106.9	105.0	110.9
1976	104.3	103.8	103.3	102.9	103.0	103.2	103.2	103.2	103.4	104.2	103.8	103.7	103.8	103.0	103.4	103.9	103.5
1977	103.8	104.2	104.2	104.7	105.2	106.3	106.2	107.2	107.7	108.3	109.0	109.4	104.1	105.4	107.0	108.9	106.4
1978	111.4	111.6	112.3	111.6	112.0	113.7	114.3	114.8	115.4	115.3	117.1	118.0	111.8	112.7	114.8	116.8	114.0
1979	119.2	119.7	118.8	121.7	121.0	122.3	122.3	123.3	124.7	125.8	126.1	126.1	119.2	121.7	123.4	126.1	122.6
1980	126.2	127.1	130.2	132.3	132.3	122.5	122.3	120.5	119.4	119.0	120.1	123.0	127.8	129.1	120.6	120.7	124.6
1981	121.7	120.7	119.0	119.0	122.3	122.4	122.5	123.3	123.4	122.1	124.5	124.4	120.5	121.2	123.5	123.7	122.4
1982	126.5	125.6	125.8	126.0	126.3	126.1	126.5	123.3	123.4	122.1	120.5	119.2	126.0	126.4	124.2	120.5	124.3
1983	117.8	117.9	116.9	115.5	114.2	114.6	115.6	114.0	114.4	114.1	115.1	116.0	117.5	114.8	114.2	115.1	115.4
1984	115.0	116.7	118.1	120.6	121.2	122.8	123.5	124.0	123.4	124.1	124.5	124.4	116.6	121.5	123.6	124.3	124.2
1985	126.5	126.7	127.5	126.9	126.4	126.6	127.6	127.6	127.6	130.1	130.1	130.1	126.0	126.4	127.4	130.1	128.3
1986	131.6	131.9	132.9	133.5	134.9	134.9	135.3	135.6	136.0	138.5	138.5	139.5	132.1	134.4	136.0	138.1	135.3
1987	140.5	141.1	142.3	140.5	141.4	141.6	141.8	142.2	141.6	143.7	143.4	142.4	141.3	141.2	141.9	143.2	141.9

Source: *Business Conditions Digest.*

C/L Ratio
Graphic History: 1952–1988

940. Ratio, coincident index to lagging index

Historical Data: 1952–1988

940. RATIO, COINCIDENT COMPOSITE INDEX TO LAGGING COMPOSITE INDEX[1] (1967=100)

Year	Jan	Feb	Mar	Apr	May	Jun	Jul	Aug	Sep	Oct	Nov	Dec		AVERAGE FOR PERIOD			
1953	119.7	119.5	120.0	117.6	115.0	113.9	114.1	111.9	109.5	108.6	106.2	103.9	119.7	115.5	111.8	106.2	113.3
1954	103.6	104.7	105.5	106.9	107.3	108.5	108.5	109.7	110.9	112.1	114.0	115.7	104.6	107.6	109.7	113.9	109.0
1955	117.7	118.2	119.8	122.2	127.3	121.7	122.1	117.2	117.2	115.8	114.1	114.8	118.6	122.2	118.8	114.9	118.6
1956	113.8	113.3	111.4	110.1	107.0	106.2	99.7	105.1	104.6	105.5	104.1	105.3	112.8	107.8	103.1	105.0	107.2
1957	103.9	105.1	104.3	102.2	101.2	101.5	92.7	99.1	94.6	94.3	91.7	89.3	104.4	101.6	97.6	91.8	98.9
1958	89.6	90.9	89.7	90.0	94.7	98.1	101.2	98.1	100.1	100.9	103.8	101.9	90.1	94.3	101.5	102.2	97.0
1959	104.5	105.8	107.0	108.6	106.8	101.7	98.1	90.4	94.3	89.1	91.2	94.3	105.8	105.7	94.1	91.5	99.6
1960	96.0	94.0	92.2	90.0	90.2	91.7	88.9	88.8	94.7	94.4	87.8	89.4	94.1	90.4	89.1	89.6	90.8
1961	87.4	87.2	88.8	90.0	91.7	94.0	94.7	94.1	95.6	97.1	99.2	95.4	87.8	91.9	95.4	97.3	93.4
1962	97.6	98.9	99.1	98.9	98.5	97.2	97.5	94.7	95.6	96.5	96.4	95.0	98.3	98.5	95.4	96.1	97.5
1963	95.6	96.2	96.3	95.9	98.5	97.0	97.4	96.1	96.4	96.6	96.5	95.8	96.4	97.1	96.4	96.4	96.2
1964	96.0	95.8	95.3	97.0	97.2	96.3	96.4	97.5	97.4	96.7	96.4	94.6	95.8	97.2	97.2	95.7	96.6
1965	98.2	98.1	98.4	97.9	96.3	98.4	98.4	97.7	98.2	98.8	98.8	95.0	98.2	98.8	99.4	97.1	99.0
1966	101.3	101.1	101.9	101.0	100.4	98.6	98.9	100.3	100.1	100.6	99.3	98.8	101.6	100.7	100.2	99.7	100.5
1967	100.1	99.2	99.6	101.1	100.0	100.1	100.3	100.1	100.2	100.6	99.3	99.3	99.3	98.8	99.3	100.2	99.7
1968	103.0	103.6	104.3	103.6	103.6	104.1	105.0	104.4	105.1	105.1	104.4	103.7	103.7	103.7	104.7	104.8	104.1
1969	104.0	104.1	104.3	103.3	102.6	102.0	102.0	102.4	101.6	100.5	100.2	96.9	104.1	102.3	102.3	100.8	102.5
1970	96.5	96.5	96.3	97.2	96.9	96.7	96.7	95.8	94.9	94.6	93.8	95.9	96.5	96.8	96.2	94.9	96.1
1971	99.5	99.7	100.0	101.8	102.1	104.4	103.0	102.1	103.0	100.7	104.7	105.9	99.9	102.8	102.8	104.7	112.9
1972	109.2	109.8	110.7	111.4	111.5	113.6	113.6	113.2	114.2	114.3	115.1	118.8	111.1	113.2	114.3	116.0	115.7
1973	118.2	118.4	118.6	116.3	116.5	115.4	114.5	113.4	113.2	110.5	108.3	102.1	116.0	110.0	108.3	101.8	108.1
1974	112.3	111.9	112.5	110.4	109.9	109.6	105.7	102.1	109.4	108.3	95.9	97.8	95.9	95.9	109.4	113.2	105.1
1975	96.0	96.3	95.3	98.4	101.2	105.8	114.2	114.2	121.9	120.9	118.2	123.2	118.4	120.9	121.9	125.6	120.6
1976	116.4	118.4	119.7	120.9	120.5	121.2	122.6	123.9	126.9	126.1	127.1	126.2	121.2	121.9	126.9	127.1	125.6
1977	123.1	123.9	125.7	128.1	126.9	125.7	126.9	126.2	119.5	123.9	127.3	119.0	122.2	126.9	127.1	126.9	126.3
1978	125.3	124.8	127.3	122.5	124.5	123.1	123.5	121.0	117.4	117.3	120.3	118.8	117.3	122.4	123.5	119.1	116.3
1979	119.4	117.7	113.7	109.7	109.9	112.4	115.6	114.9	119.2	122.1	120.3	113.3	122.4	110.7	123.5	120.3	119.3
1980	120.6	122.0	123.7	123.6	120.8	120.5	109.3	110.1	108.8	110.5	110.0	111.2	121.4	123.9	117.4	109.6	109.6
1981	109.4	111.4	110.7	109.3	109.9	108.5	109.0	126.2	108.8	105.2	114.6	112.2	120.2	118.2	108.8	110.0	124.5
1982	114.0	113.2	115.1	117.0	120.0	122.8	123.9	121.3	124.5	122.0	127.0	127.2	120.2	108.8	125.6	127.0	118.5
1983	130.0	129.0	127.9	126.5	125.2	124.4	123.8	121.7	122.3	125.4	121.2	122.1	125.1	125.4	121.2	121.2	124.5
1984	120.4	120.5	119.9	120.4	118.8	118.2	118.0	116.7	118.0	119.4	118.0	116.8	119.4	118.0	118.0	116.5	118.5
1985	115.9	115.8	114.5	117.9	116.2	115.6	115.9	115.6	116.3	116.6	116.1	117.6	115.4	116.3	116.1	116.1	116.1
1986																	
1987																	

Source: Business Conditions Digest.

Leading Index Components

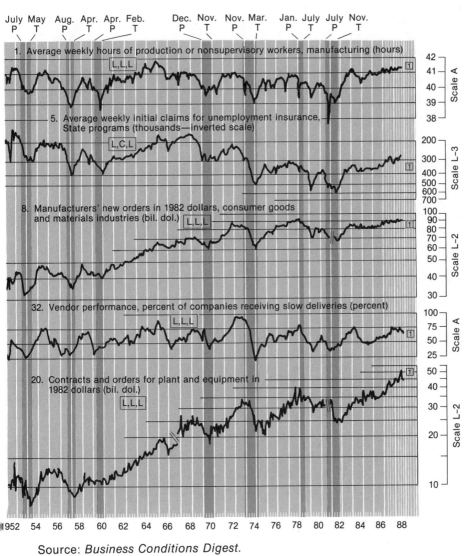

Leading Index Components (cont'd)

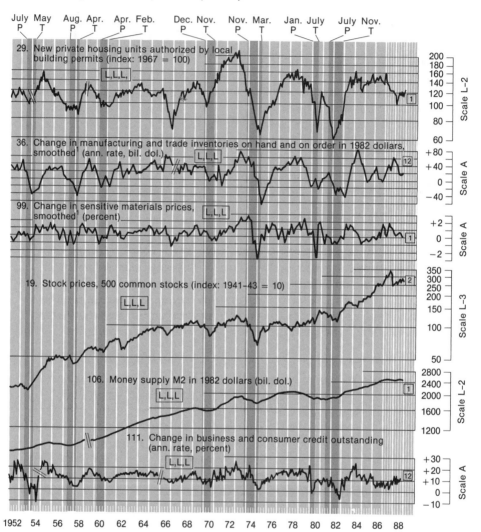

Source: *Business Conditions Digest.*

Coincident Index Components

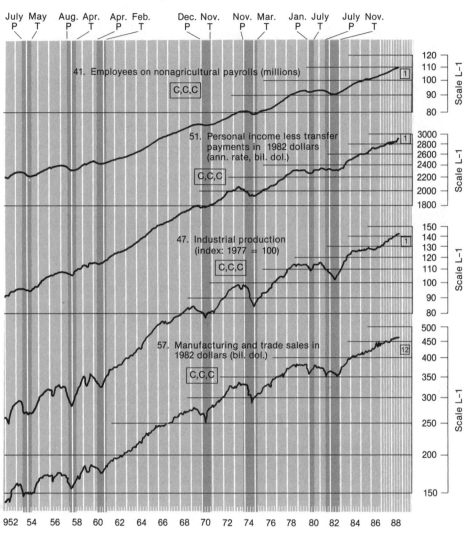

Source: *Business Conditions Digest.*

Lagging Index Components

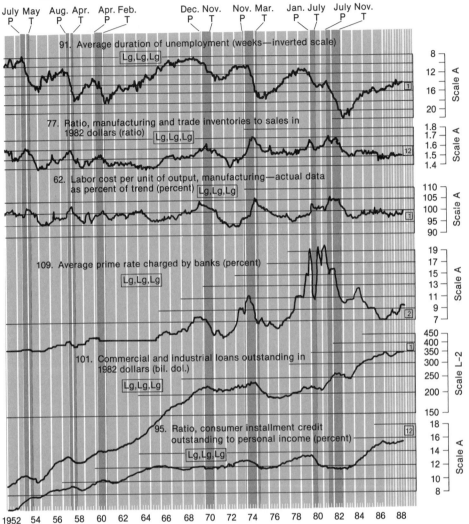

Source: *Business Conditions Digest.*

History of Primary and Partial Business Cycles: 1955–1988

Shown on the following page is the Gantt chart for 1955–1988, which displays five complete Primary Business Cycles and four partial cycles. The primary cycles, which are labeled P1, P2, P3, and so on, are shown in dark circles (●), whereas the partial or minor cycles, which are labeled m1, m2, m3, and m4, are shown in squares (■). The line of white circles (○) in Cycle P5 shows the next events that must happen to complete Cycle 5 in the future.

Following the Gantt chart, this appendix contains the actual dates and values of the turning points for each component of the Primary Business Cycle since 1955.

History of Primary and Partial Business Cycles

Primary Business Cycle Turning Points

Recession = problem

1. M2 money supply bottom
2. Stock market bottom
3. C/L ratio bottom
4. Leading indicator bottom
5. Capacity utilization bottom
6. Coincident indicator bottom
7. Official: "Expansion in progress"
8. Lagging indicator bottom
9. Consumer credit ratio bottom
10. Producer price inflation bottom
11. Consumer price inflation bottom
12.-19. All 7 interest rates and velocity of money bottom

Inflation = problem

20. M2 money supply peak
21. Stock market peak
22. C/L ratio peak
23. Leading indicator peak
24. Capacity utilization peak
25. Coincident indicator peak
26. Official: "Recession in progress"
27. Lagging indicator peak
28. Consumer credit ratio peak
29. Producer price inflation peak
30. Consumer price inflation peak
31.-38. All 7 interest rates and velocity of money peak

TURNING POINT HISTORY

Cyclical Turning Points for M2 Money Supply in 1982 Dollars

	Bottoms			Peaks	
Cycle No.	Date	Value	Cycle No.	Date	Value
P1	1/58	894.2	P1	8/59	980.8
P2	10/59	975.7	m1	6/66	1403.0
m1	8/66	1396.9	P2	2/69	1540.1
P3	4/70	1483.1	P3	1/73	1837.6
P4	1/75	1683.4	P4	1/78	1996.3
m2	5/80	1805.6	m2	9/80	1849.1
P5	7/81	1809.4	m4	1/87	2450.4
m4	12/87	2423.6	P5	?	?

Source: *Business Conditions Digest.*

Cyclical Turning Points for S&P 500 Stock Index: Values Are Monthly Averages for Daily Closing Prices

	Bottoms			Peaks	
Cycle No.	Date	Value	Cycle No.	Date	Value
P1	12/57	40.33	P1	7/59	59.74
P2	10/60	55.73	m1	1/66	93.32
m1	10/66	77.13	P2	12/68	106.48
P3	6/70	75.57	P3	1/73	118.42
P4	12/74	67.07	P4	2/80	115.34
m2	4/80	102.97	m2	11/80	135.65
P5	7/82	109.38	m3	10/83	167.65
m3	7/84	151.08	m4	8/87	329.36
m4	12/87	240.96	P5	?	?

Source: *Business Conditions Digest.*

Cyclical Turning Points for C/L Ratio Economic Indicators

	Bottoms			Peaks	
Cycle No.	Date	Value	Cycle No.	Date	Value
P1	12/57	89.3	P1	4/59	108.6
P2	12/60	87.0	m1	3/66	101.9
m1	5/67	98.8	P2	11/68	105.1
P3	11/70	93.8	P3	12/72	118.8
P4	1/75	96.0	P4	4/78	128.1
m2	4/80	109.7	m2	3/81	123.7
P5	7/82	108.4	P5	?	?
False signals	11/63	94.6	False signals	12/61	99.2
	1/87	114.5		1/84	130.0

Source: *Business Conditions Digest.*

Cyclical Turning Points for Leading Economic Indicators

	Bottoms			Peaks	
Cycle No.	Date	Value	Cycle No.	Date	Value
P1	2/58	61.6	P1	5/59	74.2
P2	12/60	70.4	m1	3/66	101.9
m1	12/66	96.4	P2	4/69	112.7
P3	10/70	104.4	P3	3/73	134.2
P4	2/75	107.6	P4	3/79	149.3
m2	5/80	130.9	m2	4/81	144.6
P5	3/82	134.7	m3	5/84	167.9
m3	7/84	163.8	m4	10/87	192.4
m4	1/88	189.2	P5	?	?

Source: *Business Conditions Digest.*

Cyclical Turning Points for Capacity Utilization Rate: Manufacturing

	Bottoms			Peaks	
Cycle No.	Date	Value	Cycle No.	Date	Value
P1	4/58	71.3%	P1	5/59	84.9%
P2	2/61	73.5	m1	10/66	91.6
m1	7/67	84.9	P2	3/69	88.1
P3	11/70	75.1	P3	10/73	87.7
P4	3/75	69.9	P4	12/78	86.5
m2	7/80	76.1	m2	7/81	79.8
P5	12/82	68.0	P5	?	?

Source: *Business Conditions Digest.*

Cyclical Turning Points for Coincident Economic Indicators

	Bottoms			Peaks	
Cycle No.	Date	Value	Cycle No.	Date	Value
P1	4/58	61.0	P1	1/60	71.9
P2	2/61	66.8	P2	10/69	112.9
P3	11/70	105.8	P3	11/73	130.7
P4	3/75	113.0	P4	7/79	151.0
m2	7/80	140.8	m2	7/81	147.6
P5	12/82	132.6	P5	?	?

Source: *Business Conditions Digest.*

Cyclical Turning Points for Lagging Economic Indicators

	Bottoms			Peaks	
Cycle No.	Date	Value	Cycle No.	Date	Value
P1	8/58	61.9	P1	6/60	79.2
P2	11/61	72.6	P2	3/70	115.1
P3	2/72	104.2	P3	12/74	121.1
P4	4/76	102.8	P4	4/80	132.3
m2	4/81	119.0	m2	6/82	126.5
P5	7/83	113.6	P5	?	?

Source: *Business Conditions Digest.*

Cyclical Turning Points for Ratio of Consumer Installment Credit to Personal Income

	Bottoms			Peaks	
Cycle No.	Date	Value	Cycle No.	Date	Value
P1	11/58	9.13	P1	12/60	10.80
P2	11/61	10.31	m1	7/65	12.64
m1	2/68	12.05	P2	2/70	12.43
P3	4/70	12.08	P3	4/74	13.27
P4	2/76	12.05	P4	6/79	13.96
P5	11/82	11.83	P5	?	?

Source: *Business Conditions Digest.*

Cyclical Turning Points for Four-Quarter Percentage Change in Producer Price Index

	Bottoms			Peaks	
Cycle No.	Date	Value	Cycle No.	Date	Value
P1	Q1, 59	0.316%	P1	Q1, 59	0.633%
P2	Q4, 61	−0.631	m1	Q3, 66	3.704
m1	Q3, 67	−0.595	P2	Q4, 69	4.638
P3	Q1, 71	2.732	P3	Q4, 74	22.484
P4	Q4, 75	4.371	P4	Q1, 80	15.641
P5	Q4, 86	−3.485	m4	Q2, 87	6.900
m4	Q1, 88	1.950	P5	?	?

Source: *Business Conditions Digest.*

Cyclical Turning Points for Four-Quarter Percentage Change in Consumer Price Index

	Bottoms			Peaks	
Cycle No.	Date	Value	Cycle No.	Date	Value
P1	Q2, 59	0.346%	P1	Q1, 60	1.730%
P2	Q4, 61	0.671	m1	Q4, 66	3.785
m1	Q4, 67	2.735	P2	Q1, 70	6.145
P3	Q3, 72	2.941	P3	Q4, 74	12.200
P4	Q4, 76	5.072	P4	Q2, 80	14.405
P5	Q4, 86	1.284	m4	Q2, 87	5.200
m4	Q1, 88	2.500	P5	?	?

Source: *Business Conditions Digest.*

Cyclical Turning Points for Prime Lending Rate

	Bottoms			Peaks	
Cycle No.	Date	Value	Cycle No.	Date	Value
P1	8/58	3.50%	P1	7/60	5.00%
P2	11/65	4.50	m1	12/66	6.00
m1	10/67	5.50	P2	2/70	8.50
P3	3/72	4.75	P3	9/74	12.00
P4	4/77	6.25	m2	4/80	19.77
m2	8/80	11.12	P4	8/81	20.50
m3	7/83	10.50	m3	8/84	13.00
P5	3/87	7.50	m4	10/87	9.07
m4	4/88	8.50	P5	?	?

Source: *Business Conditions Digest.*

Cyclical Turning Points for 91-Day T-Bill Rate

	Bottoms			Peaks	
Cycle No.	Date	Value	Cycle No.	Date	Value
P1	6/58	0.88%	P1	12/59	4.57%
P2	12/60	2.27	m1	10/66	5.39
m1	6/67	3.48	P2	1/70	7.91
P3	2/72	3.18	P3	8/74	8.74
P4	12/76	4.35	m2	3/80	15.53
m2	6/80	7.00	P4	5/81	16.30
m3	10/82	7.75	m3	8/84	10.49
P5	10/86	5.18	m4	10/87	6.40
m4	3/88	5.69	P5	?	?

Source: *Business Conditions Digest.*

Cyclical Turning Points for Federal Funds Rate

	Bottoms			Peaks	
Cycle No.	Date	Value	Cycle No.	Date	Value
P1	5/58	0.63%	P1	11/59	4.00%
P2	7/61	1.16	m1	11/66	5.77
m1	7/67	3.79	P2	8/69	9.19
P3	2/72	3.29	P3	7/74	12.92
P4	1/77	4.61	m2	4/80	17.61
m2	6/80	9.03	P4	7/81	19.08
m3	2/83	8.51	m3	8/84	11.64
P5	10/86	5.85	m4	10/87	7.29
m4	3/88	6.58	P5	?	?

Source: *Business Conditions Digest.*

Cyclical Turning Points for Long-Term T-Bond Rate

	Bottoms			Peaks	
Cycle No.	Date	Value	Cycle No.	Date	Value
P1	4/58	3.12%	P1	1/60	4.37%
P2	5/61	3.73	m1	8/66	4.80
m1	1/67	4.40	P2	6/70	6.99
P3	10/71	5.46	P3	8/74	7.33
P4	12/76	6.38	m2	3/80	11.77
m2	6/80	9.40	P4	9/81	14.14
m3	11/82	10.18	m3	6/84	13.00
P5	1/87	7.60	m4	10/87	9.61
m4	2/88	8.41	P5	?	?

Source: *Business Conditions Digest.*

Cyclical Turning Points for Corporate Bond Rate

	Bottoms			Peaks	
Cycle No.	Date	Value	Cycle No.	Date	Value
P1	6/58	3.61%	P1	10/59	5.37%
P2	3/61	4.37	m1	9/66	6.14
m1	2/67	5.35	P2	6/70	9.70
P3	1/72	7.36	P3	9/74	10.44
P4	12/76	7.90	m2	3/80	14.08
m2	6/80	11.12	P4	9/81	16.97
m3	5/83	11.24	m3	6/84	14.49
P5	2/87	8.58	m4	10/87	10.80
m4	2/88	9.43	P5	?	?

Source: *Business Conditions Digest.*

Cyclical Turning Points for Municipal Bond Rate

	Bottoms			Peaks	
Cycle No.	Date	Value	Cycle No.	Date	Value
P1	1/58	2.91%	P1	9/59	3.78%
P2	11/62	3.04	m1	9/66	4.12
m1	2/67	3.52	P2	5/70	7.00
P3	11/72	5.02	P3	12/74	7.05
P4	11/77	5.49	m2	3/80	9.17
m2	5/80	7.59	P4	1/82	13.28
m3	4/83	9.05	m3	6/84	10.67
P5	2/87	6.61	m4	10/87	8.70
m4	2/88	7.49	P5	?	?

Source: *Business Conditions Digest.*

Cyclical Turning Points for FHA Mortgage Rate

	Bottoms			Peaks	
Cycle No.	Date	Value	Cycle No.	Date	Value
P1	7/58	5.35%	P1	1/60	6.24%
P2	7/65	5.44	m1	11/66	6.81
m1	4/67	6.29	P2	2/70	9.29
P3	3/72	7.45	P3	9/74	10.38
P4	1/77	8.45	m2	3/80	14.63
m2	6/80	11.85	P4	9/81	18.55
m3	5/83	12.41	m3	5/84	15.01
P5	1/87	8.79	m4	9/87	11.22
m4	2/88	9.86	P5	?	?

Source: *Business Conditions Digest.*

Cyclical Turning Points for Velocity of Money (Ratio of Personal Income to M2)

	Bottoms			Peaks	
Cycle No.	Date	Value	Cycle No.	Date	Value
P1	6/58	1.311	P1	5/60	1.362%
P2	3/65	1.238	m1	1/67	1.302
m1	10/67	1.263	P2	4/70	1.407
P3	6/72	1.276	P3	10/74	1.389
P4	1/77	1.295	P4	7/81	1.483
m3	8/83	1.331	m3	3/84	1.374
P5	1/87	1.284	P5	?	?

Source: *Business Conditions Digest.*

Bond Yield-to-Maturity Guide

"Bond-Aid" yield-to-maturity charts were developed as a result of recognizing that:

- Intelligent decisions regarding bond investments must be based, to some extent, on the yield-to-maturity factor
- Yield-to-maturity data are *not published* in financial newspapers on a daily basis (only the current yield is provided in some publications)
- *Existing sources* of yield-to-maturity information made available to investors are either *expensive, time-consuming,* or both (i.e., computers; time-sharing systems; certain higher-priced calculators; and expensive, detailed yield tables)

These charts were designed to provide a practical and inexpensive investment aid to individual investors or money managers who wish to analyze *quickly* the price and yield aspects of bond investments with a reasonable degree of accuracy.

It is assumed that the reader is familiar with the concept of yield to maturity—the true, annualized rate of return that a bond, purchased at any price, will yield when held to maturity. A maturity value of $1,000 has been assumed throughout.

Once familiar with these charts, you will be able to:

- Find the yield to maturity of any bond, within one-tenth of 1 percent, in a matter of seconds
- Analyze specific bonds to see if they meet your own individual investment objectives
- Answer many "what if" questions with respect to future bond prices under different interest rate assumptions

No calculators or mathematical formulas are required. Detailed instructions are provided in the *Users' Guide*.

USERS' GUIDE

Finding the Yield to Maturity of a Bond

Using Bond-Aid yield to maturity charts, you need only three facts to find the yield to maturity of any bond, all of which are quoted in the financial press:

- The bond's *coupon rate* of interest
- The *year* in which the bond *matures*
- The *current price* of the bond

An example will best illustrate the procedure. Suppose that you wish to find the approximate yield to maturity of the following bond:

> **Example:** Maturity value = $1,000
> Coupon rate = $3\frac{1}{4}\%$
> Year of maturity = 1993
> Current price = $770
> Current year = 1988

- *Step 1:* Find the number of years to maturity by subtracting the current year from the year of maturity (1993 − 1988 = five years).

- *Step 2:* Turn to the appropriate yield-to-maturity chart. There is one chart for every number of years to maturity from 1 to 30. Here you should turn to Chart 5, which displays all the possible relationships between price, coupon rate, and yield to maturity for bonds with five years to maturity.
- *Step 3:* Read along the bond purchase price scale until you find this bond's price ($770) or the listed quotation (77).

Now move up the $770 line until you reach the $3\frac{1}{4}$% coupon rate line, which is read on the left-hand vertical scale. The point where the $770 and $3\frac{1}{4}$% lines meet represents your bond.

To find the yield to maturity, look to see where this point lies against the diagonal yield-to-maturity scale. If it falls exactly on a diagonal line, that line represents the yield to maturity. If it falls between the diagonal lines, you can judge the distance between those lines and closely estimate the correct yield to maturity. (Estimation to the nearest tenth is recommended.)

In this case, the point is about $\frac{2}{10}$ of the way between the 9 percent and 10 percent yield-to-maturity lines. Therefore, your estimated answer is 9.20 percent. (The actual calculated value is 9.19 percent.)

Suggestion. If you are evaluating several bonds or tracking specific bonds, it may be helpful to consolidate your findings into a table:

	From Published Quotations				From Bond-Aid Charts	
Company	Coupon Rate	Current Yield	Year of Maturity	Price	Years to Maturity	Yield to Maturity
Bond A	6.5%	7.2%	1993	$ 900	5	9.2%
Bond B	8.0	7.3	2004	1,100	16	6.9

Finding Bonds That Meet Your Investment Objectives

You undoubtedly have one or more specific objectives for your bond portfolio. Therefore, you will be seeking bonds that meet your own criteria with respect to:

1. The yield to maturity
2. Annual income
3. The cost of the investment
4. The number of years to maturity
5. The risk involved in achieving a given return

These yield-to-maturity charts can help you to assess quickly whether any given bond will meet your objectives in terms of Items 1–4. The issue of risk versus return must be left to the individual investor.

Following are three examples that illustrate the use of the charts to find bonds that meet specific investment objectives.

Example 1: Find a corporate bond maturing in ten years that gives at least a 10 percent yield to maturity.

- *Step 1:* Add ten to the current year (1988 + 10 = 1998).
- *Step 2:* Turn to the chart with ten years to maturity.
- *Step 3:* Scan the bond listings for corporate bonds maturing in 1998.
- *Step 4:* When one is found, use the coupon rate and current bond price to find the yield to maturity and see if it exceeds 10 percent.

Bond A, with a coupon rate of 8 percent and a price of $940, would have a yield to maturity of only 8.9 percent; Bond B, with a coupon rate of $7\frac{3}{4}$ percent and a price of $840, would meet your criteria with a yield to maturity of 10.4 percent.

Example 2: Find a bond maturing in eight years with a price of $700 or less that provides a 9 percent yield to maturity.

- *Step 1:* Add eight to the current year (1988 + 8 = 1996).
- *Step 2:* Turn to the chart with eight years to maturity.
- *Step 3:* Scan the bond listings for 1996 bonds selling at $700 or less.
- *Step 4:* When one is found, use the coupon rate and current bond price to find the yield to maturity and test this against your 9 percent goal.

A bond with a coupon rate of 3¾ percent and a price of $690 would give a yield to maturity of 9.4 percent.

Answering "What If" Questions

One fundamental property of a bond is that it allows you to lock in a predetermined return on investment (the yield to maturity)—*provided that you hold the bond to maturity.* However, since the market value of your bond is directly tied to prevailing interest rates, you should ask two important questions:

- What if you wish to cash in your bonds before they mature?
- What if interest rates have changed significantly by the time that you want to sell?

You can now use these charts to evaluate quickly both the downside risk and upside potential of specific bond investments. Some further examples will demonstrate some of the "what if" questions that you can now answer with relative ease.

Example 1: You can buy a ten-year bond with a coupon rate of 8 percent for $935 today. This would give you a yield to maturity of 9.0 percent. What would the market price of your bond be in three years if interest rates went up two percentage points?

In three years, your ten-year bond will have seven years remaining to maturity. If interest rates for bonds in this risk class went up by 2 percent, the price of your bond would change to whatever value gives a yield to maturity of 11 percent, (9 percent + 2 percent). Of course, the coupon rate would still be 8 percent.

- *Step 1:* Turn to the chart with seven years to maturity.
- *Step 2:* Find the point at which the 11 percent yield-to-maturity line meets the 8 percent coupon rate line.
- *Step 3:* See where this point lies against the bond purchase price scale. Here the chart shows that your bond would have a price of $860 with seven years remaining to maturity if interest levels were 11 percent.

Example 2: Using the same bond, how far do interest rates have to fall in the next two years to give you a $200 capital gain on your $935 investment?

In two years, the bond's price would have to be $1,135 ($935 + $200) to produce a $200 capital gain. In two years, the ten-year bond will have eight years remaining to maturity. The coupon rate is 8 percent.

- *Step 1:* Turn to the chart with eight years to maturity.
- *Step 2:* Use the $1,135 bond price and the 8 percent coupon rate to look up the yield to maturity. (Here it is 5.8 percent.) Therefore, the current interest level of 9 percent would have to fall to 5.8 percent, a drop of 3.2 percent, for you to obtain a capital gain of $200 in two years.

Example 3: You can receive a 10 percent yield to maturity if you buy in 1988 either of two bonds maturing in ten years:

- Bond A—Price = $955, coupon rate = $9\frac{1}{4}$ percent.
- Bond B—Price = $815, coupon rate = 7 percent.

If interest rates go down 3 percent by 1994, which bond would give you the greatest percentage profit if you decided to sell and take a capital gain at that time?

If interest rates go down 3 percent, the yield to maturity of these bonds will fall to 7 percent (10 percent – 3 percent). In six years (1994), your ten-year bonds will have four years remaining to maturity.

- *Step 1:* Turn to the chart with four years remaining to maturity.
- *Step 2:* Analyze Bond A by using its coupon rate (9¼ percent) and the 7 percent yield-to-maturity line to find the corresponding bond price, which is $1,075.
- *Step 3:* Compute your profit percentage for Bond A:

$$\frac{1,075 - 955}{955} = \frac{120}{955} = 12.56\%$$

- *Step 4:* Analyze Bond B by using its coupon rate (7 percent) and the 7 percent yield-to-maturity line to find the corresponding price, which is $1,000.
- *Step 5:* Compute your profit percentage for Bond B:

$$\frac{1,000 - 815}{815} = \frac{185}{815} = 22.70\%$$

Minimizing the Potential for Error

As you have seen in the examples, these charts quickly give you the approximate answer to many yield-to-maturity questions. The potential for error *within* any chart is quite *small* since the charts have been constructed very carefully; they can usually be read to the nearest one-tenth of 1 percent.

Therefore, the only possibility of a significant error lies in the *selection* of the appropriate chart. Without considering the *current month* and the *month of maturity,* an error of plus or minus one year is possible. (From 1988 to 1993 is five years, but January 1988 to December 1993 is almost six years, and December 1988 to January 1993 is a fraction over four years.) It should be noted that without knowing the exact date of maturity, you would face the same problem when using more expensive yield tables or a calculator.

If you know the exact time to maturity (e.g., 5.25 years), you could use the five-year and six-year yield charts and interpolate your answer for 5.25 years. If you do not know the exact time to maturity, you could use the year-to-year calculation (1988 to 1993 = five years), find your answer using the five-year chart, and then use the four- and six-year charts to see if your answer changes significantly. Although this extra effort may not require much time when using these charts, some additional information may help you to decide when the effort may be justified to meet your own accuracy requirements.

In general, an error of plus or minus one year will have a very *small effect* on the yield to maturity of *longer-term bonds,* but could *significantly affect* the yield to maturity of *shorter-term bonds.*

For a Bond

With a price of:	$900		$1,100	
And a coupon rate of:	8%	10%	8%	10%
Time to Maturity	Yield to Maturity			
2 years	14.1%	16.3%	2.8%	4.6%
3 years	12.1	14.3	4.3	6.2
4 years	11.3	13.4	5.2	7.0
5 years	10.7	12.8	5.6	7.5
8 years	9.9	12.0	6.4	8.2
10 years	9.6	11.8	6.6	8.5
12 years	9.4	11.6	6.8	8.6
15 years	9.3	11.4	6.9	8.8
20 years	9.1	11.3	7.1	8.9
25 years	9.02	11.20	7.13	8.98
30 years	8.97	11.16	7.17	9.02

This table is designed to assist you in determining when the exact time remaining to maturity may be an important factor in your decision making. It depicts the yield to maturity of four specific bonds when they are evaluated with different years to maturity. As you can see, whether the bond is a discount or premium bond, the change in yield to maturity between any two consecutive years is very significant with only 2 or 3 years to maturity, but is extremely small with 25 to 30 years to maturity.

Additional Notes

Bond Price Scales. To make these charts consistently readable and easy to interpolate, the bond price scale had to be adjusted in certain cases. As a result, *three different scales* are used, which *should be noted:*

Charts With	Have a Bond Price Scale of	And a Dollar Range of
1–2 years to maturity	20 units per $100 or $ 5/unit	$800–$1,175
3–5 years to maturity	10 units per $100 or $10/unit	$500–$1,250
6–30 years to maturity	5 units per $100 or $20/unit	$ 0–$1,500

Methodology. Bond-Aid yield-to-maturity charts were developed through a systematic mathematical analysis of the basic formula for the present value of a bond:

$$PV = \sum_{i=1}^{n} \frac{I_i}{(1 + r)^i} + \frac{FV}{(1 + r)^n}$$

where PV = the current bond price
      i = the number of years of interest payments
      n = the number of years remaining to maturity

I = the annual interest payment (in dollars)

FV = the future value or maturity value ($1,000)

r = the required rate of return or the yield to maturity

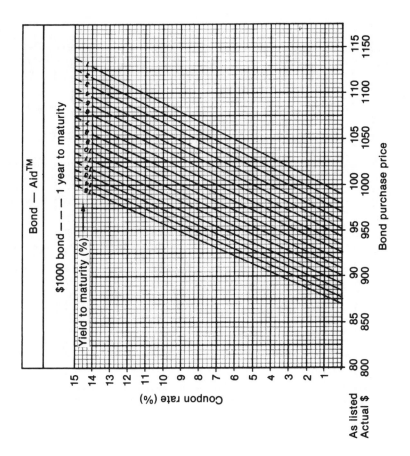

Bond — Aid™

$1000 bond — — — 1 year to maturity

Yield to maturity (%)

Coupon rate (%)

Bond purchase price

As listed
Actual $

800 850 900 950 1000 1050 1100 1150
     85   90   95   100   105   110   115

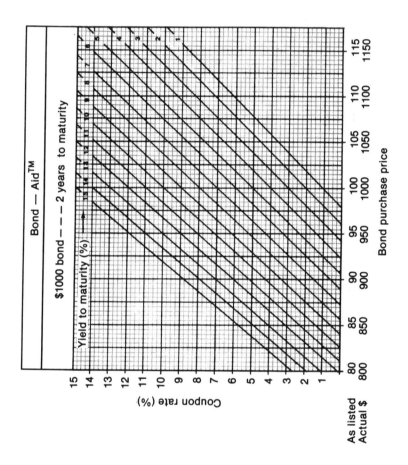

Bond — Aid™

$1000 bond - - - 2 years to maturity

Yield to maturity (%)

Coupon rate (%)

Bond purchase price

As listed
Actual $

400

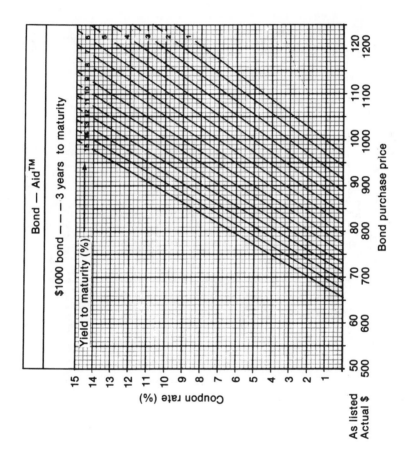

Bond — Aid™

$1000 bond — — — 3 years to maturity

Yield to maturity (%)

Coupon rate (%)

Bond purchase price

As listed   50   60   70   80   90   100 110 120
Actual $ 500 600 700 800 900 1000 1100 1200

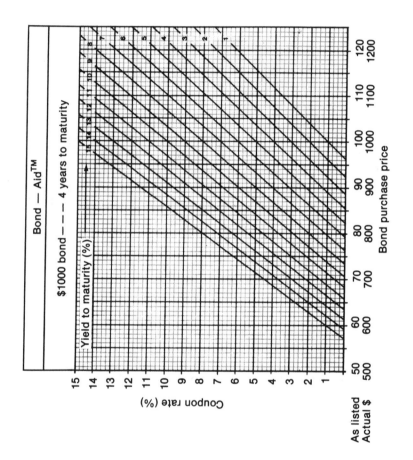

Bond — Aid™

$1000 bond – – – 4 years to maturity

Yield to maturity (%)

Coupon rate (%)

Bond purchase price

As listed
Actual $

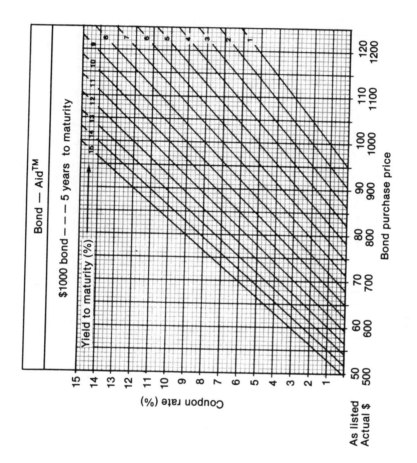

Bond — Aid™

$1000 bond – – – 5 years to maturity

Yield to maturity (%)

Coupon rate (%)

Bond purchase price

As listed
Actual $

403

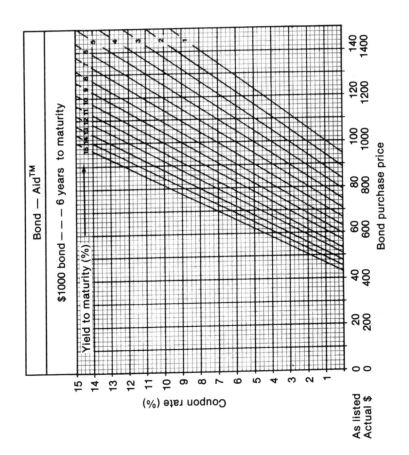

Bond — Aid™

$1000 bond – – – 6 years to maturity

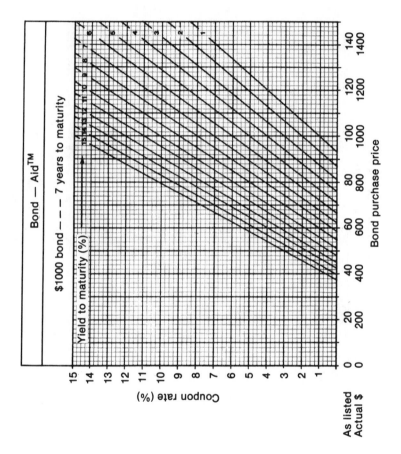

Bond — Aid™

$1000 bond — — — 7 years to maturity

Yield to maturity (%)

Coupon rate (%)

Bond purchase price

As listed
Actual $

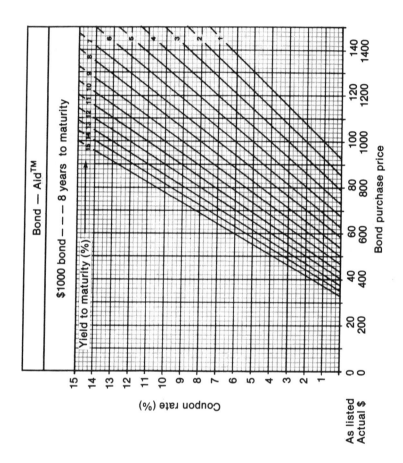

Bond — Aid™

$1000 bond — — — 8 years to maturity

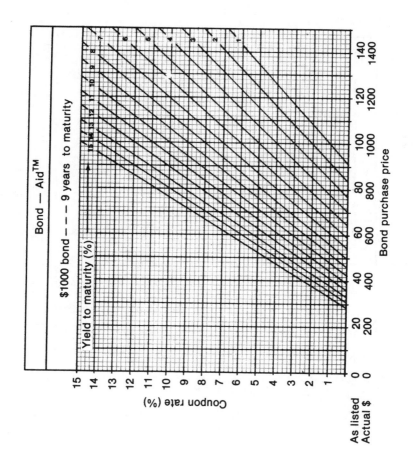

Bond — Aid™

$1000 bond – – – 9 years to maturity

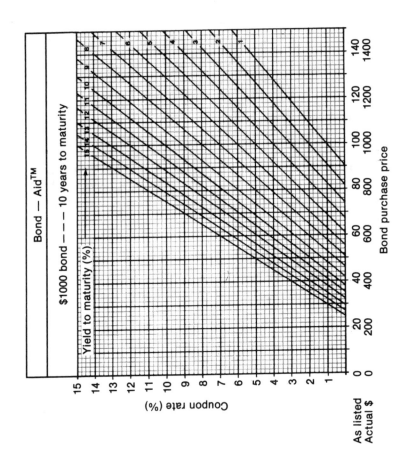

Bond — Aid™

$1000 bond — — — 10 years to maturity

Yield to maturity (%)

Coupon rate (%)

Bond purchase price

As listed
Actual $

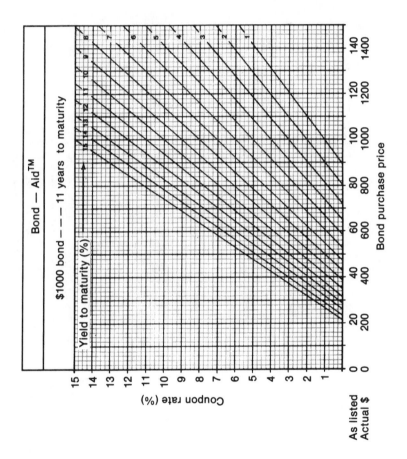

Bond — Aid™

$1000 bond – – – 11 years to maturity

Yield to maturity (%)

Coupon rate (%)

Bond purchase price

As listed
Actual $

409

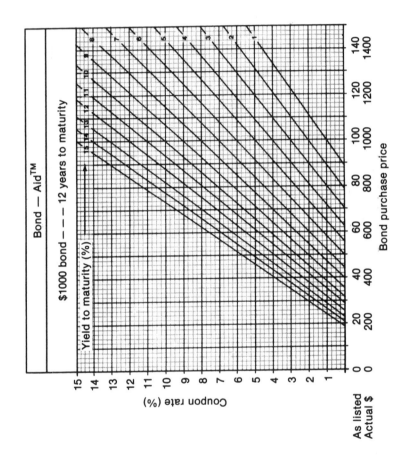

Bond — Aid™

$1000 bond – – – 12 years to maturity

Yield to maturity (%)

Coupon rate (%)

Bond purchase price

As listed
Actual $

410

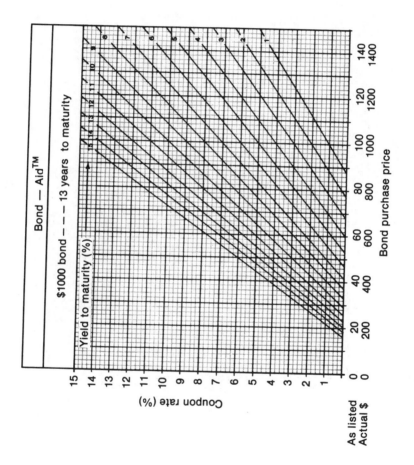

Bond — Aid™

$1000 bond — — — 13 years to maturity

Yield to maturity (%)

Coupon rate (%)

Bond purchase price

As listed
Actual $

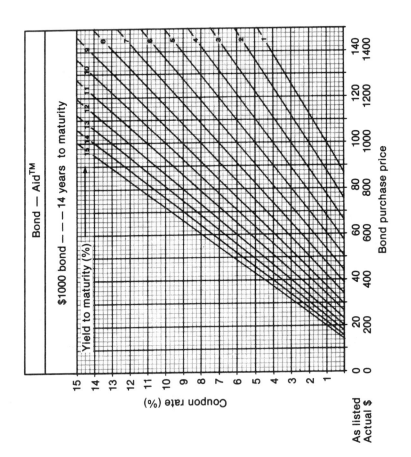

Bond — Aid™

$1000 bond — — — 14 years to maturity

Yield to maturity (%)

Coupon rate (%)

Bond purchase price

As listed
Actual $

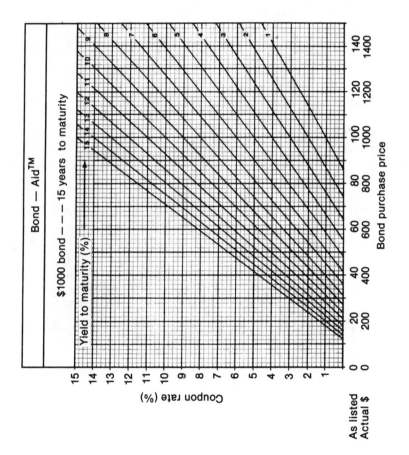

Bond — Aid™

$1000 bond – – 15 years to maturity

Yield to maturity (%)

Coupon rate (%)

Bond purchase price

As listed   0   20   40   60   80   100   120   140
Actual $ 0   200   400   600   800   1000   1200   1400

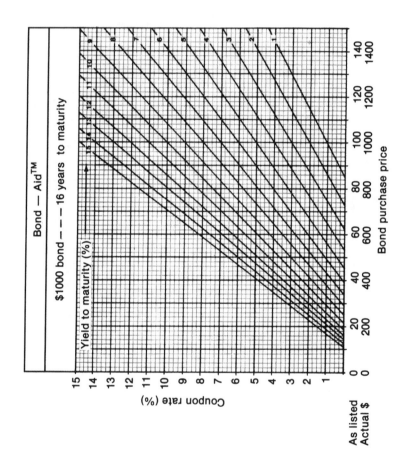

Bond — Aid™

$1000 bond – – – 16 years to maturity

Yield to maturity (%)

Coupon rate (%)

Bond purchase price

As listed
Actual $

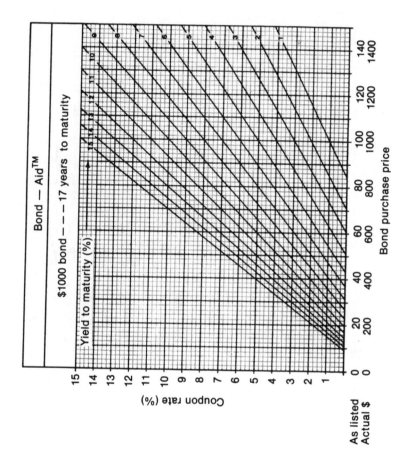

Bond — Aid™

$1000 bond – – –17 years to maturity

Yield to maturity (%)

Coupon rate (%)

Bond purchase price

As listed
Actual $

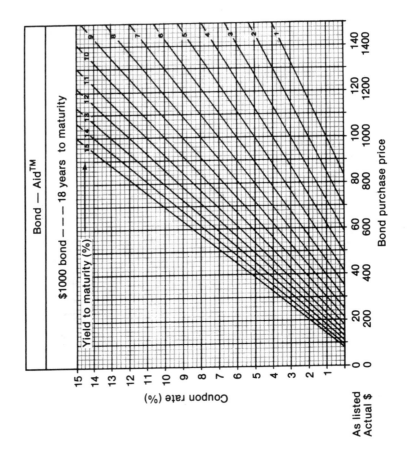

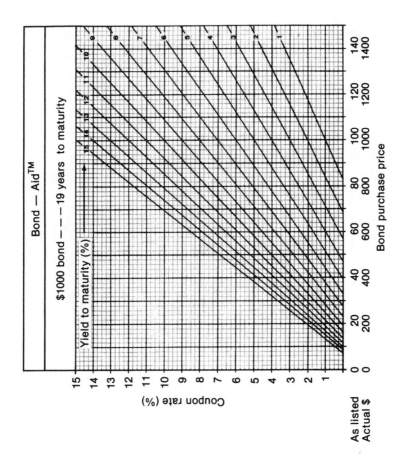

Bond — Aid™

$1000 bond — — — 19 years to maturity

Yield to maturity (%)

Coupon rate (%)

Bond purchase price

As listed
Actual $

417

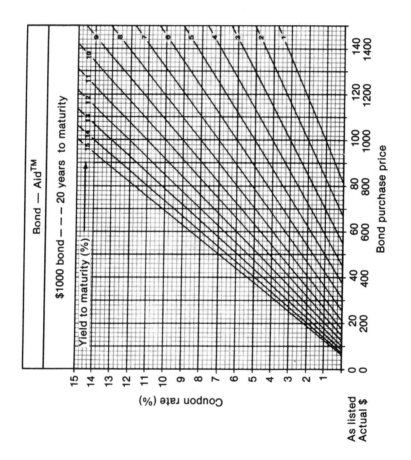

Bond — Aid™

$1000 bond – – – 20 years to maturity

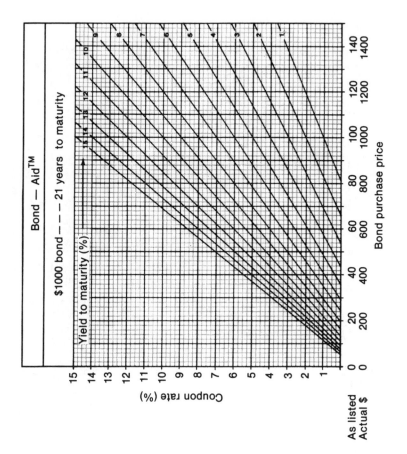

419

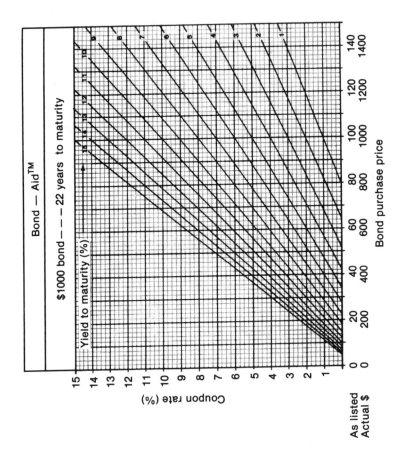

Bond — Aid™

$1000 bond – – – 22 years to maturity

Yield to maturity (%)

Coupon rate (%)

Bond purchase price

As listed
Actual $

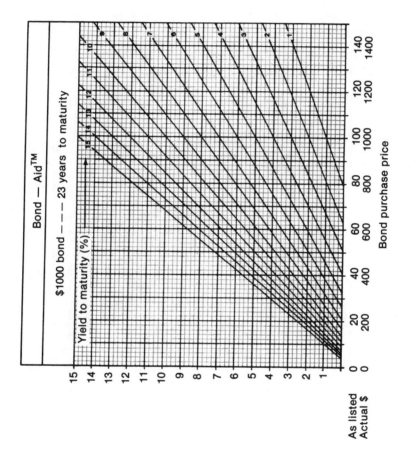

Bond — Aid™

$1000 bond — — — 23 years to maturity

Yield to maturity (%)

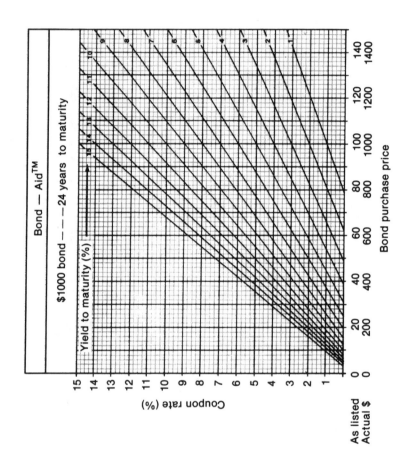

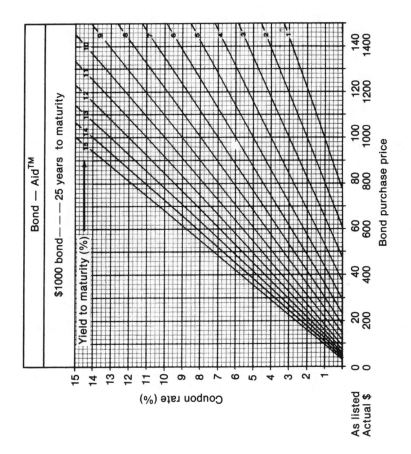

Bond — Aid™

$1000 bond — — — 25 years to maturity

Yield to maturity (%)

Coupon rate (%)

Bond purchase price

As listed
Actual $

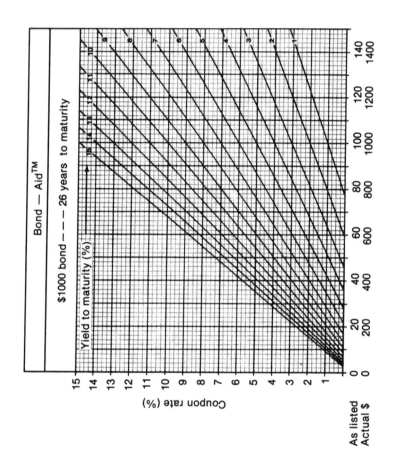

Bond — Aid™

$1000 bond – – – 26 years to maturity

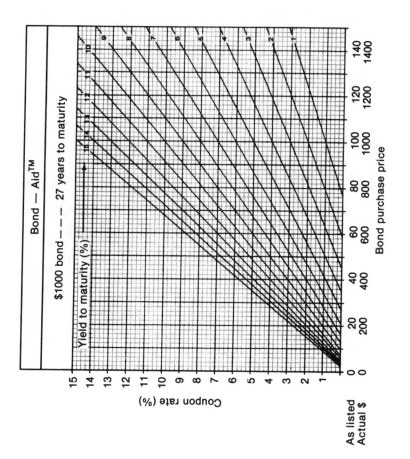

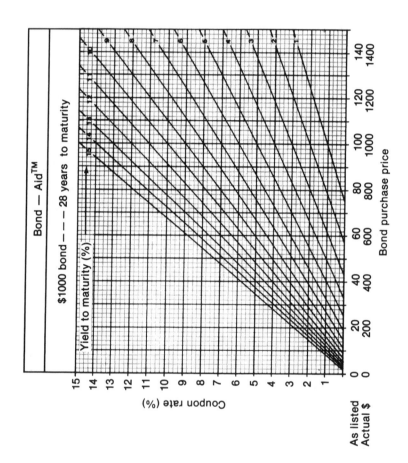

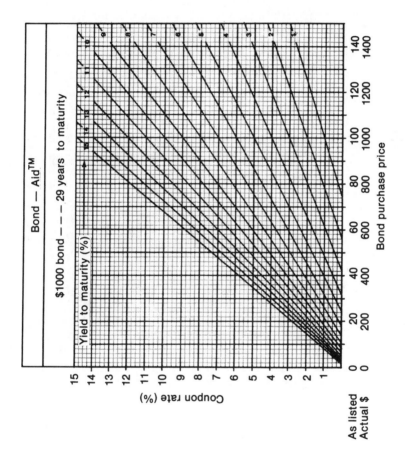

Bond — Aid™

$1000 bond — — — 29 years to maturity

Yield to maturity (%)

Coupon rate (%)

Bond purchase price

As listed
Actual $

427

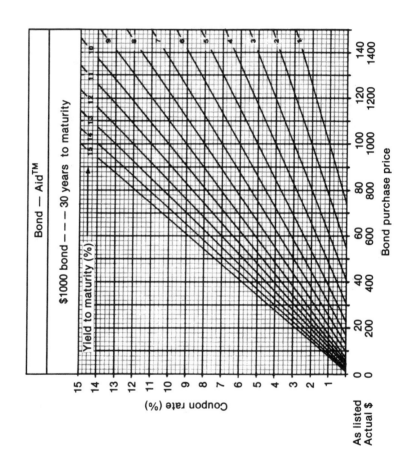

Appendix E

The Stock Market Valuation Map

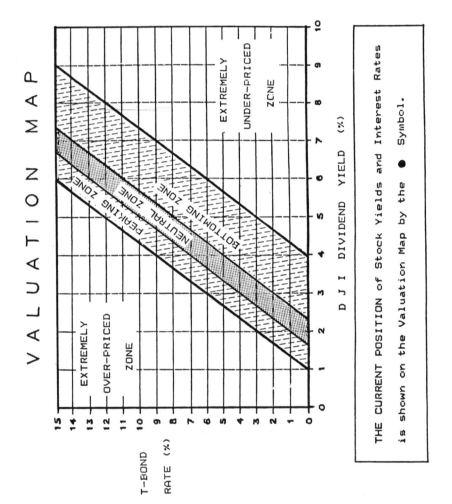

V A L U A T I O N   M A P

THE CURRENT POSITION of Stock Yields and Interest Rates

is shown on the Valuation Map by the ● Symbol.

The *Business Cycle Monitor*

PURPOSES AND GOALS

The *Business Cycle Monitor* is published monthly on a subscription basis by the Business Cycle Research Company. The purpose of the *Business Cycle Monitor* is to track the progress of each business cycle and advise investors on where we are and what the next events in the cycle will be.

The specific goals of this advisory service are to:

• Get long-term investors into the stock, bond, and gold markets at *major bottoms*

• Keep investors in each market while the fundamentals are still positive

• Get long-term investors *out* at major tops

• Let investors recognize the difference between short-term "technical" adjustments (such as the technical stock market plunge of September 11–12, 1986) and major market turning points (such as the crash of October 1987) throughout each cycle

In each issue, the *Business Cycle Monitor* provides:

- Our updated position in the current business cycle based on the latest economic and financial data
- Our current position on the stock market valuation map
- Updates on each component of the Primary Business Cycle
- Specific "buy," "hold," and "sell" recommendations for stocks, long-term bonds, and inflation hedges such as gold based on our position in the business cycle
- Early warning signals as we approach major turning points
- Special reports on unique situations and opportunities as they develop

As an example of the format of this newsletter, as well as the practical application of the methods discussed in this book, we've included in this appendix the *Business Cycle Monitor* that was issued on September 15, 1987—one month before the crash of 1987!

Business Cycle Monitor: Subscription Information

3-month trial subscription	$ 45.00
6 months	$ 75.00
12 months	$120.00

Please make checks payable to:

The Business Cycle Research Company
Exchange Park
P. O. Box 45684
Dallas, TX 75245

Refund policy: Subscribers may cancel at any time and receive a full refund on unmailed issues.

SUBSCRIPTION ORDER FORM

Please send check to:
Business Cycle Research Co.
Exchange Park
P. O. Box 45684
Dallas, TX 75245

MONEY-BACK GUARANTEE
I may cancel within three
months and receive a FULL
REFUND on all unmailed
issues.

Please enter my subscription
to ***THE BUSINESS CYCLE MONITOR***
at the introductory price of:

_____ $120 for 12 monthly issues

_____ $75 for 6 monthly issues

_____ $45 for a 3-month trial
subscription

Name _____

Address_____

City _____ State _____ Zip _____

SEPTEMBER 15, 1987, ISSUE

THE BUSINESS CYCLE MONITOR
SEPTEMBER 15, 1987

I. SUMMARY

We have jumped to Phase # 19 of the Primary Business Cycle, as shown in the Chart below.

Last month the Stock Market reached new peaks and the dividend yields reached a
60 Year low point. Since then, the market has fallen off sharply during the part
of the Business Cycle where a Stock Market Peak is to be expected. We believe that this
is a significant Market Peak and that investors should completely exit the Stock Market
at this time.

The Economic Cycle Indicator and the Leading Indicators should reach their peaks in the
near future, confirming, in spades, a Major Peak in the Market and the Economy. If these
economic indicators continue to grow for several months, then the Stock Market could
stage one last rally. However, the upside potential is both limited and speculative and
we recommend against any stock purchases for the foreseeable future.

Interest Rates will remain in an uptrend during this Phase of the Cycle, which means that
Bond prices will remain in a downtrend.

Gold prices have a $400 floor with some upside potential.

Recommendations.

At this point in the Cycle, we recommend NO investments in Stocks and NO investments in
Bonds, a limited position in Gold and a significant building of reserves in Cash.
Our comments on Stocks, Bonds, Gold, and specific portfolio recommendations are found on
pages 5 - 8 of this report.

MAJOR TURNING POINTS	THE CURRENT BUSINESS CYCLE
	1981 | 1982 | 1983 | 1984 | 1985 | 1986 | 1987 FUTURE
1 MONEY SUPPLY BOTTOMS OUT	
2 STOCK MARKET BOTTOMS OUT — B U Y	
3 LEADING INDICATORS BOTTOM OUT	
4 ECON. CYCLE INDICATOR BOTTOMS OUT	
5 COINCIDENT INDICATORS BOTTOM OUT	
6 ECONOMY BOTTOMS OUT:RECESSION ENDS	
7 LAGGING INDICATORS BOTTOM OUT	
8 INFLATION BOTTOMS OUT	
9-16 VELOCITY AND ALL 7 INTEREST RATES BOTTOM OUT	
17 MONEY SUPPLY PEAKS	
18 ECON. CYCLE INDICATOR PEAKS	
19 STOCK MARKET PEAKS ——— S E L L	
20 LEADING INDICATORS PEAK	
21 COINCIDENT INDICATORS PEAK	
22 ECONOMY PEAKS: RECESSION BEGINS	
23 INFLATION PEAKS	
24 VELOCITY PEAKS	
25 LAGGING INDICATORS PEAK	
26-32 ALL 7 INTEREST RATES PEAK	

● = Completed Turning Points

II. MONTHLY BUSINESS CYCLE UPDATE.

A. The Money Supply

The M-2 Money Supply continued its decline last month, for the <u>sixth</u>
consecutive month. This decline, however must be attributed to Mr.
Greenspan, and not Mr. Volcker. Last month we said that it was
inconceivable that Mr. Greenspan would loosen the reins on the Money
Supply in the next several months. All visible signs now appear to
bear out that conclusion, and we predict that you will see more of the
same in the months ahead.

History shows that continued restraint in the Money Supply will:

    1) Slow down the Economy, which will affect corporate profits
    2) Keep Inflation at moderate levels
    3) Put upward pressure on Interest Rates
    4) Reduce the growth rate in Gold prices.

MONEY SUPPLY --- M 2

B. The Economy

The Leading and Coincident Economic Indicators continued their steady rise
last month, and the Economic Cycle Index also moved up again.

The Economy, as a whole, continues to move ahead at a slow pace, but some foreboding
signs are now appearing very clearly. Both Housing and Autos, two mainstays in the
Economy, are faring poorly, and will not improve as interest rates move up even higher.
Further, the Personal Savings Rate is now at a <u>37 Year low</u>, at 3.0 %. When people begin
to save more again, Consumer Spending and the Economy will receive a serious jolt.
Also, Consumer Credit, which has been driving the Economy since 1983, has now peaked
out, suggesting that the end of the expansion is near.

All of this coincides perfectly with of current position in the Business Cycle.

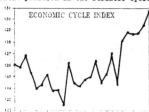

C. Inflation

Inflation is moderating now, as a result of the declining Money Supply.
While the Inflation Rate for Raw Material Prices increased, Producer Prices,
and Consumer Prices rose at a slower pace. We expect the resolve of the FED
to suppress any further dramatic increases in inflation, even at the expense
of higher Interest Rates and a possible recession.

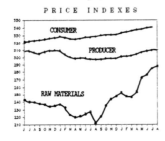 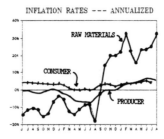

D. Interest Rates.

Interest Rates moved up sharply last month as the Money Supply was reduced.
The long-term direction of Interest Rates will continue to be UP as long as
inflation continues to rise, even modestly, and the FED keeps the Money Supply
in check.

SHORT-TERM INTEREST RATES

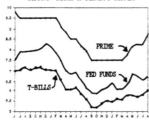

The Velocity of Money, our key confirming
indicator of Interest Rate movements, also
rose again last month, confirming the upward
pressure on future Interest Rates.

LONG-TERM INTEREST RATES

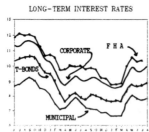

E. The Outlook for Stocks

The average price of the S & P 500 rose to 329.31 in August.

However, since the S & P hit its recent peak of 336 on August 25, it has
declined sharply --- closing yesterday at 323. Over the same period, the
Dow has fallen over 100 points.

If you followed our recommendation of last month, and had a limit order
to sell your stocks at 5 % below their values in mid-August, your are now
out of the Market. Our recommendation is that you stay out of this market
over the foreseeable future.

The Stock Market situation is this: We are now in Phase # 19 of the
Business Cycle, in which the Money Supply has peaked, and the Stock Market
has peaked, while the Economy, Inflation, and Interest Rates are now climbing
toward their ultimate peaks. While no two Business Cycles are exactly the
same, we know that the peaks in the Economic Cycle Indicator (Phase # 18),
the Stock Market (Phase # 19), and the Leading Indicators (Phase # 20) occur
over a short time span --- usually, but not always in that exact order.

We see very little upside left in the Stock Market at this time, and while
it may rally on a technical basis later on , we believe that the tide has
turned and that the bear market preceeding the next recession has now begun.
The Economic Cycle Indicator and the Leading Indicators will reach their
peaks in the next few months.

The yield on the S & P 500 Stock Index bottomed out on August 31 at 2.64 %,
the lowest yield in over 60 years. Since then the yield has risen back to 2.82 % as
the Stock Market declined in the last two weeks.   The table below shows the
dates of the most significant Stock Market Peaks in the last 80 years, along with
the S & P 500 yield at those Market Peaks, along with the yields of recent months.

DATE OF MARKET PEAK	S & P 500 YIELD
September, 1929	2.93 %
October, 1965	2.91 %
November, 1968	2.92 %
January, 1973	2.69 %
August 31, 1987	2.64 %
Sept. 14, 1987	2.82 %

- 4 -   Based on our position in the Business Cycle and the extremely low yield on the
S & P 500, we recommend a complete exit from the Stock Market at this time. We
believe that any recovery in Stock prices from here will be short-lived and that
the Stock Market doesn't represent a prudent long-term investment now.

F. <u>THE OUTLOOK FOR GOLD</u>

Gold Prices stabilized in the $450 to $460 range in the last thirty days,
and closed at $459 yesterday.

Tensions in the Persion Gulf have eased somewhat in recent days and the
Iranian attacks on neutral oil tankers have proven to be insignificant
in terms of closing down the flow of oil or directly attacking a U.S. ship.

Oil prices have declined over the last month, confirming the reduced
liklihood of a serious oil curtailment caused by a military incident.
Iran has apparently realized that if it cannot defeat Iraq in 7 years
of fighting, then it would not be militarily wise to engage in a war with
the U. S. at the same time.

In earlier MONITORS, we've outlined the three dominant forces governing
the future direction of Gold prices:

  1. The decline of the Money Supply -- which is <u>bearish</u> for Gold
     prices over the longer term since inflation will be held to
     moderate levels by a tight Money Supply.

     As seen on Page 2, the Money Supply continues to decline, and
     therefore continues to put downward pressure on Gold prices.

  2. The continuing moderate rate of inflation -- which is only
     moderately <u>bullish</u> for Gold.

     As seen on Page 3, the inflation rate is still quite modest
     and, therefore, continues to represent only a modest bullish
     influence.

  3. The potential for a political or military confrontation with
     Iran in the Persian Gulf -- which remains the <u>dominant, driving force</u>
     behind the recent price increases (whenever the Persian Gulf hits
     the top of the news), and price decreases (whenever war news
     disappears from the headlines).

     As indicated above, the military confrontation scenario appears
     less likely at the moment.

The other fundamental factors influencing Gold prices, specifically, massive
international debts, and unstable currency markets will continue to provide a
floor for Gold in the $400 per ounce range with "crisis" potential at any time.

Therefore we continue to recommend a 10 % allocation of funds to Gold at
this time.

G. THE OUTLOOK FOR BONDS

Driven by significant Interest Rate increases across-the-board, the
Bond Market took a beating last month, and our bench-mark long-term
Treasury Bond dropped from $109 on August 15 to $102 yesterday. The
recent increase in the Prime Rate to 8.75 % (up 1/2 a point, not just
1/4) is a significant warning of more to come.

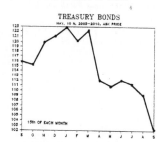

TREASURY BONDS
MAY, 10 %, 2005-2010, ASK PRICE

15th OF EACH MONTH

Since our "SELL" recommendation of late last year, when our bench-mark
Bond was at $120, we've seen almost a 20 % decline in long-term Bond prices.
At this time, we continue to advise against purchasing or holding Bonds.

The key to the future of Bond prices still lies in the future policies of the
FED under the direction of Mr. Greenspan, and we continue to expect a tight-money
policy to prevail in the coming months. As we near the 1988 elections, it is
reasonable to expect a looser money policy to generate an expansionary psychology
as people cast their votes, but for now, expect tight money from the FED.

Our assessment of the driving factors behind Bond prices remains unchanged
and continues to suggest upward pressure on interest rates and downward pressure on
Bond prices in the future.

1. A <u>tight-money</u> policy will necessarily put upward pressure on Interest Rates.

2. The moderate rate of <u>inflation</u> will keep interest rates in an upward trend,
   and Bond prices in a downward trend.

3. The widening <u>Trade Deficit</u>, if not improved soon, will weaken the Dollar, and
   the Bond Market will decline further.

4. The <u>Budget Deficit</u> will not improved in the months ahead, and if the FED
   continues a tight-money policy, the huge borrowing needs of the Government
   will force interest rates up and Bond prices down.

5. The<u>Persian Gulf</u> situation could cause an oil crisis similar
   to those of 1973 and 1979, which would dramatically drive
   inflation and interest rates up, and Bond prices down.

Until one or more of these factors show a positive change, we continue to recommend
that Long-term Bonds be avoided at this time.

III. <u>RECOMMENDED INVESTMENT PORTFOLIO AS OF SEPTEMBER 15, 1987.</u>

As indicated in earlier MONITORS, Turning Points #18, #19, and #20 usually occur together within a short time span. We believe that Turning Point #19, <u>the Peak in the Stock Market, has now occurred.</u> The Turning Points in the Economic Cycle Indicator and the Leading Economic Indicators will, therefore, occur in the very near future.

Accordingly, we advise investors to allocate their funds according to the recommended Portfolio for Phase #19 of the Business Cycle.

As shown in the table below, we recommend a complete exit from the Stock Market, no investments in Bonds, a limited position in Gold, and all remaining funds invested in Cash.

```
-------------------------------------------------
|   Recommended Portfolio Percentages           |
|-----------------------------------------------|
| STOCKS  |  BONDS  |  GOLD   |  CASH  |
|-----------------------------------------------|
|   0 %   |   0 %   |  10 %   |  90 %  |
-------------------------------------------------
```

M O D E L   P O R T F O L I O

BASED ON BUSINESS CYCLE TURNING POINTS

	MAJOR TURNING POINTS	RECOMMENDED PORTFOLIO ALLOCATION			
		STOCKS	BONDS	GOLD	CASH
1	MONEY SUPPLY BOTTOMS OUT	60%	40%	–	–
2	STOCK MARKET BOTTOMS OUT	80%	20%	–	–
3	LEADING INDICATORS BOTTOM OUT	80%	20%	–	–
4	ECON. CYCLE INDICATOR BOTTOMS OUT	80%	20%	–	–
5	COINCIDENT INDICATORS BOTTOM OUT	80%	20%	–	–
6	ECONOMY BOTTOMS: RECESSION ENDS	80%	20%	–	–
7	LAGGING INDICATORS BOTTOM OUT	80%	20%	–	–
8	INFLATION BOTTOMS OUT	80%	–	20%	–
9	1st INTEREST RATE BOTTOMS OUT	70%	–	30%	–
10	2nd INTEREST RATE BOTTOMS OUT	70%	–	30%	–
11	3rd INTEREST RATE BOTTOMS OUT	70%	–	30%	–
12	4th INTEREST RATE BOTTOMS OUT	70%	–	30%	–
13	5th INTEREST RATE BOTTOMS OUT	70%	–	30%	–
14	6th INTEREST RATE BOTTOMS OUT	70%	–	30%	–
15	VELOCITY OF MONEY BOTTOMS OUT	70%	–	30%	–
16	7th INTEREST RATE BOTTOMS OUT	70%	–	30%	–
17	MONEY SUPPLY PEAKS	20%	–	10%	70%
18	ECON. CYCLE INDICATOR PEAKS	–	–	10%	90%
19	STOCK MARKET PEAKS	–	–	10%	90%
20	LEADING INDICATORS PEAK	–	–	10%	90%
21	COINCIDENT INDICATORS PEAK	–	–	10%	90%
22	ECONOMY PEAKS: START OF RECESSION	–	–	10%	90%
23	INFLATION PEAKS	–	–	–	100%
24	VELOCITY PEAKS	–	–	–	100%
25	LAGGING INDICATORS PEAK	–	–	–	100%
26	1st INTEREST RATE PEAKS	–	20%	–	80%
27	2nd INTEREST RATE PEAKS	–	40%	–	60%
28	3rd INTEREST RATE PEAKS	–	60%	–	40%
29	4th INTEREST RATE PEAKS	–	80%	–	20%
30	5th INTEREST RATE PEAKS	–	80%	–	20%
31	6th INTEREST RATE PEAKS	20%	80%	–	–
32	7th INTEREST RATE PEAKS	40%	60%	–	–

CURRENT POSITION → (at 19)

IV. TELEPHONE SWITCH INVESTMENT STRATEGY.

In the tables below, we have identified the only five Mutual Fund families that we could find that 1) provide investors with the opportunity to invest in Stock, Bond, Gold, and Cash Funds, 2) allow virtually unlimited switching between these four types of funds at minimum cost, 3) are either NO-LOAD or LOW-LOAD Funds, and 4) have small opening balance requirements.

We recommend that investors establish accounts with any one of the five Mutual Fund Companies listed below, and then allocate their money to that Company's Stock, Bond, Gold, and Cash Funds, based on our recommended percentages as shown on the previous page. As we move through each business cycle, we will change the recommended percentages in each investment category, based on our position in the Business Cycle.

SPECIFIC INFORMATION ON EACH FUND MANAGER					
	FIDELITY	FRANKLIN	LEXINGTON	UNITED	U S A A
SALES LOAD	0% TO 3% DEPENDING ON FUND	4%	NONE	NONE	NONE
REDEMPTION FEE	1%	NONE	NONE	2%	NONE
MINIMUM TO OPEN	$1000 TO $2500	$100	$1000	$100	$1000
TELEPHONE SWITCHING ABILITY	AFTER 4 SWITCHES PER YEAR, COST INCREASES	UNLIMITED	UNLIMITED BUT MUST STAY IN FOR 7 DAYS	AFTER 12 SWITCHES PER YEAR, COST GOES TO $50/SW.	UNLIMITED
COST PER SWITCH	$10	$5	$0	$5 UP TO 12 SWITCHES / YEAR	$5
AVAILABLE THROUGH BROKERS	NO	YES	NO	NO	NO
PHONE NUMBER	800-544-6666	800-632-2180	800-526-0056	800-824-4653	800-531-8000

RECOMMENDED MUTUAL FUNDS FOR TELEPHONE SWITCHING BASED ON THE BUSINESS CYCLE				
MUTUAL FUND COMPANY	SPECIFIC FUND IN EACH INVESTMENT CATEGORY			
	GROWTH STOCKS	BONDS	GOLD	CASH
FIDELITY	Magellan	G N M A	Select American Gold	Cash Reserves
FRANKLIN	Equity	U.S. Gov't Securities	Gold	Money Fund
LEXINGTON	Growth	G N M A Income	Goldfund	Money Market Trust
UNITED SERVICES	Good and Bad Times	U.S. GNMA	New Prospector	U.S. Treasury Security
U S A A	Growth	Income	Gold	Money Market Fund

The BUSINESS CYCLE MONITOR is published monthly by the Business Cycle Research Company, Exchange Park,P.O. Box 45684, Dallas, Tx. 75245. Subscription Rates: $ 120 for 12 months, $ 75 for 6 months, $ 45 for 3 month trial subscription. This report contains our interpretation of information from external sources that are considered to be reliable, but neither the accuracy of the information, nor our interpretations and recommendations, are guaranteed by the Business Cycle Research Company. Neither the information nor any opinion expressed constitutes a solicitation for the purchase or sale of any securities referred to herein.

Index

A

Actual economic bottom, as event in Primary Business Cycle, 102
Actual economic peak, as event in Primary Business Cycle, 104
Adjustments, partial cycles and, 111
Allocation step
    Business Cycle Money Management System, 334–42
    portfolio allocation limits, 334–36
    principle of, 334
    rules for, 336
Analysis step, Business Cycle Money Management System, 306, 313–31
Annual rate of return, bonds, 213
Annual tax revenues, definition of, 148
Apparent consumption, 44–45
Apparent supply of goods, 45–46
Asset allocation, 11
Assets for living, 307–9

B

Balance of trade, dollar and, 174
Banking certificates of deposit (CDs), 196
Bank loans, 57
Bartering, 25, 292
Base case scenario, 362–64
    alteration of, 363–64
Board of Federal Reserve Governors, 61–62
Bond-Aid, 389–428
Bond investments, 210–17
Bond market effects, of exchange rate movements, 177–80
Bond prices, sources of data, 315
Bonds
    annual rate of return, 213
    general investment rule, 216
    linkage between stocks and, 218–26
    price of, 211, 213–15

C